CANADA AMONG NATIONS 1993–94

GLOBAL
JEOPARDY

CANADA AMONG NATIONS 1993–94

GLOBAL JEOPARDY

Christopher J. Maule
and
Fen Osler Hampson
Editors

THE NORMAN PATERSON SCHOOL
OF INTERNATIONAL AFFAIRS

—

Carleton University Press
Ottawa — Canada
1993

ISBN   0-88629-203-4 (paperback)
ISBN   0-88629-202-6 (casebound)

Printed and bound in Canada
Carleton Public Policy Series 12

Canadian Cataloguing in Publication Data
The National Library of Canada has catalogued this publication as follows:
   Canada among nations
      1984–
      Annual.
      1993–94 ed.: Global jeopardy
      Each vol. also has a distinctive title.
      Produced by the Norman Paterson School of International Affairs of
      Carleton University.
      Includes bibliographical references.
      ISSN 0832-0683

      ISBN   0-88629-202-6 (1993–94 ed., bound)
      ISBN   0-88629-203-4 (1993–94 ed., pbk)

1. Canada–Foreign relations–1945– –Periodicals.   2. Canada–Politics and govern-
ment–1984– –Periodicals.   3. Canada–Politics and government–1980–84–Periodicals.
I. Norman Paterson School of International Affairs.
FC242.C345   327.71   C86-031285-2
F1034.2.C36

Distributed by   Oxford University Press Canada,
                 70 Wynford Drive,
                 Don Mills, Ontario,
                 Canada. M3C 1J9
                 (416) 441-2941

Cover design: Aerographics Ottawa

Acknowledgements

Carleton University Press gratefully acknowledges the support extended to its
publishing programme by the Canada Council and the Ontario Arts Council.

The Press would also like to thank the Department of Communications, Government of Canada, and the Government of Ontario through the Ministry of Culture,
Tourism and Recreation, for their assistance.

Table of Contents

Introduction

Down and Out in Ottawa and Charlottetown

Trade Wars

The Road from Rio

New Agendas for Global Change

List of Figures, Tables and Exhibits

List of Contributors

Nigel Bankes is associate professor of law in the Faculty of Law, University of Calgary, and is chair of the Canadian Arctic Resources Committee.

Andrew Cohen is a foreign affairs and international economics writer and columnist for the *Financial Post*.

Fanny Demers is associate professor in the Department of Economics, Carleton University.

Michel Demers is associate professor in the Department of Economics, Carleton University.

Terry Fenge is executive director of the Canadian Arctic Resources Committee.

Nancy Gordon was Director of Public Programs at the Canadian Institute for International Peace and Security, and is now Director of Communications at CARE.

Fen Osler Hampson is associate professor in the Norman Paterson School of International Affairs, Carleton University.

Michael Hart is senior advisor, trade policy studies, Department of External Affairs and International Trade Canada.

Brian L. Job is professor, Institute of International Relations, University of British Columbia.

Sarah Kalff is senior policy advisor, Canadian Arctic Resources Committee.

Frank Langdon is professor emeritus, Institute of International Relations, University of British Columbia.

Albert Legault est professeur au département de science politique de l'Université Laval et directeur du programme d'études stratégiques au Centre québécois de relations internationales.

Christopher Maule is professor in the Department of Economics and Director of the Norman Paterson School of International Affairs, Carleton University.

Lynn K. Mytelka is professor in the Department of Political Science, Carleton University.

Geoffrey Pearson was the Executive Director of the Canadian Institute for International Peace and Security, 1984–88.

Evan Potter is a doctoral student in the Department of International Relations at the London School of Economics, and is editor of the *Canadian Foreign Policy Journal*.

David Runnalls is Director, Environment and Sustainable Development Program with the Institute for Research on Public Policy.

Clyde Sanger is director of Communications with the North-South Institute.

Michael Shenstone is a foreign affairs consultant and a research associate with the Norman Paterson School of International Affairs, Carleton University.

Mark Zacher is professor, Institute of International Relations, University of British Columbia.

Glossary

Acronyms for *Canada Among Nations 1993–94*:

AEPS	Arctic Environmental Protection Strategy
AES	Arctic Environmental Strategy
AGNU	Assemblée Générale des Nations Unies
AIEA	Agence internationale de l'énergie atomique
ANVAR	Agence nationale pour la valorisation de la recherche (France)
APEC	Asia Pacific Economic Co-operation
ASEAN	Association of South East Asian Nations
ASICs	application specific integrated circuits
AUCC	Association of the Universities and Colleges of Canada
BCSD	Business Council for Sustainable Development
CANZ	Canada Australia New Zealand group
CCIC	Canadian Council for International Cooperation
CEREM	Centre de Recherche et des Études sur les Entreprises multinationales (France)
CFCs	chlorofluorocarbons
CFSI	Canadian Foreign Service Institute
CIDA	Canadian International Development Agency
CIIPS	Canadian Institute for International Peace and Security
CIS/CÉI	Commonwealth of Independent States
CPCU	Canadian Preparatory Committee for UNCED
CSCE	Conference on Security and Co-operation in Europe
DAC	Development Assistance Committee (OECD)
DAIEs	developing Asian industrial economies
DEAITC	Department of External Affairs and International Trade Canada
DEW	Distant Early Warning (NATO)
DND	Department of National Defence (Canada)
DOC	Department of Communications (Canada)
EAEC	East Asian Economic Caucus
EAEG	East Asian Economic Grouping

EC	European Community
ECE	Economic Commission for Europe
ECOMOG	Economic Community Monitoring Group
ECOWAS	European Community of West African States
EFTA	European Free Trade Association
EHS	European Monetary System
EMU	European Monetary Union
EPA	Environmental Protection Agency (United States)
ESPRIT	European Strategic Program for Research and Development on Information Technology
EUREKA	European Research Co-operation Agency
FAMOS	flexible manufacturing projects
FDI	foreign direct investment
FNUC	Force des Nations Unies à Chypre
FORPRONU	Force de protection des Nations Unies
FTA	Free Trade Agreement
FUNU	Force d'Urgence des Nations Unies
G-7	group of the seven most industrialized countries
GATT	General Agreement on Tariffs and Trade
GDP	gross domestic product
GEF	Global Environment Facility
GNP	gross national product
GRC	Gendarmerie Royale Canadienne
GST	Goods and Services Tax (Canada)
HDTV	high-definition television
ICC	Inuit Circumpolar Conference
ICRAF	International Council for Research in Agro-Forestry
IDA	International Development Assistance (World Bank)
IDRC	International Development Research Council (Canada)
ILO	International Labour Organization
IMF	International Monetary Fund
IRIS	Institute for Robotics and Intelligent Systems (PRE-CARN Associates)
ISTC	Industry, Science and Techology Canada

ITAC	International Trade Advisory Committee
ITC	International Trade Administration and International Trade Commission (United States)
ITO	International Trade Organization
IUCN	International Union for the Conservation of Nature and Natural Resources
JESSI	Joint European Semicron Silicon Initiative
LRTAP	Long Range Transfrontier Air Pollution Convention
MERCOSUR	Southern Cone Common Market
MDN	Ministère de la défense nationale
MFA	multi-fiber arrangement
MIPRENUC	Mission préparatoire des Nations Unies au Cambodge
MIT	Massachusetts Institute of Technology
MTN	multilateral trade negotiations
NAFTA	North American Free Trade Agreement
NATO	North Atlantic Treaty Organization
NDP	New Democratic Party (Canada)
NGO	Non-governmental organization
NIEs	new industrial economies
NORAD	North American Air Defense Command
NPCSD	North Pacific co-operative security dialogue
NRC	National Research Council of Canada
NSF	National Science Foundation (United States)
NTT	Nippon Telegraph and Telephone
OAS	Organization of American States
ODA	official development assistance
OECD	Organization for Economic Cooperation and Development
OIHP	Office International d'Hygiène Publique
ONU	Organisation des Nations Unies
ONUMOZ	Operation des Nations Unies au Mozambique
ORCI	Office of Research and Collection of Information (UN)
OTAN	Organisation du traité de l'Atlantique du Nord
PAFSO	Professional Association of Foreign Service Officers (Canada)

PBS	Public Broadcasting System (United States)
PCTE	portable common tool environment
PECC	Pacific Economic Co-operation Council
PER	Political and Economic Relations Program (DEAITC)
PMO	Prime Minister's Office
R & D	research and development
SAGIT	Sector Advisory Groups on International Trade (DEAITC)
SALT	Strategic Arms Limitation Talks
SIPRI	Stockholm International Peace Research Institute
SMEs	small and medium sized companies
SRC	Science Research Council
UN	United Nations
UNCED	United Nations Commission on Environment and Development
UNCLOS	United Nations Conference on the Law of the Sea
UNCTAD	United Nations Conference on Trade and Development
UNEP	United Nations Environment Program
UNHCR	United Nations High Commissioner for Refugees
UNRWA	United Nations Relief and Works Agency
UNTAC	United Nations Transitional Authority
USC	Unitarian Service Committee
VLSI	very large scale integration
WCPA	Canadian Press Newswire
WCS	World Conservation Strategy
WEU	Western European Union
WHO	World Health Organization
WMO	World Meteorological Organization

Dedication

Over a number of years, the late George Hampson made donations to the Resource Centre of the Norman Paterson School of International Affairs at Carleton University. After a distinguished career in Canada's diplomatic service, he retained a continuing interest in promoting the interdisciplinary study of international affairs in Canada. On behalf of the School, I would like to express my deep appreciation for his generosity and the assistance that he provided to faculty, staff and students.

Christopher J. Maule

Preface

This is the ninth volume on Canada in international affairs produced by the Norman Paterson School of International Affairs. The book contains an analysis and assessment of aspects of Canadian foreign policy and the setting that shapes that policy, focusing on the period since the beginning of 1992. Our intention is to contribute to the debate about appropriate choices for Canada by calling on the services of academics and other experts from across the country.

The theme of this edition is "Global Jeopardy" because of the many risks that have appeared in the post-Cold War world — civil wars, ethnic conflict, famines, refugees, the partition of states and the formation of new countries, environmental threats, AIDS, mounting trade disputes, the failure to complete the Uruguay Round of trade negotiations, and a prolonged economic recession in the major industrialized countries. No country is immune from at least some of these threats, and Canada has to navigate the international shoals while being buffeted by constitutional winds at home. This volume attempts to assess the impact of external events on Canadian foreign policy at a time of domestic political uncertainty and a prolonged recession which is being accompanied by economic restructuring.

Financial support for this volume has been provided by the former Canadian Institute for International Peace and Security, the Military and Strategic Studies Program of the Department of National Defence, the Dean of Social Sciences and the Dean of Graduate Studies and Research at Carleton University, and the Norman Paterson School of International Affairs.

Brenda Sutherland has guided the editors and goaded the authors. Her advice and efficiency in shaping the manuscript have been invaluable and once again we would like to express our sincere appreciation to her. Continuous liaison with the authors over the year was maintained by Janet Doherty who also organized the authors' workshop in December. Our thanks to her for this and for making all the calls that the editors avoided! Once again Carleton University Press is the publisher and we are pleased to acknowledge the assistance of Anne Winship, Steven Uriarte and Noel Gates. We would also like to thank Pauline Adams, Jean Daudelin and Elizabet Filleul for assistance with the final manuscript and

Christina Thiele for undertaking the typesetting. Finally we would like to offer our best wishes to the editors who will follow us to produce the tenth volume of a series that is increasingly being used in classrooms.

Fen Osler Hampson
Christopher J. Maule
Ottawa, March 1993

INTRODUCTION

1   Global Jeopardy

Fen Osler Hampson
Christopher J. Maule

GLOBAL JEOPARDY IS THE TITLE of this year's volume of *Canada Among Nations*. As in the TV game show, the problem that confronts Canadian foreign policy decision-makers is not that there is a shortage of answers. Rather it is a matter of asking the right question. The question, as we see it, is how should Canada address the mounting challenges of global competition and new threats, such as those presented by the environment and refugees, at a time of shrinking fiscal resources and continuing political uncertainty at home?

We argue that choices cannot be avoided and that there is a need to manage the linkages not only between different areas of foreign policy but also between domestic and international issues. For example, national economies are increasingly exposed to the gusts of global competition and the unpredictable flows of capital and investment across national borders. Canada is no exception. Our economic exposure is greater than that of most countries, given the importance of international trade to our economic health and survival as a nation.

The winners in global competition are those countries which can mobilize human and capital resources in order to take advantage of opportunities offered by new technology and the reorganization of production in a context of stiff global competition. This requires domestic co-operation between government, business, and labour, as well as international co-operation between national governments in opening and enlarging markets and ensuring that global competition remains fair. Existing international regimes will have to be renegotiated and amended and new ones created.

As the economy becomes more open, we will also have to address issues of human rights, guest workers, and the consequences of a freer flow not just of capital and investment but also of labour, as workers migrate to locations where there are jobs.

Just as the nineteenth and the early twentieth centuries brought a wave of European immigrants to North America, the latter part of the twentieth century is seeing an influx of immigrants from Asia, Latin America, and other parts of the Third World. Too often immigration is viewed as a problem for industrial societies, rather than an opportunity. Many of the advanced industrial countries, like Canada, confront the twin problems of an aging work force and the growing demands on social services made by a population which is living longer. Immigration is a way of replenishing the work force with individuals who are young and still productive. Indeed, without this infusion of migrants, the advanced industrial economies will continue to experience economic decline. But the distinction between political refugees and economic migrants is increasingly blurred. Because of the vast number of people now on the move globally, new conflicts are erupting between and within societies about ways of dealing with refugees and migrant workers. Canada is not immune to these pressures, although it is only just beginning to come to grips with the problems posed by the long-term consequences of international migration.

Another dimension of global risk is the environment. It is increasingly evident that humanity is gambling with global weather patterns and the health of the biosphere more than ever before. Ozone depletion in the upper atmosphere is the most extreme example of the unanticipated dangers of certain economic and industrial policies, but it is by no means the only one. The loss of species, the accumulation of hazardous wastes in the plant and animal food chain, the loss of arable lands and forests present fundamental new challenges both at home and abroad.

Diminishing Threats, New Challenges

With the end of the Cold War and bipolarity, the military threats to Canada from outside have diminished dramatically. It can be argued that even at the height of the Cold War, the threat to Canadian security was limited because nuclear weapons lent an element of stability and predictability to the superpower relationship. Although "uncertainty" has become the watchword of the post-Cold War period, the contours of change and risk are now well defined. They include the all too familiar litany of woes that threaten the

"new world order," including growing political and ethnic unrest in much of the former Soviet Union and the countries of East
and Central Europe; the attendant dangers of nuclear proliferation
coupled with the potential loss of control of nuclear stockpiles in
the territories of the former Soviet Union; regional conflict in the
Third World; the rise of regional powers which have sought to fill
the void brought about by the collapse of bipolarity and the decline of the superpowers; deteriorating environmental conditions
on a global scale; and the threat of pandemic diseases like AIDS.

Some of these new threats are concentrated and specific (e.g.,
ethnic conflict in the Balkans), but others are latent and diffuse (e.g.,
climate change or loss of biodiversity). Few threaten Canada's vital interests in the short run though all pose longer-term challenges
to global order and stability. The foreign policy agenda is crowded
with a growing array of challenges, all of which command attention and have the potential to consume vast resources. There is
no easy way to assign priorities to this list, in spite of the urgency
of doing so at a time of shrinking budgets, mounting deficits, and
growing public debt. The challenge is not one of doing "more
with less" but doing "less with less" — i.e., cutting programs and
deciding where to allocate increasingly scarce resources.

In 1992–93, the government began to confront this dilemma,
albeit haltingly, occasionally disingenuously, and with a constant
eye to its own domestic interests. Examples include the decision
to close the policy councils, to pull back Canadian forces from
Europe, to reallocate peacekeeping commitments by withdrawing
from Cyprus, to cut and rechannel foreign aid, and to reorganize the Department of External Affairs and International Trade
Canada (DEAITC). One cannot quarrel with the government's need
to cut spending, focus priorities, and bring order to a foreign
policy bureaucracy that to many Canadians seemed bloated, inef-
ficient, and increasingly ill-equipped to perform its analytical and
management functions. One can quarrel with the way cuts were
implemented, the priorities that were assigned, and the haphazard
way the government approached reorganization and streamlining
issues in the bureaucracy. Did it make sense to hive off immigration from DEAITC just at the time when immigration and refugee
issues were becoming key matters of foreign policy? Did it make
sense to close down foreign policy think-tanks and cut funding for
research on the questionable grounds of fiscal austerity? Does it

make sense to redirect foreign aid from the Third to the Second World? All of these questions are debated in this volume and deserve widespread discussion.

Admittedly, there is little consensus on how to assign priorities and allocate increasingly scarce resources, although a variety of views and suggestions are offered here. Moreover, it is difficult to assign priorities when issues force themselves on to the foreign policy agenda without warning. Old priorities can easily be upset by a rapid turn of events. Consequently, an effective foreign policy requires an ability to adapt to new challenges, rather than attempts to set in concrete priorities liable to be upset later on. The current system of decision-making is neither flexible nor especially well-suited to meet these challenges. There is widespread agreement among the authors in this volume that the current *process* of foreign policy decision-making is in a shambles, in spite of recent efforts to return to a "back to the basics" approach, as reflected in the decision to rid DEAITC of certain functions in the areas of immigration, culture, and communications.

Our contributors raise troubling questions about the continued marginalization of DEAITC in foreign policy decision-making and the fractured policymaking process. At a time when international issues are merging with matters of domestic policy—in such areas as trade, monetary policy, environmental policy, immigration, communications, or peacekeeping—policy co-ordination among relevant agencies and interests is weak. How best to restore coherence and focus to Canadian foreign policy? A number of answers are provided here, although all point to the need to make DEAITC more relevant to the business of government by upgrading the quality, training, and skills of its officers, by bringing the department into closer contact with its clients, and by strengthening the role of the Secretary of State for External Affairs and the Department's senior officials in the formulation of policy. Above all, one, not three or four ministers, must be in charge of foreign policy. To paraphrase Harry Truman, it's high time the buck stopped somewhere.

A number of dilemmas confront Canada in the 1990s. Many observers have pointed to the renewed possibilities for this country to re-assume its middle power role in international relations now that the Cold War is over. Canada never relinquished this

role, although bipolarity restricted Canada's freedom of manoeuvre once the Cold War was in full swing. The end of the Cold War,
the collapse of one superpower and the declining influence of the
other, and the proliferation of new issues, actors and agendas in
international politics have made the international system more
complex and unruly. If Canada is to exert its influence globally,
it will have to choose its issues carefully and muster the requisite
skills and resources to make its influence felt. There are many
chessboards in international diplomacy, and Canada may not be
able to play effectively on every one. The danger of playing every
game is the dissipation of diplomatic energy and with it the failure
to develop an effective strategy.

A second dilemma is that the world is discovering Canada at
a time when Canadians are less able to take up major responsibilities because of economic and political difficulties at home. Latin
Americans, for example, are looking to Canada to play an interme-
diary role in the Western Hemisphere in order to provide leverage
and exercise a moderating force on Washington. For many years,
Canada played such a role between Washington and London and
Paris (during the height of the Suez crisis, for example, Ottawa was
able to talk to both sides at a time when British and French actions
threatened to tear the Atlantic Alliance apart). Although Canada's
decision to join the Organization of American States (OAS) and to
develop closer economic and political linkages with Latin America
is shifting the country closer to the Western hemispheric orbit, it
remains to be seen whether Canada can move Washington in the
direction preferred by its partners to the South. Much will depend
on the attitude of Latin America to the Clinton Administration,
and the development of Canada's own relationship with the new
president and Congress.

A third dilemma arises because Canada's long-standing commitment to multilateralism is being called into question by the
declining capacity of international institutions to manage a wide
array of challenges. The essays in this volume document the failures of the General Agreement on Tariffs and Trade (GATT), the
questionable outcomes of Rio and international negotiations on
the environment, and the difficulties of peacekeeping in a situation where the United Nations finds itself unable to cope with the
proliferating demand for more peacekeepers. Part of the problem
of international co-ordination lies in the growing number of states

in the international system, the complexity of the issues, and the mobilization of interest groups within and across borders. But international institutions are also plagued by problems of legitimacy and efficacy; their administrative and financial reform is essential and Canada should lead the way. At the same time, it will be important to build public support by showing how these international institutions affect Canada's domestic interests and why Canada cannot resolve global problems on its own.

A fourth dilemma is the continued pressure of the political timetable and agenda on foreign policy. In spite of efforts by the government to focus public attention on the economy and to turn Canadians away from constitutional navel gazing to the outward challenges of the global economy, it was the election of Bill Clinton to the American presidency that set the mood for political change at home. The question "whither Canada?" became "whither Mulroney?" The prime minister's inability to shake off his rock-bottom standing in the polls had pundits and fellow Conservatives whispering that it was time for him to go. On February 24, 1993, Mulroney announced his resignation, fuelling speculation about the outcome of a summer leadership convention and further diverting the attention of Canadians from the outside world.

Political uncertainty at the federal level was compounded by growing uncertainty in Quebec about the future of the Liberal government and its premier, whose renewed health problems increasingly appeared to be life-threatening. The prospect of a Quebec election in 1994 which might bring to power a separatist government has revived Canada's constitutional malaise in a different forum. These uncertainties, dictated by electoral timetables, have diverted attention from the economy and the deficit and led to a paralysis in all areas of policymaking.

Canadian Foreign Policy: the Constitution and the Economy

Canada spent most of 1992 navel gazing, as it debated amendments to the constitution which ended up with the Charlottetown Accord in July and were rejected in a country-wide October referendum. While no one, except supporters of the Parti Québécois, wants to renew discussion of these issues, a time bomb is ticking that could set off a chain reaction, following a federal election in 1993 and a subsequent election in the province of Quebec. Fanny and Michel Demers discuss alternative outcomes for Canada as well as Quebec and the rest of Canada, and link these to Canada's international economic relations. They raise troubling questions for Canadian foreign policy about the problem of the twin deficits and the implications of a further devolution of federal powers, with or without Quebec separation.

How Canada manages its domestic affairs is important to foreign investors, especially when its public and private international indebtedness expressed as a percentage of Gross Domestic Product (GDP) is, at 40.4 percent, the highest of any of the group of seven most industrialized countries (G-7), and its current account deficit as a percentage of GDP is, at 4.5 percent, the worst of the G-7. This means that Canada is currently borrowing from abroad almost 5 percent of its GDP in order to finance its current account deficit and is thereby testing the willingness of foreigners to loan and/or invest in Canada. At some point, their largesse may end, and, as the C.D. Howe Institute and others point out, this may require Canada to borrow from the International Monetary Fund (IMF) and submit to imposed structural adjustment policies for the first time in the country's history. The result would be drastic cuts in education, social services, defence, aid, entitlement programs, and transfers to the provinces. Present fiscal medication would seem like a band-aid in contrast to the drastic and radical surgery that might follow. As Fanny and Michel Demers point out, the consequences for domestic and foreign policy would be profound, if Canada was forced to take medicine similar to that administered to Ireland, Italy and Sweden during their recent financial and currency crises.

In discussing present cuts to government spending programs, critics of cutbacks misread the conditions of the times and hark back to an era when times were better. In the context of Canadian foreign policy, the central challenge is to manage resources and select priorities that are in keeping not only with Canada's national interests but the country's diminished fiscal capacity. To enable Canadians, at the very least, to understand why certain cuts have been made, a vigorous national debate is needed to define priorities which too often have been left to political fashion or to the pruning shears of Treasury Board and the Department of Finance.

Ironically, at the very time when a vigorous public debate on foreign policy is required, the government has withdrawn funding from the Canadian Institute of International Peace and Security (CIIPS) and other think-tanks that provided commentary on foreign and domestic policy at low cost. Geoffrey Pearson and Nancy Gordon describe the demise of CIIPS and evaluate the contribution it made to the discussion of foreign policy. The importance of this topic is not just historical. It raises questions about the viability of government-funded agencies as instruments for critical evaluation of government policies; about the past and future adequacy of universities to perform this task; and about the structure of, and need for, such agencies in the future. One implication of the chapters by Evan Potter and by Pearson and Gordon is that existing foreign policy-making structures are not well equipped to devise policies or provide leadership for dealing with turbulent world events including the widespread recession in industrialized countries.

The G-7 countries ended 1992 with unemployment rates averaging 8.5 percent, ranging from 2.2 percent in Japan to 11.8 percent in Canada. Without Japan the lowest rate was 7.1 percent. Miraculously, Japan never seems to experience high unemployment even when its industrial production shrinks by 6 percent, as it did in 1992. The ability to predict economic change a year hence is limited. Last year the Organization for Economic Cooperation and Development (OECD) predicted GDP growth in 1992 of 3.1 percent for Canada and 2.2 percent for the United States. Actual growth rates were 1.5 percent and 1.7 respectively, and other OECD countries experienced substantially lower growth rates than those forecast a year previously. Next year is supposed to be much better, but that was also the case last year when the estimates for the G-7 countries were an average of 43 percent higher than what was actually realized.

The economic news on the trade front was mixed. The North American Free Trade Agreement (NAFTA) was signed by all three countries in December but remained to be ratified by the respective governments, all of which faced domestic pressures and possible changes in political leadership. The GATT negotiations for the Uruguay Round remained incomplete and uncertainty prevailed, with the possibility of trade wars erupting, particularly over agriculture. Mixed signals continued to come from Washington and the new Clinton Administration about the direction of U.S. trade policy. The inexperience of Mickey Kantor, the new trade representative, and his protectionist-sounding statements also sent jitters through the trading partners of the United States.

Against this background, Michael Hart discusses the new items that are likely to be the subject of future trade negotiations. Whatever the outcome of the present talks, firms will continue to trade across borders with more or less help from governments. The discussion focuses on the restructuring that is taking place within firms which straddle markets as they adjust to sourcing from and selling into foreign markets. The operations of multinational enterprise do not coincide with the boundaries of nation states and therefore weaken the ability of national governments to manage their economies. Decisions made by the governments of the world's largest trading powers, the United States, Japan, and members of the European Community (EC) will continue to make a major impact on the system, while smaller countries will be forced to respond.

The pursuit of international business is now being conducted not just by firms with a traditional hierarchical structure, but by enterprises that create a web of relationships with other firms by way of licensing and flexible contractual arrangements. Lynn Mytelka examines the nature of these strategic alliances and indicates how Canadian firms can enter into such alliances to the benefit of Canada.

Canada and the Environment

The environment has been on the agenda of international conferences since the 1972 Stockholm Conference on the Human Environment. Since then the stakeholders have set out their positions, North versus South, energy producers versus energy consumers, countries and groups with and without forests, fish, and the industries that use these products. The complexity of environmental problems begins with the measurement of the condition of the environment, the rate of change taking place, and the consequences of change. It ends with knowing what to do about it and how to mobilize the political will to act domestically and internationally. The problem is that unborn generations do not have a seat at the bargaining table. Would today's decision-makers act differently if they believed in reincarnation and thought they would be back on Earth a hundred years from now?

The lead-up to the Earth Summit at Rio, its debates and aftermath are examined by David Runnalls, Clyde Sanger, and Nigel Bankes, Terry Fenge and Sarah Kalff. Sanger focuses on the implications for development; Runnalls examines the agreements that were reached; while Fenge looks at environmental co-operation among the circumpolar states in the Arctic. The debate at Rio illustrates the major bargains that have to be struck. Countries such as Canada (and in earlier times those in Western Europe), that have built their economies on the exploitation of renewable resources such as lumber, without doing a particularly good job of renewing them, are now asking developing countries, like Brazil, to save their forests. The response is predictable: to ask for massive financial assistance from the North to assist development that makes less intensive use of natural resources. To this the Northern response is also predictable. In the eyes of the South, as Sanger points out, the environment and development are seen as the environment versus development.

The world is becoming more aware of environmental threats and the trade-offs that are involved. Although the results of Rio fall well short of the organizers' aspirations, and those of many non-governmental organizations which staged their own conference at Rio, several key agreements were signed which address the problems of climate change and biodiversity. Furthermore, the sterile confrontation between North and South, which characterized much of the development debate in the 1970s, gave way to a more positive and co-operative spirit and a breakdown of traditional divisions between industrialized and developing countries. Canada played a leading role at the conference in helping to bridge the gap between North and South and advancing the agenda on key issues like fisheries and biodiversity.

New Challenges

Mark Zacher's chapter provides needed historical perspective for the changed nature of the threats facing mankind at the end of the twentieth century, as distinguished from those of previous eras. Aside from military threats, the greatest hazards to human life in the past were diseases, especially cholera, smallpox, yellow fever, and malaria. In 1918–19, influenza caused over 20 million deaths worldwide, far more than had resulted from the first World War. Many of these diseases have been controlled or virtually eradicated by a combination of public health policies, medicines, testing, international agreements, and improved living standards. In fact, disease as an environmental threat has been reduced since the first World War. Similarly, the threat of global war has diminished with the advent of nuclear weaponry and the end of the Cold War.

Compared to previous generations, citizens of the advanced industrial democracies enjoy relative stability and prosperity. Indeed, one of the sad ironies of modern environmental threats is that, if they were causing deaths in the First World, more direct action would be taken. The onslaught of AIDS could become a modern version of previous lethal diseases. AIDS may generate Malthusian-type disasters in certain parts of the world, such as Africa and those parts of Asia where the sex tourism industry flourishes. Behind these problems is the fact that there are over five billion people on the earth today compared to 2.5 billion in 1950. By 2050 the world's population could double again to an estimated 10–12 billion people. With the bulk of the world's population in developing countries having a disproportionately small share of global GDP, the demands for development, the threat of famine, and the need for disease control, will pressure more people to move from poor to rich areas. Most of the threats discussed in this year's volume can be linked directly or indirectly to population pressures. Michael Shenstone takes a direct look at the problem of immigration and refugees and the attempts by Canada to deal with this situation by the introduction, in 1992, of major amendments to the 1976 Immigration Act. Shenstone examines both the root causes of the problem and the way in which Canada and the international community are approaching solutions.

A renewed role for the United Nations in peacekeeping is a result of ethnic conflict, famines, and the pressures of population. However, the UN is inadequately funded to deal with all the requests made to it and has inadequate authority to enter conflicts as peacemaker. Moreover, national support for the UN and for peacekeeping will dissolve once casualties occur and UN-sponsored troops perform combat roles and missions. Albert Legault discusses the financial constraints facing the UN as the new Secretary-General tries to cope with its peacemaking role. Canada has had extensive experience in peacekeeping on behalf of the UN, and can offer advice and support. The timing is right for the Department of National Defence, which has faced cutbacks in recent years, to reassess its own priorities. An expanded peacekeeping role may boost public support for national defence, although politicians will look for others to help foot the bill.

As for regional aspects of Canadian foreign policy, Canada as a nation of the Pacific and the Atlantic has to develop and manage a policy with respect to these two major regions of the world, which have been and still are the source of most of Canada's immigrants. Frank Langdon and Brian Job examine Canada's trans-Pacific relations, while Andrew Cohen focuses on Canada's role in the North Atlantic Treaty Organization (NATO) and the new Europe.

What portfolio of policies and strategies will address the global risks that Canada confronts in the 1990s? Each author gives recommendations for the specific issues covered in this volume. All agree that trade-offs and choices are better defined now but are no less difficult. From their analysis and recommendations it is clear that Canada will have to handle a number of linkages between trade and environmental policy, immigration and labour policy, fiscal and foreign policy, defence policy and our contribution to international peacemaking. At the same time, accountability and authority in foreign policy decision-making must be restored so that the tough choices can be made in a period of fiscal restraint.

DOWN AND OUT IN
OTTAWA AND CHARLOTTETOWN

2   From Constitutional Debacle to Economic Restructuring

Fanny S. Demers and Michel Demers

Markets open to trade, and minds open to ideas, will become the sole battlefields.

Victor Hugo

IN THE REFERENDUM held on October 26th, 1992, Canadians rejected the Charlottetown Accord, a compromise laboriously negotiated, supported by all eleven first ministers, the native leaders, all three federal political parties and business and labour leaders, and designed to end three years of constitutional uncertainty. In spite of an unprecedented degree of consensus among Canada's elites, the Accord crashed on the rocks of a nation-wide referendum. In recent years, the vain efforts to bring about constitutional reform drained a considerable amount of Canada's energy away from other concerns such as the recession, the budget and current account deficits, the adoption of measures to smooth out the period of structural adjustment following the adoption of the Canada-U.S. Free Trade Agreement (FTA) and, more generally, concerns about Canada's competitiveness in world markets.

No internal problem is devoid of external ramifications in today's global economy. The constitutional debacle had a number of serious international consequences for Canada. Political uncertainty about the status of Canada, together with the existence of numerous opportunities for investors worldwide, reduced Canada's attractiveness for foreign direct investment. Political uncertainty also made financial markets nervous, resulting in a run on the Canadian dollar, first in the spring of 1990 when the ratification of the Meech Lake Accord became doubtful, and more recently, when the "no" forces began to gain ground and establish themselves in the lead in the weeks preceding the October 26th referendum. Evidence of the lack of confidence in Canada by international markets abounds: in August alone, foreigners liquidated $4.7 billion in various Canadian securities including bonds, stocks and money market funds. The capital flight was even larger in September and October. As a result of two months of constitutional debate, the Canadian dollar fell by 3.5 cents relative to the U.S. dollar, lending and borrowing interest rates rose by 2 percent, and the value of Canadian corporations diminished by 5 percent. Investment and consumer spending were adversely affected by the higher interest rates and by a loss of confidence. As a result, the recovery was substantially delayed.[1]

Since early 1993, we have finally witnessed a shift of attention from the constitutional debacle to economic restructuring, with the debate over the North American Free Trade Agreement (NAFTA) and the implications of the Clinton administration's economic policy agenda for Canada. In this chapter, we explore the economic challenges facing Canada and ask whether Canada will be able to confront these challenges effectively. An affirmative answer ultimately rests on strong political leadership and national unity. Although Canada's ability to perform and survive in the next century is in jeopardy, this paper suggests a number of alternatives which could avert outright disaster.

Economic Challenges in the Aftermath of Charlottetown

The new international order is characterized by an unprecedented degree of economic interdependence. The last decade witnessed both a strengthening of existing regional initiatives towards trade liberalization (in the context of the European Community and the European Economic Area) and the formation of new free trade areas, such as the FTA and the more recent NAFTA which includes Mexico. The wave of regional trade liberalization initiatives culminated in the "Enterprise of the Americas" project proposed by the Bush administration. This project was intended to eventually encompass all countries of the Western hemisphere in a free trade agreement, and, in fact, negotiations have been initiated with Chile.

The NAFTA was signed in October 1992. According to Hufbauer and Schott, it should expand Canada's trade with Mexico by 30 percent by 1995. Although some have expressed concerns about labour adjustment due to the difference in per capita incomes between Mexico and its two partners, the NAFTA, like the

FTA before, could help Canadian firms compete more effectively against foreign firms in North America and in world markets. Under the NAFTA, Canadian and American firms will be allowed to compete for government procurement of major Mexican state enterprises such as the Mexican state oil company (PEMEX), the Federal Electricity Commission (CFE), and the National Railways of Mexico (Ferronales), as well as for other government purchases. In particular, the opening of the Mexican market for financial and telecommunication services will be especially attractive to Canadian firms specializing in these niche markets. To meet this new challenge, however, Canadian firms will need a well-trained labour force.

For Canada, as for other industrialized countries, competitive advantage lies in industries with relatively high technological content which require a highly skilled labour force. Human resources and the capacity to innovate are recognized as the key determinants of a competitive economy. In addition, financial stability, as well as free access to markets, is also essential to competitiveness. But Canada faces a threat under both these heads. First, the government's failure to adequately control the budget deficit and the current account deficit has put Canada's financial stability in greater danger than is widely recognized. Second, the Clinton Administration's protectionist tendencies may pose a threat to Canadian export industries as well as to Canada-U.S. trade relations. The recent shift in U.S. trade policy is not only endangering the realization of the Enterprise of the Americas project and the successful completion of the Uruguay Round of the General Agreement on Tariffs and Trade (GATT), but is also casting doubt on the smooth functioning of the FTA and the ratification of the NAFTA.

The Prosperity Initiative and Competitiveness

Regional and multilateral initiatives toward freer trade are generating ever-increasing cross-country trade and economic linkages which are forcing countries into a race for the competitive edge. Improving competitiveness has become an overriding economic concern for all governments of the Western world.

With the advent of freer trade and the increased international flow of goods and services, the labour force of each country is in direct competition with that of others. In addition, some declining sectors have shrunk further, leading to economic dislocations in the form of business bankruptcies and higher unemployment. These problems have been accentuated by the recession. Quite apart from international pressures, the fast pace of technological change is forcing firms, even in more traditional sectors, to restructure and innovate, thereby increasing their demand for skilled workers. Rapid technological change also implies that workers' skills become obsolete at a much faster rate, thereby requiring frequent retraining to maintain their employment potential.

As pointed out by Alexis Jacquemin,

> Technology is one of the most decisive factors for industrial competitiveness in the 1990s. . . . Because of their wide-ranging contribution to the increased productivity potential of all factors of production — from labour, capital, materials and energy to inventory stock control, organization and management, quality control and marketing — new technologies are the main determinant of industrial competitiveness. This fact explains why all sectors, regardless of product or service produced, are faced with the task of mastering state-of-the-art technology.[2]

Bill Clinton won the presidency of the United States on a mandate of "change". The message of the American people indicated support for structural adjustment programs such as training programs for dislocated workers, a rethought and redesigned educational system better suited to current needs, better infrastructure and more advanced telecommunications networks, and an "industrial policy" aimed at promoting those industries that are deemed to be capable of successfully competing in international markets. Similar concerns are being voiced in Canada as well as in the European Community.

In an economy open to international commerce such as Canada's, where exports amount to 26 percent of gross domestic product (GDP) — the second highest ratio in the group of the seven most industrialized countries (G-7), after Germany — maintaining a high standard of living requires the ability to compete in international markets. In addition, Canada's prestige as a member of the G-7 and as an influential participant in the shaping of economic and security decisions at the international level — an example of which is its active role in the peacekeeping missions of the United Nations — also rests on its ability to maintain a growing and competitive economy.

In the past nine years, the federal government has embarked on a comprehensive package of structural reforms, the first phase of the so-called "Competitiveness Agenda". It includes the FTA and NAFTA, the general sales tax (GST) and tax reform, privatization and deregulation, fiscal restraint and the pursuit of price stability.[3] All of these policies were designed to make the Canadian economy more competitive, that is, to improve its ability to produce goods and services more efficiently than its trading partners.

Under the "Prosperity Initiative," the Canadian government launched a broad popular consultation, marking the second phase of its competitiveness agenda. The report of the McCamus-Drouin committee, "Inventing our Future: An Action Plan for Canada's Prosperity," released shortly after the October 26th referendum, called for co-operation by government, the private sector and the public to improve Canada's performance in the areas of training, education and innovation. In addition to formulating specific recommendations for the federal and provincial governments and business, the report urged joint federal-provincial initiatives to eliminate interprovincial trade barriers, co-ordinate technical and financial support programs for private firms, and reform social security programs, such as unemployment insurance, so as to eliminate work disincentives. Furthermore, since high budget deficits have a detrimental impact on the rate of investment and thereby reduce the growth potential and consequently the competitiveness of an economy, it also called for federal-provincial action to reduce budget deficits and achieve spending cuts.

The Twin Deficits

The downgrading by Standard and Poor's of a small percentage of Canada's external debt in October 1992 was a warning signal that Canada's high budget and current account deficits, as well as its total debt, have to be brought under control. The combined federal and provincial debt has reached $665 billion or 96 percent of GDP, while the foreign debt amounts to $300 billion. Total federal and provincial deficits amount to $58 billion or 8.4 percent of GDP while the current account deficit is $30 billion and Canada's external interest service ratio is tending toward that of highly indebted countries such as Brazil and Mexico. On both the debt-to-GDP ratio and the deficit-to-GDP ratio, Canada fails the Maastricht test for membership in the European Monetary Union (EMU), which requires ratios of at most 60 and 3 percent of GDP, respectively. These norms are fast becoming the international community's implicit acid test for sound financial performance. Canada has joined the club of highly indebted nations in the company of Belgium, Italy, Ireland and Greece. However, unlike Canada, these countries do not rely as heavily on the international financing of their debt. In fact, Ireland and Belgium run current account surpluses!

Furthermore, high interest rates, resulting in part from the political risk premia imposed on Canadian debt, have contributed to raising the interest payments on debt, thus swelling both the government deficit and the Canadian current account deficit. As a result of the dynamics of interest compounding, the accumulation of the debt has acquired a momentum that will be difficult to break. In spite of forecasts of low inflation and real growth of 4 percent, the current term structure of the debt imposes a severe constraint on the government. Even though interest rates have fallen somewhat, debt-financing costs have not been substantially affected because 50 percent of the government's financial liabilities are in fixed-term assets with interest rates as high as 9 to 10 percent. Such a state of affairs could strongly tempt a future federal government to seek a monetization of the debt by raising the inflation rate, with harmful consequences for Canada's credibility in financial markets and for the long-run performance of the economy. As Ed Neufeld puts it, when you ask foreign investors "why, despite everything, [do you] still buy Canadian bonds, many say: 'We like Canadian monetary policy. We have confidence in your currency' . . . If confidence were to go, you'd face a totally different attitude from foreign investors toward Canadian debt."[4]

Since a large part of Canadian debt is held by foreigners, the confidence of international investors is of paramount importance.[5] Yet, as demonstrated by the currency crises in European markets since September 1992, investor confidence is difficult to maintain. Uncertainty about the provinces' financial management capabilities, apprehension about the magnitude of the current account deficit and the results of upcoming federal and provincial elections could have grave consequences for Canada. Given the great fluidity of financial capital, the confidence of domestic investors in

Canada is also crucial. Elections in Quebec, or bad news with respect to the budget deficit in Ontario or in Ottawa, could provoke a major financial crisis, necessitating deep financial adjustments.

There are obvious parallels between Canada's situation and those of Italy, Sweden and Ireland, which have all faced recent financial and currency crises. Italy and Sweden had to commit themselves to cutting their deficit-to-GDP ratios in half which has led to drastic budget cuts with dire social implications. The high Canadian deficit and debt-to-GDP ratio point to the urgent necessity of pursuing a policy of "fiscal prudence" now, if Canada is to avoid such draconian measures in the future.[6]

The efforts toward deficit reduction have, so far, sought to accommodate Canadians' desire for a Swedish-style welfare state. The depth and unexpected duration of the recession, accompanied by unexpectedly high unemployment insurance payments and unexpectedly low personal and corporate income tax revenues, have further thwarted the government's efforts to reduce the deficit. Nevertheless, the operating balance of the federal government has shown a small surplus for the past few years. In fact, the operating budget shows a small surplus of 1 percent for the 1992–93 fiscal year while the trade balance is in surplus, so that the so-called "twin-deficits" are largely a consequence of federal interest payments on the debt and of the provinces' operating deficit amounting to 3 percent of GDP. In view of the already high taxation levels in Canada (the ratio of taxes to GDP is approximately 8 percent higher than in the U.S.), it will be difficult if not impossible to raise taxes further without impairing the competitiveness of Canadian firms and the productivity of the work force. Consequently, cutting spending is the only way to attack the twin deficit problem effectively. To this end, the federal and provincial governments will have to collaborate. The required measures would range from greater reliance on user fees — to control health care costs — to more efficient approaches to regional development, and would include reductions in personal and intergovernmental transfers. Effecting substantial spending cuts, however, is a politically sensitive issue, requiring a broad national consensus that is not easy to achieve, due to the influence of special interests in the Canadian political process. With appropriate leadership it may be possible to sensitize Canadians to the urgency of adopting the reforms that are needed to avoid the kind of situation Sweden and Italy have faced.

U.S. Protectionism

Another challenge for Canada is to maintain secure access to the U.S. market in spite of mounting U.S. protectionism. The U.S. is currently undergoing a period of industrial restructuring. Congress is under pressure from both industry and labor to impose protectionist measures, several of which are targeted at Canadian industries. The severity and length of the current recession, as well as the election of a Democratic President, may reinforce this tendency. The new Clinton administration has raised the spectre of protectionism. Laura Tyson, head of the Council of Economic Advisors, is a long-time advocate of industrial policies, and Mickey Kantor, the U.S. Trade Representative, is relatively inexperienced in matters of trade policy. The future direction of U.S. trade policy is anyone's guess.

To the extent that the Clinton Administration is able to control the U.S. budget deficit, while offering more education and training programs and reforming health care in fulfilment of the Democrats' policy platform, it may be able to keep in check protectionist forces lobbying Congress and the executive branch. If it fails in this endeavour, Canada could become the target of more extensive attacks by U.S. protectionist lobbies.

An added concern is the future of U.S.-Japan and U.S.-EC trade relations. The recession that started in Canada and the U.S. in 1990 is now affecting Europe and Japan. As the U.S. economy starts to recover, its trade deficit with Japan and Europe will increase while Japan, hit by the recession, is experiencing a rising trade surplus with the U.S. This could easily foster a new wave of Japan-bashing, with Canada being hurt in the crossfire. Recently, the three U.S. automakers announced that, contrary to their initial intention, they had decided against filing a complaint of unfair trading against their Japanese counterparts. The reason they gave for this change of heart is that President Clinton intends to address the imbalance in trade flows between the U.S. and Japan.[7] Although the anti-dumping suit was in fact never filed, the Japanese are likely to alter their behaviour and exercise voluntary export restraint for fear that American automakers may change their mind again in the future. Furthermore, the move by the U.S. government to ban its purchase of products made in the European Community (EC) in the areas of telecommunications, water, energy and transportation, in retaliation for the EC's local content rules, could have repercussions on Canadian firms in these sectors if the EC in its turn retaliates.[8]

Recent months have seen several instances of U.S. protectionism directed at Canada. In November 1992, the U.S. imposed countervailing duties of up to 59 percent on steel imports from twelve countries including Canada, arguing that steel production was being subsidized in these countries; this was followed by the imposition in January 1993, of temporary anti-dumping tariffs of up to 109 percent on steel products from nineteen countries including Canada. Also in January 1993, a second extraordinary challenge was mounted by the U.S. in the pork case, where the binational panel's authority in ruling on the magnitude of the countervailing duties was questioned. In a recent case involving Canadian exports of durum wheat, the Canadian industry was accused by the U.S. agricultural lobby of selling below acquisition cost. The binational panel supported the Canadian view with respect to the calculation of costs, though it refused to rule before knowing the results of an independent audit of the Canadian Wheat Board's pricing behaviour. The panel's favourable stance towards the Canadian position drew the ire of several U.S. senators, notably Senator Kent Conrad of North Dakota, who argued the FTA was "no free-trade agreement at all ... [T]here are enough loopholes in this agreement to drive hundreds of Canadian grain trucks through," and Senator Max Baucus of Montana, vociferous opponent of the Canadian lumber industry, who asserted that Canada's grain-trade cheating would even "put Japan to shame."[9]

A united Canada has more weight in settling its trade disputes with the United States than one which is fragmented. The size and strength of the Canadian economy exerts an important influence on international trade negotiations, as well as on the management of international economic relations with our other trading partners, including the Uruguay Round of the GATT negotiations.

In the Canada-U.S. FTA, Canada was able to win exemptions for the cultural industries, import quotas for supply-managed farm sectors, and yet had to accept very few obligations regarding foreign investment regulation. Canada obtained a binational panel review mechanism which has overturned a number of decisions by the U.S. International Trade Administration and International Trade Commission, without imposing any restrictions on Canadian domestic subsidies. Other important elements of federal industrial policy, such as the Autopact, and a broad range of provincial policies, such as provincial procurement policies, were left intact under the FTA. The tariff-rate-quotas negotiated in the FTA and NAFTA, combined with drawback provisions, are providing, and will continue to provide, significant benefits to the textile and apparel industry. Clearly, a fragmented Canada would not be able to defend so forcefully its vital interests in trade negotiations.

Can Canada Cope? The Dilemmas of Weakened Political Leadership and National Disunity

In recent years, structural policy changes as well as changes in international trade relations have altered the shielded environment to which Canadians had grown accustomed, requiring substantial adjustments on the part of Canadian firms and workers. Canadians have been left with a sense of insecurity and a fear of change, which has created a propitious environment for the proliferation of interest groups which, through the media, can influence public opinion. The cacophonous and often strident demands of conflicting interest groups have paralyzed the political decision-making process and thwarted the exercise of leadership by political elites.

The Conservative government is highly unpopular and a replacement for departing Prime Minister Brian Mulroney has yet to be chosen. Jean Chrétien and Audrey McLaughlin do not so far appear capable of quenching the electorate's thirst for change, as Bill Clinton has done south of the border. The Conservatives may have difficulty finding a leader who can hold together the coalition of Quebec nationalists and Westerners which has been their key to victory in the past two elections. It is also unclear whether a successor to Prime Minister Mulroney will adhere to past policies. The degree of uncertainty will be even greater if the Liberals are elected. Will Canada ask for the renegotiation of the NAFTA? Will the GST be dropped in favour of another tax that could harm the export sector? Will the Liberals' economic policy orientation be dominated by protectionists or by the free trade and open market policies favoured by some Liberals such as Roy MacLaren and

Paul Martin? Will the next federal government be a captive of interest groups, yield to their pressures to increase spending, and thus abandon any attempt at deficit control? Splinter groups such as the Reform Party and the Bloc Québécois will feed on public discontent and may benefit from the current uncertainty and political vacuum. In such a climate of uncertainty there may be little political will to tackle Canada's profound fiscal and deficit problems.

Threats to National Unity

The prospects for resolving the constitutional deadlock that Canadians face in the aftermath of the referendum on the Charlottetown Accord also look grim. Jacques Parizeau, leader of the Parti Québécois, which is currently ahead in the opinion polls in Quebec, predicted that the post-election House of Commons would look like a "real Italian parliament," with five parties represented but none of them strong enough to form a majority government. "We'll be faced with the weakest federal government ever, just months before a Quebec election. It will be an extraordinary opportunity and we musn't let it slip away . . . We will achieve independence by June 24th 1995."[10]

The Bourassa government has been losing steam after two mandates, the recession, and several scandals involving Bourassa's credibility as an able defender of Quebec interests. Nevertheless, the high support (43 percent) garnered by the Charlottetown Accord in spite of these setbacks reveals the importance of Mr. Bourassa's role in defending federalism. The void in federalist political leadership in Quebec, following the unexpected resurgence of Premier Robert Bourassa's illness, and his likely departure from the political scene, has made the national unity issue resurface after the demise of the Charlottetown Accord. These unfortunate circumstances in Quebec, together with the upcoming federal elections, do not bode well for the preservation of national unity and for the confidence of international financial markets. The search for Bourassa's successor will be a key in shaping the political landscape. The pro-Allaire sovereignist forces will surely attempt to influence the outcome, and if unsuccessful, could try to form a splinter group promoting Allaire's model of "wimpish sovereignty," and thus take votes away from the Quebec Liberal Party.[11]

Should the Parti Québécois win the next provincial election, a referendum on sovereignty is sure to follow, putting Quebeckers between the Scylla of sovereignty and the Charybdis of a refusal of sovereignty which would leave them with little credibility in the process of bargaining with the rest of Canada. This dilemma may well force a majority of Quebeckers (even those who are not hard core separatists) to vote in favour of independence.

But even if the political disintegration of Canada never takes place, the mere possibility that it could might prompt financial markets to raise the premium on federal and provincial government debt as well as on the debt of Canadian private and public enterprises. In the next section we examine the implications of a break-up. We then discuss possible strategies that might enable Canada to survive in the twenty-first century.

Implications of Political Fragmentation

Quebec and the rest of Canada jointly own a common federal debt of $450 billion and assets of unknown value.[12] The sharing of the debt and assets and the method of transferring Quebec's share remain difficult and controversial questions. Several methods have been suggested. The secretariat of the Bélanger-Campeau Commission established Quebec's share of the federal debt on the basis of the percentage of federal revenues collected in Quebec in recent years, that is, 22 percent. After making a number of adjustments (for instance, assets and pension funds), the secretariat concluded that Quebec should only accept 16.6 percent of the federal debt. Another method would allocate the debt burden according to the historical benefits derived by each province and would attribute 32 percent of the debt to Quebec. The gap between these two methods is $62 billion, or $9,000 per citizen of Quebec. Other criteria, such as the share of Quebec's population or gross domestic product would attribute 25.4 percent and 23.2 percent of the debt respectively to Quebec. It is certain that any negotiations on how to share the federal debt and assets would be acrimonious and cause shock waves in international financial markets.

Without a political union and fiscal transfers it would be impossible to maintain a monetary union between an independent

Quebec and the rest of Canada. The break-up of Czechoslovakia is a good example. Although the Czech and Slovak republics initially agreed to maintain a monetary union for a six month period, that is, until July 1993, cracks began to appear in January. In the acrimonious debates following the separation of Quebec, the odds might well be against monetary union with the rest of Canada. What would Quebec's options be then? Pierre-Paul Proulx argues that a consensus exists in Quebec according to which Quebec would relinquish any margin of manoeuvre in monetary policy (as limited as it might be), and adopt a Quebec "*piastre*" pegged to the Canadian or U.S. dollar or both.[13] Would a fixed exchange rate suffice to prevent speculation against the Quebec "*piastre*"?

Could one convince financial markets of the credibility and strength of this new currency which would not have the reputation of other currencies like the Canadian and U.S. dollars? It is well documented that as soon as financial markets doubt the credibility of an exchange rate, this lack of confidence creates uncontrollable speculative attacks. For example, during the recent French referendum on the Maastricht Treaty, the Bundesbank alone spent U.S. $39 billion and the four largest European central banks together spent U.S. $100 billion in order to defend the exchange rates in the European Monetary System (EMS). These efforts were in vain since Britain was forced to withdraw the pound from the EMS in spite of a rise of more than five percent in its interest rates. Italy withdrew the lira temporarily from the EMS and was forced to undertake severe cuts in its social programs in order to control its budget deficit. Spain devalued its currency by 5 percent, while Ireland has had to devalue its currency by 10 percent. The EMS has been under continuous strain due to the delays in the ratification of the Maastricht Treaty. The very fate of the Treaty is uncertain in the face of mounting opposition in Britain, thus putting in doubt the realization of the EMU and further impairing the stability of the EMS.

All of these events in Europe indicate that any attempt to peg the "*piastre* québécoise," while facing the numerous shocks which are bound to hit the Quebec economy in its accession to independence, would be difficult if not impossible to sustain. An independent Quebec would have neither an independent monetary policy nor a credible currency.

The Canadian dollar would not be immune from this turmoil. It too would be the currency of a new country backed by a lower GDP (75 percent of the previous one). The Canadian dollar would be seriously weakened by the high budget and current account deficits and by acrimonious discussions over how to divide the federal debt and assets and over monetary union. Indeed, the move toward political disintegration could trigger a financial crisis forcing deep budget cuts both in Quebec and in the rest of Canada.

While Canadian monetary union would clearly be in jeopardy in the event of political disintegration, equally problematic would be the preservation of the economic union between Quebec and the rest of Canada, at least in its current form. The tariff equivalents of the current Canadian quotas on milk and cheese reach up to 300 percent. In addition, Quebec presently holds 48 percent of the Canadian quota for industrial milk. If Quebec became independent, why would Ontario purchase its dairy products from Quebec at double the U.S. price? Other sectors of the Quebec economy such as textiles and apparel are also protected by high tariffs and by quotas imposed under the Multi-Fiber Arrangements (MFA) which, as a whole, grant a level of protection ranging between 50 and 70 percent. The rest of Canada would not have any interest in maintaining this high level of protection for Quebec exports towards the rest of Canada after independence.

It therefore seems likely that the Canadian customs union and common market would not stand following the break-up of the Canadian political union. At best, there might be a free trade area between Quebec and the rest of Canada, including rules of origin on products and border controls, a multiplicity of countervailing duties and anti-dumping actions. It is precisely these obstacles to the free movement of goods and services that the European Community seeks to eliminate with the completion of the single market. The breakdown of the Canadian economic union would seriously hamper the competitiveness of the many firms that rely heavily on the Canadian market.

Not only would the Canadian economic union be imperilled, but Quebec's participation and that of the rest of Canada in the FTA and the NAFTA would be thrown into question. A study prepared by Ivan Bernier for the Bélanger-Campeau Commission recognized the necessity of renegotiating the FTA if Quebec became independent. A recent report of the United States International

Trade Commission (ITC) in Washington confirmed that Quebec would need to obtain the approval of Congress before joining the FTA and NAFTA. According to the ITC, Quebec is currently protected from "the full rigours of the FTA" which is only directed at the federal government and not at sub-national governments. For example, the public purchases of Hydro-Quebec are exempted from the FTA and NAFTA, whereas, in order to join NAFTA, Mexico had to allow Canadians and Americans to compete with Mexican firms for procurement by PEMEX, Mexico's petroleum firm, as well as by other firms in the energy sector. It is therefore certain that Quebec would no longer benefit from the protection it currently enjoys if it were to become independent and the conditions of its admission to the FTA and NAFTA had to be negotiated. All of Quebec's policies would be scrutinized: procurement, subsidies, industrial policy in general, the operations of the Caisse de Dépôt, the management and tarification of its natural resources, as well as its environmental policies. Furthermore, the U.S. government might force Quebec and the rest of Canada to reach an agreement on the sharing of the debt and assets as a precondition for Quebec's accession to NAFTA.

Canada succeeded in obtaining a range of exemptions from the NAFTA because it could credibly threaten to withdraw from negotiations in the event that the NAFTA compromised advantages obtained under the FTA. An independent Quebec would suffer from a major disadvantage. It would not have any plausible fall-back position. Since it would be obliged to accept the conditions dictated by the U.S., Americans would seek to extract numerous new concessions. This tendency might be strengthened by a Democratic administration, prone to yield to protectionist pressures. Finally, whereas during the Cold War the U.S. might have been more conciliatory towards Quebec due to national security interests, this constraint has disappeared with the collapse of the Soviet Union.

Any new concessions Quebec would have to make in order to join the FTA and NAFTA would undoubtedly provoke domestic opposition from those groups hurt by them. This would further delay Quebec's full participation in the North American free trade zone. The disintegration of Canada might also lead to calls in the U.S. Congress for repeal of the grandfather safeguards in the Auto Pact, to remove the exemption of the cultural industries, and even to renegotiate the FTA. This situation would fuel the already strong opposition to free trade in Canada and jeopardize the rest of Canada's participation in the FTA and NAFTA.

In conclusion, in the disintegration-of-Canada scenario, both Quebec and the rest of Canada would face severe economic trauma with several shocks occurring simultaneously: a collapse of the Canadian monetary union and of the Canadian common market and customs union; higher risk premia on debt due to low investor confidence, which would require severe budgetary retrenchment; bitter debates over the sharing of the federal debt between Quebec and the rest of Canada; and a renegotiation of the FTA and the NAFTA.

In the meantime, what would happen to the competitiveness of the Canadian economy? Where would foreign and Canadian investors locate if not in Mexico, where they would enjoy guaranteed access to the U.S. market and adequate political stability?

Canadian Strategies

What initiatives should the current, or a future, federal government pursue in order to address Canada's economic challenges and, at the same time, reverse the dangerous trend towards political fragmentation? The Charlottetown Accord sought to achieve a modest devolution of powers designed to eliminate costly duplication of government services and increase administrative efficiency; to circumscribe federal spending power in areas of provincial jurisdiction; to designate training as a provincial responsibility; to sign and constitutionalize intergovernmental agreements in regional development and telecommunications; and to improve the functioning of the economic union. Many of these measures would have had a beneficial impact on Canada's competitiveness. Even though the Accord has failed, policymakers still have the option of using extra-constitutional means of achieving some of the objectives pursued by constitutional reform, namely, more efficient government, better policy co-ordination across different levels of government and a strengthening of the Canadian economic union.

Administrative Arrangements

In the past, many innovative policies did not arise from constitutional amendments but from administrative arrangements. For example, federal-provincial co-operation has allowed Quebec to obtain fiscal compensation in return for setting up its own hospitalization program, or to have its own approach to the management of public pension funds, which has led to the creation of the *Caisse de Dépôt et Placement* designed to promote the economic development of Quebec. Such an approach underlies the Cullen-Couture agreement on immigration, which gives a greater say to Quebec in the selection of immigrants.

The federal government could similarly negotiate administrative arrangements allowing a greater role for provinces in training, thus enabling them to develop a comprehensive approach to human resource development through the integration of training with education. Such a move is necessary, given the new world trend towards a knowledge-based economy. Empirical studies indicate that human capital endowment and a highly-skilled labour force are some of the key determinants of faster growth.

Regional development is another area where better federal-provincial co-ordination would be fruitful. While federal involvement is usually necessary in large-scale regional development projects because of financing requirements or the resulting externalities, in many other cases a provincial or local government can devise programs that are better suited to provincial or local needs.

Another area in which federal-provincial co-ordination will be of crucial importance is in the control of the twin deficits. As was mentioned above, provincial budgets, which have traditionally shown a surplus in the past, are now an important element in the country's deficit, amounting to almost 3 percent of GDP. Controlling the deficit and the debt, and averting the danger of a financial crisis, will be impossible without policy co-ordination between different levels of government.

A Stronger Canadian Economic Union

Canada should adopt policies to enhance the functioning of a "single Canadian market" in a way that is consistent with the spirit of Canadian federalism.[14] There are three important objectives that must be pursued: elimination of interprovincial discrimination, promotion of provincial policy harmonization, and securing effective provincial participation in international agreements.

There currently exist a number of discriminatory practices that impede the functioning of the Canadian common market. One obvious example is procurement practices at both the federal and provincial levels, where local suppliers are often favoured. Any out-of-province bid for public procurement may be either rejected outright, or in-province and local bids may be favoured by a ten percent preference margin. In addition, federal procurement practices sometimes restrict bids by region.

Beyond initiatives to remove explicitly discriminatory measures, there is also a need to develop better ways of implementing common standards among provinces and of harmonizing policies in several areas. For instance, product and environmental standards, financial services regulations, professional standards and occupational licensing should be harmonized across provinces. As a result of the current lack of harmonization, interprovincial labour mobility is hindered even when there exist mutually beneficial opportunities. A qualified unemployed auto mechanic or electrician trained and licensed in one province may not be allowed to fill a vacancy in another province without pursuing a complete retraining and recertification program. Furthermore, firms operating across different provinces are obliged to satisfy different sets of provincial regulations, as, for example, in the case of the environment, which is a joint federal-provincial jurisdiction. This lack of harmonization leads to inefficiencies and limits the competitiveness of Canadian firms by preventing them from taking full advantage of economies-of-scale.

The need is not so much for adopting uniform standards — which seems to be recommended by the Prosperity Initiative Report — as for innovative mechanisms based on mutual recognition, as in the EC. Under the principle of mutual recognition, the regulations and standards adopted by one member state have to be recognized by all other member states of the EC. By encouraging the search for the most efficient policy, such an approach would be more conducive to policy innovation and to competitiveness.[15]

Canada's credibility in international trade agreements depends on its ability to implement these agreements. More effective provincial participation in international agreements could be offered as a *quid pro quo* for greater provincial co-operation in treaty implementation. As the recent GATT disputes over wine and beer illustrate, the federal government is already subject to international obligations with respect to provincial policies, but has no constitutional authority to enforce international agreements. It took threats of trade retaliation by the European Community and the United States to begin a breakdown of long-standing interprovincial barriers to trade in wine and beer. Indeed, GATT or FTA panels appear to be the only effective mechanism for limiting discriminatory provincial trade barriers. This question will become more important as international agreements begin to deal more with services, investment and environmental issues.

Strategic Alliances

In January 1992, in a joint effort, the federal and Ontario governments rescued the commuter aircraft manufacturer De Havilland, a subsidiary of Boeing, which was in financial difficulty. The aerospace industry accounts for one-fifth of all research and development (R & D) conducted in Canada. As indicated by federal Industry Minister Michael Wilson, the government assistance was given "in recognition of the strategic importance of the industry." By providing a combined $540 million in subsidies ($240 million by the federal and $300 million by the provincial government), the two governments permitted Bombardier, a Quebec aerospace and transportation firm, to acquire a controlling interest in De Havilland. The government of Ontario invested an additional $49 million to acquire 49 percent of the firm's equity. As argued by De Wilde, temporary government assistance to the highly successful and internationally competitive Bombardier operating in specialized niche markets may be a fruitful way of improving Canada's competitiveness by capitalizing on Canada's comparative advantage.[16] It may also be an important way to strengthen national unity by fostering interprovincial relationships. The proposed fast train between Windsor and Quebec City provides another opportunity for strengthening interprovincial infrastructure and national unity.

Conclusion

Canada faces many challenges in the years ahead, not the least of which is that of positioning itself in the race for competitiveness. Canada's prestige as a member of the G-7 countries, and as an influential participant in economic and security decisions at the international level, depends on its ability to sustain a growing and competitive economy. Achieving a better competitive position is itself dependent on resolving the national unity issue and maintaining the integrity of the Canadian economic union. This chapter has proposed some extra-constitutional means of strengthening national unity while promoting the competitiveness of the Canadian economy. Federal-provincial co-operation will also be necessary to attack another fundamental challenge, the twin deficits. Finally, preserving national unity is also a key to handling Canada's second fundamental challenge, countering U.S. protectionism in order to secure access to the American market. Whether or not Canada can extricate itself from its crippling constitutional dyspepsia and confront its fundamental challenges at the dawn of the next millennium, will depend to a critical extent on strong political leadership and on the ability to take a pragmatic approach to achieving desired goals.

3

A Question of Relevance: Canada's Foreign Policy and Foreign Service in the 1990s

Evan Potter[1]

Barring any significant adaptation of the Department, the Canadian foreign service will not serve as an effective instrument of Canada's national interests.

THE POST-COLD WAR ERA marks a profound shift in international relations. The collapse of the Soviet Union, the rise of ethnic conflicts and the use of military intervention for humanitarian aims present new challenges that will require a fundamental rethinking about the way in which Canadian foreign policy is co-ordinated both at the domestic and international levels. The old question as to how Canada could play a mediating role between the Cold War powers—the United States and the former Soviet Union—has given way to a new one: How can Canada best respond to a world in which nations are simultaneously fragmenting ethnically and politically while consolidating economically? That is, how best to define Canadian interests in a world which a *New York Times* writer recently epitomized as one in which "ethnic-cleansing" zones and free trade zones exist side by side?

This "paradigm shift" and the continuing communications revolution have tended more and more to limit the purview of traditional diplomacy. One of the most telling signs of this new age of diplomacy has been the localization of "high" and "low" politics, that is, political/security and trade issues, at the executive level—the White House, the Prime Minister's Office (PMO), or the Chancellery. This has come about as a result of the increasingly policy-oriented discussions among national leaders in bilateral, regional and multilateral security and economic fora. At the same time, the diffusion of foreign policy interests has created a situation in which the key issues of finance, overseas development assistance, fisheries, and the environment, to name a few, are being managed by expert line departments. In an environment where a premium is put on the quick formulation and articulation of policies, it is not altogether surprising that embassies are increasingly bypassed in the communications loop. As one senior External Affairs official has confided: "foreign offices have become post offices where only the form, rather than the function, of foreign policy survives."

In this new era of diplomacy a number of important questions have been raised in framing the debate about Canada's role and the relevance of the Canadian foreign service. Most prominent is the question of whether the Department of External Affairs and International Trade Canada (hereafter referred to as either DEAITC or the Department) has the right tools to perform the tasks required of it in this new, demanding environment of centralized decision-making and more rapid policy formulation. Some of the ancillary questions posed in this paper concern the relevance of the Department in the conduct of government business. Should DEAITC continue to bleed away its functions to other government departments or should it maintain its own specialists? How relevant are Canada's missions to current international issues? The chapter concludes that barring any significant adaptation of the Department, the Canadian Foreign Service in the coming years will not serve as an effective instrument of Canada's national interests.

The Environment of Canadian Foreign Policymaking

The international environment within which Canada is operating is steadily becoming more complex and demanding. It has a number of dimensions. First, interstate relations are based more on economic rivalry than ideological or military competition. Second, the interdependence of international issues has contributed to a merging of external and internal policies, and to more complex relationships between bilateral and multilateral objectives and priorities. Third, the proliferation of states in recent years and the need for speedy reactions to international events has multiplied the number of diplomatic activities and therewith the number of diplomatic problems for Canada. Finally, the convergence of "high" and "low" policy means that politicization of economic/trade issues will increase.

At the same time, the domestic environment in which DEAITC has to exercise its mandate has become more complicated. Other federal government departments are making strong representations of their interests as part of Canada's foreign policy agenda, and there is pressure from each province to extend its domestic interests. Meanwhile, native groups, ethnic organizations, and other special interest groups are presenting themselves in the international arena to pursue their own objectives.

At the bureaucratic level, the declining influence of DEAITC is routinely documented and charted by the print and electronic media, but some of the harshest and perhaps most constructive criticism about the Department and the management of Canada's foreign policy comes from within. It can be found in *bout de papier*, the quarterly magazine of Canada's diplomatic service, published by the Professional Association of Foreign Service Officers (PAFSO), the union representing non-managerial rotational members of the foreign service. Most of the criticism, both internal and external, is long-standing and structural, and therefore pertains not only recent Canadian foreign policymaking. Before we examine more closely the impact of the domestic and bureaucratic environments on the foreign service, some of the major Canadian foreign policy objectives over the past year will be reviewed.

The "New Internationalism"

Under the rubric of the "new internationalism," External Affairs Minister Barbara McDougall has sought to recalibrate Canada's foreign policy approach to the post-Cold War environment.[2] Underpinning this term is the notion that the nation-state is not what it once was. As a result of the irreversible erosion of national sovereignty in recent decades — through economic globalization and the telecommunications revolution — familiar subjects on the foreign policy agenda, such as military security and trade practices, have had to make room for new ones such as respect for human rights, good governance, and the advancement of women. In short, there is greater co-operation across a wider front — economic, political and security.[3] A "co-operative security" policy approach, that is, increased international co-operation on such diverse issues as the environment, population migration, terrorism and the interdiction of drug trafficking, is only one dimension of this "new internationalism." Multilateral institutions such as the United Nations (UN) are singled out as the ideal instruments to foster international co-operation on a cross-section of international issues over the long term.

What is "new" about the "new internationalism" is that it links global and regional security to the domestic issues that were once outside the purview of foreign affairs. Countries today are drawn into each other's internal affairs in ways unimaginable a few years ago. The key point about the "new internationalism" is that viable structures for the preservation of peace cannot be established successfully without an understanding of, and respect for, human rights and democratic principles. Over time this means the creation of a new lexicon of international relations in which the terms "non-interference" and "non-intervention" need to be redefined, or possibly dropped. Human rights violations are now not only legitimate subjects of concern for one nation-state when dealing with another, but also serve to promote enforceable measures by the international community.

In light of the theory, the past year's conduct of Canadian foreign policy can be characterized as a disciplined approach using "preventive diplomacy" to head off global problems. In addition to the major Canadian foreign policy initiatives such as aid to Central and Eastern Europe and the former Soviet Union, nuclear non-proliferation, and enhancement of the role of the United Nations in securing peace and security there have been peacekeeping/peacemaking roles in the former Yugoslavia and new thinking about Canada's policy towards Latin America.

The past year has seen a substantial increase in Canadian aid to Central and Eastern Europe, the Baltics, Ukraine and Russia. It became increasingly evident that the initial hopes for a quick transition to democracy and free markets were not going to be realized. The Canadian government had to prepare itself for longer-term, instead of short-term, objectives. From a bureaucratic perspective the focus changed: not only was the financial assistance increased, but the government also had to broaden its horizons in terms of the recipients of the aid. In other words, the government had initially planned for a larger amount of aid to a smaller number of republics, but it soon became evident that Canadian interests— strategic, political, economic and commercial—were engaged in other republics as well, and this caused a dispersal of efforts.[4]

An increase in funding for technical assistance programs from $25 million to $100 million over three years, aimed chiefly at Russia, Ukraine and Kazakhstan, was announced at the time of Boris Yeltsin's visit to Ottawa in June 1992.

The assistance allocated for Central Asia and the Trans-Caucasus remained very limited. From a practical standpoint Canada can get more return on its assistance by helping a republic such as Georgia, than it can through, say, its assistance to Ukraine and Russia, for the simple reason that in a smaller country modest levels of assistance can go further.[5] As a modest but encouraging start the Canadian Government has committed $1 million to a program of technical assistance for the Republic of Georgia.

Another foreign policy issue championed by Canada in 1992 was that of nuclear proliferation. At the Munich Summit (July 1992) Canada outlined a strategy to counter proliferation. Specifically, it was decided that the safety of nuclear power reactors in Eastern Europe and the former Soviet Union had to be addressed; this issue was distinguished from strategic arms limitation, which is a matter involving Russia, Ukraine, Belarus, Kazakhstan and the United States. Steps were taken by Canada to create a bilateral program in the nuclear field with the countries of Eastern Europe and the former Soviet Union. The Munich Summit also created a multilateral nuclear fund to which Canada is contributing.

As a traditional supporter of the UN, Canada contributed to and welcomed the most recent proposals set out in UN Secretary-General Boutros-Ghali's "Agenda for Peace." Prompted in part by an increasingly vicious civil war in the former Yugoslavia, the Secretary-General's report articulated an expansion of the range of tools available for conflict resolution as well as new approaches. Until the report's publication, the post-Cold War international relations lexicon had lacked a commonly accepted vocabulary to define the management and alleviation of the "new" dimensions of global insecurity (e.g., unchecked population growth, crushing debt burdens, barriers to trade, poverty, disease, oppression and famine). The Secretary-General's report provided a framework for understanding how, if successful, four integrally related elements of constructive interference — "preventive diplomacy," "peacemaking," "peacekeeping" and "peace-building" — could secure peace among nations and peoples in the spirit of the UN Charter.[6]

Conflict prevention, entailing policy formulation, diplomacy and action is an area in which Canada has internationally recognized expertise. Having the second largest contingent of peacekeepers in the world (after France), deployed in 13 missions, this country has had ample opportunities over the past year to test itself at global flashpoints as disparate in their natures as Somalia, Cambodia, Croatia, and Bosnia-Herzegovina. But the year did not witness only expansion in Canadian peacekeeping actions; after a 28-year presence the government announced the forthcoming withdrawal of Canadian peacekeepers from Cyprus. Nevertheless, with the four elements of conflict resolution becoming a growth industry in the 1990s, it is unlikely that there will be a shortage of global hotspots to which these Canadian peacekeepers could be redeployed.

Two fundamental questions arise from this discussion of Canada's role in conflict resolution. The first concerns the rationale for putting Canadian lives at risk in places such as Bosnia-Herzegovina, where ceasefires are repeatedly violated and peacekeepers are caught in the crossfire. This can be answered in part by pointing out that as professional soldiers Canadian peacekeepers put their lives on the line as part of their jobs.

The second question, though, should prompt a more fundamental debate about Canadian defence policy. In light of ongoing resource constraints, that is, the underfinancing of the army (the service branch that carries the heaviest load in UN peacekeeping operations) and a multi-year capital acquisition program (e.g., frigates and military helicopters), will Canada be able to afford to project its interests internationally through peacekeeping? Should Canadian taxpayers be expected to support Canadian peacekeepers in the former Yugoslavia as they did in Cyprus? In addition, different crises will require different and potentially more costly combinations of peacekeeping and peace-building strategies. As the "Agenda for Peace" report indicates, for peacemaking and peace-building to be truly successful, there must be comprehensive post-conflict efforts to "consolidate" peace, running the gamut from repatriating refugees, monitoring elections and reforming government institutions to clearing tens of millions of land mines, and providing technical assistance to revive agriculture. But who will pick up the tab, especially when there are no governmental institutions to reform or strengthen, as is the case in Somalia, where the civil society that *does* exist is based on pre-medieval clan politics?

Although Canada prides itself in paying its UN dues on time and in full (unlike the United States and Russia, which are in arrears) and has underwritten the costs of its peacekeepers in Cyprus, how much more of a financial burden should it be expected to bear? Obviously, there are no easy answers to these questions; nevertheless, they would certainly benefit from more public debate, as called for by the Liberal Party.[7]

Loosening Transatlantic Bonds

Canada is gradually distancing itself from Europe.[8] The withdrawal of Canadian troops is seen by some observers as a defining characteristic of this process; so is the failure of the Conference of Security and Co-operation in Europe (CSCE) to develop a key role. The reason for this gradual withdrawal is that the traditional policy of anchoring Canadian interests in "Atlanticist" institutions — the CSCE and the North Atlantic Treaty Organization (NATO) — has lost its resonance in a post-Cold War world. Relations with the third pillar of Canada's European policy, the European Community (EC), have improved since the issuance of the EC-Canada Transatlantic Declaration in late 1990, a declaration that has injected more political will into bilateral relations. For instance, formalized "regular" bilateral meetings at the high political level allowed Prime Minister Mulroney in 1992 to meet with the Presidents of the European Commission and the European Council in Ottawa to discuss, among other things, Canada's continuing concern about EC overfishing in the North Atlantic; this represents an advance beyond the previous practice of conferring with EC representatives on the periphery of international meetings of heads of state, e.g., the G-7. Although there is now greater recognition in Ottawa of the EC as a *bona fide* international actor, Canada's adoption of more balanced ties with Brussels as an integral element of its European policy approach are unlikely to make up for its waning influence in Europe. Of course, the gradual Canadian withdrawal is not entirely one-sided. West Europeans, beset by the challenges posed by Maastricht and the turmoil of economic and political liberalization in the East, have themselves become more inward-looking and distracted.

Canada's role in Europe has become the subject of spirited debate in the upper echelons of DEAITC. One senior Departmental official has commented that Canada was "fortunate" to have Yugoslavia tearing itself asunder because it gave Canada a "European vocation," one that was, of course, entirely unplanned. It was thus "fortuitous" that Canadian troops stationed in Germany could be mobilized for duty as peacekeepers in Croatia and Bosnia-Herzegovina. Another senior official countered that this line of argument rested on a false supposition, namely, that a Canadian military presence in Europe is necessary for Canada to have a European role. According to the second official, Canada's participation in two World Wars is testimony enough that Canada will always have a role in European affairs. In other words, it is immaterial whether Canadian peacekeepers leave for Yugoslavia from Baden-Soellingen or Valcartier to project Canadian interests in Europe.

The central issue here is not so much Canada's physical presence in Europe as a symbol of its European role as it is the changing nature of threats in the international system. Thus, the Yugoslav operation is in reality a kind of fig-leaf for Canada's European role. The cement of the trans-Atlantic alliance, like that of most alliances, has always been the external threat. The end of the Cold War has erased the focal point of the trans-Atlantic alliance: the spectre of a large, hostile, military, anti-democratic power in the centre of Europe, embodied first in the Nazis and later in the Communists. With the dissipation of the old external threats, the real question today is whether the spillover or potential spillover of numerous ethnic conflicts will require Canada to continue to have a seat at the European table. It may therefore turn out that the "new" basis for Canada's European policy will be one that integrates its European interests more fully into a global co-operative security approach. Canada's multilateral institutional affiliations would then be identified less with European institutions and more with global ones, like the UN.

Reinforcing Canada's gradual disengagement from Europe is the continuing pressure of globalization, which has meant that economic, rather than military, competition is the primary basis on which nation-states relate to one another in the post-Cold War era. Faced with a 27 percent drop in Canada's share of world trade over the last two decades, the Conservative Government under

Prime Minister Mulroney has positioned Canada strategically by negotiating first a Free Trade Agreement with the United States, and then a North American Free Trade Agreement (NAFTA) to include Mexico, while simultaneously pursuing the completion of the multilateral Uruguay Round negotiations. What do these initiatives portend for Canada's future "key relationships"?[9] First and foremost they signify a desire to integrate Canada more fully into a North American market. In addition, in the light of new thinking on the possible extension of the NAFTA to other parts of Latin America, Canada is increasingly seeing its economic future in the Americas.

The Domestic Front

In spite of the radical transformation of the international system since 1989, DEAITC appears to have had difficulty in explaining to Canadians why its work in this "new era" of diplomacy is relevant to their day-to-day interests. In other words, the Department has not justified its existence in terms that the average Canadian will understand and accept. Recognition that this state of affairs was becoming increasingly debilitating for the management of external relations has led, in the past year, to a repositioning of the Department's role within the federal bureaucracy. Before we discuss this repositioning it will be useful for us to review some of the perennial image and structural problems facing DEAITC.

The Canadian media's extensive coverage of improper conduct by Departmental personnel with respect to travel claims and housing allowances has been a continuing source of concern and frustration for the Department, and has in no way enhanced its image. Another factor that has contributed to the devaluation of the Foreign Service is its failure to maintain rigorous standards of professional skill. Until the official opening of the Canadian Foreign Service Institute in the fall of 1992, there were few opportunities for officials to participate in continuing educational programs that were structured to meet their specific needs and that reflected the changing nature of diplomacy.

Furthermore, the Department, in the course of its history, has been reluctant to reform its analytical and management processes with a view to encouraging constructive debate and dialogue. The

symptoms of this reluctance include a lack of legitimate channels for dissenting opinions and the poor quality of reporting
from Canada's posts abroad.[10] As a follow-up to the Corporate
Review final report (June 1990), which had not specifically addressed the role of Foreign Service members responsible for "po-
litical/economic" affairs, the Department commissioned a comprehensive audit of its Political and Economic Relations Program
(PER), the final report of which was tendered in December 1991.
The report examined the way in which the PER Program (as distinct
from the trade, aid, or immigration programs) was responding to
the double impact of reduced resources and increased workload.[11]
Among its findings were weaknesses in information management,
which created problems between DEAITC and its clients (e.g., the
public, the provinces, other government departments), within the
Department in Ottawa, and between Headquarters and Canadian
diplomatic missions abroad. In addition, the report stated that
effective policy formulation and implementation was being frus-
trated by deficient management processes. It concluded that, since
the PER program is a vital component of the Department's functions, these problems had the potential to undermine Canada's
ability to protect and pursue its interests abroad.

Constrained by the reduction in its resources, DEAITC has had
difficulty shedding functional or area responsibilities, and the result has been a weakening of the focus and thrust of Canadian
foreign policy. This decline is apparent in many policy areas.
Aid policy, which is now one of Canada's most important tools
in its relations with the expanding developing world, has been
managed and controlled by the Canadian International Development Agency (CIDA).[12] Critics have pointed out that there are also
other fields where this decline is obvious, such as multilateral relations policy, immigration policy, security and intelligence policy.[13]
In the area of trade development, managed by the Trade Commissioner Service, recent findings suggest that the Department's
trade development programs and services should be designed to
reduce dependence on government support rather than entrench
it; that access to programs and activities will need to become more
selective and differentiated; and that current resources and activities are over-concentrated in mature markets (e.g., Europe) with
diminishing marginal rates of return.[14]

In the conduct of its relations with other government departments, DEAITC has been able to secure few allies in the interdepartmental power centres in Ottawa, where it is viewed as unable to provide sufficient specialist expertise. Finally, there is the failure of ministers and some senior public servants to respect Canadian traditions of ministerial and public service responsibility. Related to this, and certainly brought to the fore by the Al-Mashat episode, is the general disaffection between the political level and the public service in Ottawa.

The image and structural problems discussed above clearly demand change, without which a healthy future for the Foreign Service, and by extension the sound management of Canada's foreign relations, cannot be predicted. It is, however, a testament to the professionalism of the Foreign Service that in spite of the deep-seated nature of some of its problems, it was still able, during the past year, to provide effective support to its Ministers, to the Prime Minister and to the government as a whole for the purpose of presenting Canadian foreign policy positions (e.g., peacekeepers to the former Yugoslavia, aid to Somalia, support of Haiti's ousted President Aristide) in a positive light.

In general, foreign policy does not appear to be a controversial part of the Conservative Government's policy agenda. Fairness, however, makes it necessary to state that this appearance may be due in part to: 1) the decrease in the number of independent institutes and agencies that could provide regular comment and criticism with regard to the government's security and international trade policies (as part of the 1992 federal budget both the Canadian Institute for International Peace and Security and the Economic Council of Canada were dissolved — see Chapter 4); and 2) the relative lack of sustained and nuanced analysis of *Canadian* foreign policy thinking and approaches by the Canadian media, which display a preference for exposing and reporting corporate scandals.

In the new world order, the mark of a successful foreign ministry will be what one senior official has described as "the successful marriage of information/intelligence; policy capacity; coherence in implementation; and effectiveness in the delivery of communications." If such a marriage can be consummated it may alleviate some of the Department's structural problems.

Departmental Repositioning: "Back to Basics" vs. the "Central Agency" Vision

Over the past decade, since the re-organization in 1982, DEAITC has pursued a program of steady expansion. The past year, however, has been marked by a decided contraction. In the aftermath of the February 1992 federal budget, the decision to "streamline" the Department's operations, by transferring its responsibility for the delivery of four programs to other federal departments and agencies, was greeted with disbelief by the rank and file Foreign Service members.[15] In an open letter to Departmental employees on February 26th, the Under-Secretary of State for External Affairs, Reid Morden, explained the decision as "consistent with the themes announced by the Minister of Finance in the budget," and aimed at sharpening the focus of the Department's core mandate or, in short, getting "back to basics." The new corporate direction exhibited a double thrust. DEAITC would now (1) focus on international political and economic interests and trade policy and development and (2) improve service to the public, strengthen program effectiveness and accountability, eliminate duplication and reduce program overlap.

In institutional terms "back to basics" entailed the transfer of the Department's immigration role to Employment and Immigration Canada, the cultural and academic and cultural relations program to the Canada Council, international expositions to Communications Canada, and the international sports program to Fitness and Amateur Sport. It was felt that "greater operating efficiencies" would result from strengthening and clarifying accountability by linking policy formulation and program delivery.[16] All well and good, except that this decision was arrived at with (1) no prior consultations with the affected employees, and (2) did not explain how DEAITC would continue to maintain a degree of policy control as implied by the 1983 Government Organization Act (of which Part One is designated as the Department of External Affairs Act). Indeed, this repositioning of DEAITC appears to lay to rest the vision of the Department as a central agency within the federal bureaucracy, the expressed desire of Allan Gotlieb, among others, when he was Under-Secretary of State in the late 1970s and early 1980s.

With regard to the first point, the decision to transfer the immigration role was, in the words of PAFSO president, Donald Mackay, "arrived at in secret . . . and dropped like a bomb in our midst."[17] In unusually undiplomatic, pointed language he declared in a letter to Minister McDougall that the decision to transfer was "taken in *concert* with, but not *part of* [Mr. Mackay's emphasis] the 1992–93 budget process," and that therefore explanations "relying on the budget process for a total lack of consultations were disingenuous at best." He went on to write that "unveiling the announcement [of the move] in the dead of night by posting press releases in elevators, [was] to display an unheard of disrespect for the Department's employees."[18] Complementing the official PAFSO reaction, the corridor discussions in the Pearson Building reverberated with more nuanced explanations for the move of the immigration role in particular, many of them centring on the thesis that, in addition to helping the refocusing of the Department's priorities, this transfer was also a "convenient" way of ensuring that any future "Al-Mashats" would land squarely in the lap of Employment and Immigration and not "embarrass" the Secretary of State for External Affairs or the Department.[19]

On the second point, it is worth exploring the vision of DEAITC as a central agency when the Department was developing into a "full service" institution in an attempt to secure its role as the lead articulator and co-ordinator of foreign policy advice to the government. By jettisoning this "full service" role in favour of a more targeted approach it appears that the Department is conceding that its earlier attempts to maintain its relevance were producing less than satisfactory results. Several years of successive budget cuts have left DEAITC with declining resources spread more and more thinly over a growing number of issues and functions, some of which, such as immigration, academic relations and sports have their own specialist agencies and departments within the federal government. This situation has strengthened outside perceptions of the Department "as being all over the map" and not having a niche in the conduct of government business. Yet in trying to reposition itself the Department is caught in a fundamental dilemma: how can it reconcile the need to enhance its relevance by streamlining with the equally important need of maintaining — if not increasing — its control of, and role in, the production of the government's foreign policy outputs to ensure a coherent articulation of Canada's foreign policy interests. This latter objective would seem to be more readily achievable by a central agency.

It can be argued that before the "back to basics" program, the Department always had been a kind of central agency. The fact that the Under-Secretary of State has long been a member of the Clerk of the Privy Council's Co-ordinating Committee of Deputy Ministers (a committee largely constituted of the heads of central agencies) is one sign that this status is recognized at the heart of the federal bureaucracy. But most public servants, when they speak of "central agencies," mean those agencies that have authority to make rules applicable to the entire public service, such as the Privy Council Office, Treasury Board, the Public Service Commission, and the Department of Finance. They would, according to former Under-Secretary of State James Taylor, be more likely to see DEAITC as a combined ministry of foreign affairs and international trade, perhaps organizationally unique among government departments, but a regular government department nonetheless, one more among many.[20] This is exactly the status of the Department as a result of its latest re-organization. Of course, other things being equal, it could still be argued that the fact of having three ministers at the head of the Department in and of itself reinforces its role as a central agency. There are many examples of departments having two ministers, but it is a rare department that has three.

Taylor concludes his observations with the statement that these arrangements — central agency functions and the reporting relationship to three ministers — guarantee the Department access and influence, but are not of themselves a guarantee of a coherent foreign policy. The existence of many masters (the Prime Minister, the Deputy Prime Minister, and three Ministers), who may have competing objectives, compounds the confusion about the manner in which the Department should exercise a degree of policy control, as implied by the 1983 External Affairs Act. Because of constraints on their time and divergent agendas, rarely do the three portfolio ministers of the Department sit down with their deputies all at the same time so that they may consider the Department's affairs together.

The essential point is this: it is not the number of ministers that matters; it is their Cabinet seniority and access to the Prime Minister.[21] What exists is a Cabinet decision-making process that is opaque in the sense that the formal Cabinet decisions are only the tip of the iceberg; government policy is often made by the Prime

Minister or one or two other ministers, and it is not always easy to keep abreast of such decisions and trace their roots to particular government departments.

The "back to basics" philosophy raises other questions, besides those discussed above. It can be criticized as representing a narrow vision that does not take into account the multitude of activities that characterize state-to-state relations.[22] Indeed, the diffuse character of international issues makes it anachronistic to conduct diplomatic relations in the 1990s on the basis of "traditional" concerns such as military relations and international trade. Furthermore, the "back to basics" philosophy would require DEAITC to relinquish any role in regard to the other non-traditional issues now on the international agenda, such as the advancement of women, the environment, efforts to contain the spread of AIDS, and the international co-ordination of monetary policy. What would the Department do on these issues — act as a post box and reservation service abroad? Other government departments would then present Canada's international position abroad on all such issues, without any guarantee that Canada would be pursuing a foreign policy in which individual strategies served to mutually support the country's international objectives. In the final analysis DEAITC is still the only federal department that can fulfil the critical overview function and highlight the interlinkages between and among the policy nodes in Canada's foreign policy machinery.

Reaching Outside and Inside: Democratizing Canadian Foreign Policy and the Birth of a Foreign Service Institute

In a 1989 article, John Kirton pointed out that, because of changes in Canada's demographic composition, widely different groups would in the coming years put to the test our ability to form consensus on directions in Canadian foreign policy.[23] He noted that Canada's world view would be defined increasingly by particular ethnic groups which would place "demands" on Canadian foreign policy. But there will not only be pressure from ethnic groups. In the post-Cold War era it is the set of interlinked issues that go under the name of "co-operative security" that have gained ascendancy on the public policy agenda. This means that the government can also expect increasing demands for participation in the foreign policymaking process to come from non-government organizations such as churches, community organizations, and environmental watch groups, to name a few.

There is overwhelming pressure from the central government agencies (such as the Privy Council Office and the Public Service 2000 study team), especially in light of the constitutional consultations that preceded the national referendum on the Charlottetown Accord, for government to get closer to its clientele by engaging in a more regular, structured, consultative process. An Inter-Departmental Working Group on Consultations has been established to investigate the means of creating this more open policy process. The idea and implementation of consultative frameworks is not a radically new one.

Since 1986 DEAITC has held regular consultations through its permanent advisory committee system — the International Trade Advisory Committee (ITAC) and the Sector Advisory Groups on International Trade (SAGITs) — thereby permitting an ongoing, confidential, two-way flow of information and advice between the government and the private sector on international trade matters. This committee system is now going through a transition since the policy initiatives for which it was designed — the Canada-U.S. Free Trade Agreement, the NAFTA, and the multilateral trade negotiations (MTN) — have now either been completed or, as in the case of the MTN, will be completed or will fail in the near future. In light of the increasingly nebulous distinction between the domestic and international arenas, the next stage in the evolution of the ITAC and SAGIT structures is to use them for consultations on emerging issues such as competition policy, trade and the environment, and trade development. DEAITC officials can draw on the positive experience of the ITAC and SAGIT structures, and given the pressure to democratize the policymaking process, they have been examining how the "lessons" of the ITAC and the SAGITs could be extended Department-wide so that "formal," "structured" and "ongoing" consultations could begin to take place with a broader spectrum of interest groups on a larger number of interlinked foreign policy issues, including human rights and overseas development assistance.

The Department is therefore displaying a will to reach out and open up the foreign policymaking process, by fostering the spirit of ITAC and the SAGITs in other sectors of its activity, though not necessarily through similar structures. On the other hand, its creation of the Canadian Foreign Service Institute (CFSI) in the past year can be seen as an effort to reach within itself and provide its personnel with the tools necessary to deliver high levels of service in a period of rapidly changing technological, economic and international political conditions.

Through the CFSI, the Department will ensure that its employees receive a common basis of experience and then have their skills upgraded throughout their careers. The largely *ad hoc* way in which officers have traditionally learned how to become diplomats is no longer tenable and is being replaced by a more structured approach. Support staff, mid-career officers and senior managers will also be rotated through the Institute. The various functional and geographic Bureaux that make up the organization of the Department will also be able to ensure that the Institute provides training tailor-made to its needs. Finally, the Institute's location may in the medium- to long-term also lead it to assume an additional role as a centre for research into Canadian foreign service priorities, although it is not clear at this stage whether such a role would be associated with, or distinct from, the applied research on Canadian foreign policy that is undertaken by the Policy Planning Staff.

Lastly, the Foreign Service Officer Exchange Program, a reciprocal arrangement whereby Canadian diplomats serve for a year in the foreign services of New Zealand and Australia, is apparently a very useful learning exercise both for the participants and the Departments involved. As resource constraints cause Canada to downsize and possibly close some of its diplomatic posts abroad, it makes sense for Canada to be able to utilize these alternate sources of information-gathering. Although there has been no indication that the exchange program will be expanded beyond Australia and New Zealand, some DEAITC officials talk wistfully of one day serving in the heart of the U.S. foreign policy establishment at State, Defense, and the National Security Council.

The "Triangle" of Canadian Foreign Policymaking

It has been argued in this chapter that, in addition to organizational repositioning to increase DEAITC's relevance, another critical factor is the interaction between Ministers and senior officials and their access to the Prime Minister and his thinking. There is a triangular relationship between the stature of the Secretary of State for External Affairs, patterns and directions in Canadian foreign policy, and the stature of the Department within the foreign policy bureaucracy. By the end of his tenure as Secretary of State for External Affairs, Joe Clark had carved out a niche for himself with respect to a number of foreign policy "files" such as South Africa, Central America and the Pacific Rim, all of which enhanced his stature, and by extension that of the Department, in the management of Canada's external relations. But whereas Clark had seven years to grow in his portfolio it may still be premature — with just two years passed — to pass judgement on the impact of Secretary of State McDougall.

Nevertheless, it can be said that under McDougall's stewardship there has been a breakdown in this triangular relationship. Observers both inside and outside the Department give the Minister high marks for her handling of individual issues (e.g., calling for UN reform), but they note that what is appropriate for day-to-day management does not necessarily translate into a coherent overall foreign policy. The most trenchant criticism appears to be that she has not put an identifiable stamp on her foreign policy in those areas where the Prime Minister, as the primary actor in the management of Canadian foreign policy, would allow her scope for initiative. It has already been mentioned that foreign policy formulation is increasing localized at the PMO, where the Prime Minister has staked out for himself the G-7, non-proliferation of weapons of mass destruction, the restoration of democracy in Haiti, and aid to Eastern Europe and the former Soviet Union. In addition, there was Michael Wilson, as International Trade Minister, stickhandling NAFTA and the MTN, and Monique Landry (now replaced by Monique Vézina) overseeing Canada's relations with developing countries. It therefore becomes difficult, as one senior DEAITC official has pointed out, to see in Secretary of State McDougall's actions "any identifiable pattern that has meaning in foreign policy terms."

At the bureaucratic level, Reid Morden assumed the title of Under-Secretary of State for External Affairs — the Department's top civil service position — at a particularly difficult time. His appointment came in the wake of the Al-Mashat episode, which had highlighted the growing politicization of the public service and had fundamentally altered the relationship between ministers and their deputies. Morden was to preside over substantial budget cuts.

Regarded by his officials as a manager's manager rather than a visionary, the Under-Secretary has moved away from the "Star chamber-like" management of the Department favoured by his predecessor, de Montigny Marchand, who had alienated some of his senior officials. There are now daily 8:30 a.m. operations committee meetings on the eighth floor of the Pearson Building, attended by the Under-Secretary, the Executive Assistant to the Deputy Minister for International Trade, all the Department's Assistant Deputy Ministers and the chiefs of staff of the three Ministers. An indication of the Under-Secretary's "no nonsense" operating style was amply demonstrated in his first meeting with his senior officials, when he told them not to bother pouring themselves coffee — the meeting wouldn't last that long. Commenting on changes in the Department since Morden's arrival, DEAITC officials point out that, on the one hand, the Under-Secretary has tightened procedures, improved operational competence and has had to make some very difficult decisions, such as inviting some senior diplomats to retire early, in order to fulfil Treasury Board requirements (arising from the February 1992 Budget) to reduce the number of senior public service managers (EXs) at DEAITC. On the other hand, the Department seems to suffer from policy constipation. As one official commented wryly: "There is no horizon beyond the next 24 hours."

Conclusion

How can and should Canada respond to the simultaneous processes of ethnic division and economic integration, in order to maximize its influence, and protect and promote Canadian values globally? As this chapter has pointed out, the "paradigm shift" makes it necessary to have a realistic understanding of how much power, or influence, Canada has. This country will not have as much influence at the European table as it did in the past. Canada may, however, be able to restore its global influence, given sufficient domestic political will, by re-deploying its resources to preventive diplomacy, peacekeeping, peacemaking and peace-building actions. In the economic arena, one of the major questions for the future is what impact the new Clinton Administration will have on the "special relationship," and whether any changes in that relationship will modify Canada's steady economic evolution as a nation of the Americas.

The ability of Canada to project its interests globally also depends of course on the quality of its diplomats and the respect accorded them both domestically and internationally. The restructuring of the Department over the last year was intended not only to improve but, in certain cases, to change the co-ordination, oversight, and programming of its activities. It reflected an effort to change the role of External Affairs within Canada's foreign policymaking machinery, to make it more relevant in the business of government. The question remains whether the imperatives of foreign policy, in which international relations and domestic policy are increasingly fused, can be reconciled effectively with the Department's streamlining approach. Under these conditions it may prove difficult for the Department to maintain its role as the primary articulator of Canadian foreign policy.

4

Shooting Oneself in the Head:
The Demise of CIIPS

Geoffrey Pearson and Nancy Gordon

It will cost the government $2.5 million less annually, because instead of having the Canadian Institute for International Peace and Security, we will have officials within the Department of External Affairs doing the same job.[1]

THE ABOVE QUOTATION contains the last words pronounced over the grave of the Canadian Institute for International Peace and Security (CIIPS) before the government majority in the House completed the burial ceremony for it and five other research/advisory bodies at the end of November, 1992. They were sacrificed, it was said, to help reduce the burden of government on the economy, although a total saving of $22 million out of a budget of about $160 billion raised obvious questions of priorities. Might not equivalent savings have been found elsewhere? While it is not our purpose to explore this question here, we think the story of the birth and death of CIIPS may help others to do so, perhaps in the context of the appropriate role of public advisory and research bodies, or as part of the wider issue of who benefits from public spending.

In 1983–84, as the Trudeau era drew to a close, the Prime Minister embarked on a journey that was to take him round the world in a search for common ground between Washington and Moscow, then apparently on the verge of nuclear confrontation. The final outcome of that quest was the establishment by Parliament, in June 1984, of the Canadian Institute for International Peace and Security. The concept of such an organization was described in the Speech from the Throne on December 7, 1983 as follows:

> Improving the climate among nations requires knowledge, creativity, and a determination to find solutions. Reflecting Canada's concern about international tensions, the Government will create a publicly funded centre to gather, collate and digest the enormous volume of information now available on defence and

arms control issues. Fresh ideas and new proposals, regardless
of source, will be studied and promoted.[2]

This concept was born in the office of the Prime Minister, not in
the main Departments concerned (External Affairs and National
Defence). It had its genesis in what Mr. Trudeau had said was "the
difficulty all of us experience in trying to know what is going on
in the world — to know it and to understand it in a manner that
is accurate, that provides the ground for useful action."[3] Public
support for his peace initiative, then at mid-point, had impressed
him with the need for independent, knowledgeable and accessible
sources of information and analysis on issues of international security, sources that would bring to bear a Canadian perspective on
such issues at a time when images of the 'evil empire' dominated
the media. There was, for example, only one full-time Canadian
correspondent in Moscow in 1983.

An Act to establish the Canadian Institute for International
Peace and Security was put before Parliament on April 16, 1984,
after close consultation with the leaders of the opposition parties.
Those consultations had led to the strengthening of the Institute's
independent status by making the appointment of its Directors
subject to nomination by non-governmental organizations, and
only after "consultation by the Minister with the Leader of the Opposition in the House of Commons and the leader of every other
recognized party . . ."[4] The Leader of the Opposition, Mr. Mulroney, insisted that the Institute be protected from "prevailing
political winds" and that its financing be guaranteed through public means.[5] Moreover, unlike the Economic Council and the Science
Council — established in 1963 and 1966 respectively (and also to
be abolished in 1992) — which were required to advise the Minister on various and specific aspects of their fields of work, the
Institute was not put under any obligation to proffer advice either to the Minister or to Parliament, although it might do so if
requested. This difference may be explained both by the general-
ity of the subject matter — international peace and security rather
than problems of Canadian policy — and by the process of consultation with Parliament and the public which the government
began in the spring of 1984.

As well as entrenching the independence of the new Crown
Corporation, this process of establishment resulted in a broadening of the purposes of the Institute by adding to its mandate

the study of "conflict resolution," and by requiring it to "study and propose ideas and policies" in addition to fostering research, and disseminating information. These ideas were put forward by many of the forty witnesses who appeared before the Standing Committee on External Affairs and National Defence at the end of May, and were adopted by the Committee, which recommended the following statement of purpose:

> The purpose of the Institute is to increase knowledge and understanding of the issues relating to international peace and security from a Canadian perspective, with particular emphasis on arms control, disarmament, defence and conflict resolution, and to foster, fund and conduct research on matters relating to international peace and security; promote scholarship in matters relating to international peace and security; study and propose ideas and policies for the enhancement of international peace and security; and collect and disseminate information on, and encourage public discussion of, issues of international peace and security.[6]

This mandate reflected the broad diversity of opinion in Canada about the priorities to be attached to the study of the different aspects of international peace and security. It encompassed the advocacy of specific policies as well as the analysis of competing policies, and it committed the Institute to distinct activities — fostering *and* conducting research, and encouraging discussion *as well as* disseminating information.

A study of comparable institutes in other countries, done in the Department of External Affairs before the legislation was introduced in Parliament, had found no similar mix of purposes. Most were concerned solely with research, and although they usually published material of a kind accessible to the public, they had no mandate to foster research elsewhere, or to encourage public discussion by the granting of funds for such purposes. The Stockhom International Peace Research Institute (SIPRI) is an example of an institution with this more limited, research-oriented mandate. The study also found, however, that the Canadian public was less well served than the European or American publics in this field of research. Universities, by and large, gave it low priority, and the media relied chiefly on American expertise. While the Canadian government did provide modest funds for military and strategic studies and some support for research on disarmament, non-governmental organizations (NGOs) generally welcomed the prospect of an institution that would have wider responsibilities, provided it did not divert funds already available to them. This was also a concern of witnesses from universities, and it strengthened the case for guaranteed funding of the Institute by Parliament (a guarantee subsequently provided in the Act for each of the following five years, and "in each fiscal year thereafter, five million dollars," or more).[7]

The Initial Period

While assured of its independence, the new Institute was still faced with a formidable array of disparate tasks, none of which were clearly defined. It would have to find its own way.

Its path was charted by the first Board of Directors appointed on August 15, 1984, after due consultation with the opposition parties. Three of the seventeen places were left vacant, to be filled later by the Executive Director and two persons from outside Canada. William Barton, former Canadian Ambassador to the UN, was elected Chairman, and in December, Geoffrey Pearson, after some soul searching, was elected Executive Director.[8] The delay in Pearson's appointment reflected a debate over the chief purposes of the Institute that was bound to arise between Board members, half of whom were proud to be known as peace "activists," a point of view regarded by the remainder with varying degrees of skepticism. Having just returned from three years in Moscow, Pearson was well aware of the concerns of the first group but not persuaded that radical measures of disarmament or substantial change in Canadian policies would be feasible, even if they might be desirable in the long run. In any event, the first priority was to establish the structure and plan the activities of the Institute, and on these matters, agreement was reached without great difficulty.

Programs were established on research, public affairs and information, each overseen by a Board committee. About half of the annual budget, set initially for 1984–85 at 1.5 million dollars, would be spent on grants for research and public affairs, and these funds in turn would be equally divided between the two programs. Emphasis would be placed on job mobility for research purposes through the appointment of fellows, and of interns as visitors to CIIPS, rather than the creation of a permanent staff. Publications might include a newsletter or magazine, as well as more specialized papers and an annual yearbook or guide. The library would be "state of the art," permitting access to data bases and possibly a "hot line," but including a wide selection of periodicals and a smaller collection of books. The Institute would not advocate specific policies; instead, it would try to provide the contextual background of policy, including the possible consequences of alternative decisions. Relations with similar institutes in other countries would be cultivated, in part by holding an annual conference to which foreign scholars and others would be invited. The staff would be held to a maximum of thirty for the initial years (it eventually reached about forty, some of whom were part-time visitors).

Given the climate of the times, it was appropriate that the research program give early attention to East-West relations, including the nuclear balance, the Strategic Defence Initiative (SDI) and arms control negotiations. The first annual conference focused on "challenges to deterrence,"[9] and in 1986 joint projects were arranged with SIPRI on a comprehensive test ban, and with Chatham House on Western arms control policies[10] An agreement with the Soviet Institute for the Study of the USA and Canada to exchange up to five scholars a year served to fill a long-felt need amongst Canadian students of Soviet foreign policy. In response to requests from the Secretary of State for External Affairs, studies of nuclear freeze options and of trends in continental defence were prepared and later published.[11] Close attention was also paid in the first years to the dimension of conflict resolution in the mandate of the Institute; the situation in Central America and the Caribbean basin was the subject of a series of round tables, and a conference took place in Jamaica on the security of small states in the Caribbean.[12] Grants for research totalling over $600,000 were made in 1985–86 to some 60 scholars or organizations.

In the field of public affairs, or public programs as the Board named it, a series of publications was begun, a survey of peace education in schools and universities was undertaken, and planning began for a teachers' guide to the main issues. During the first two years, 160 grants, (averaging $5000 per grant), were awarded to groups and individuals to support conferences, publications, and events relevant to the mandate. Most of the applicants represented the "peace movement" broadly defined, and this fact led some observers to perceive a bias in the approach of the Institute.

This was not so. Grants were made in response to applications, of which 90 percent came from those critical of current policies. Some of the resulting projects contributed little to public understanding, but on the whole, they helped to raise the level of public debate. Experience led to a wider spectrum of applicants and to more rigorous criteria for approval. In addition, the staff began to search out organizations with national mandates for public education and to enter into joint projects with them. These included co-operation with libraries to develop a common database and to improve access to bibliographies.

Subsequent Development

Research Activities

After the first flush of activity and as the Institute developed, members of the Board and staff had to face questions of both content and process. In the area of research a number of factors had to be considered. What subjects should be studied? Should the work take place in-house or externally? If the former, how and where could the Institute find staff? If the latter, how could the results form a part of the Institute's output?

A number of considerations influenced the answers to these questions. The availablity of staff was a primary concern. The first research director, David Cox from Queen's University, was an active participant in the discussions which led to the formation of the Institute. He was able to take an extended leave from Queen's, and remained at the Institute from early 1985 until September 1987. A number of interns or research assistants were hired — usually students who had completed a first or second degree and were continuing in the field — but recruiting for the more senior positions was difficult. Scholars were reluctant to abandon tenured positions at universities for the fledgling and as yet unknown "think-tank," although they found conditions at the Institute much to their liking. The Institute experimented with part-time arrangements with Carleton, brought professors on sabbatical to the Institute for one or two years, initiated a program with the Departments of External Affairs and National Defence to have a member from each of their staffs in residence for a year, and for its more permanent staff, with one or two exceptions, hired junior scholars.

The public policy debate, the views of the Board, and the interests and knowledge of staff, guided the substance of Institute studies. Institute research continued to focus on the hard issues of arms control, disarmament and defence, but under the rubric of conflict resolution a number of new fields were explored. Given the Canadian experience, peacekeeping and the UN played a large part, with major studies undertaken on Cyprus and Lebanon, and on the UN's role in Namibia, for example.[13]

The Namibia project illustrates one of the formats the Institute developed to good effect: Institute staff gathered together a number of people who knew something about a subject, but who came to it from different perspectives and from different backgrounds, and who had different roles. Academics, journalists, members of NGOs, officials, and parliamentarians, exchanged ideas during Institute projects; there was a sharing of experience as well as views. That catalyzing role was an important contribution in a field where groups tend to talk only to themselves. It also broadened the discussion from a concentration on specialized detail to one which might have more general application and interest.

By mid-1988, threats to the natural environment and the consequent challenges to security came to be considered an appropriate area for Institute study, although the decision to stretch the mandate to this field was by no means unanimous. Two major projects contributed to this work; both were joint undertakings by the research and public programs sections. The first involved a series of meetings with a selected group of physical and natural scientists, along with economists, social scientists and officials, to discuss threats to global security—environmental, military, economic and political. The Institute sponsored the publication of a book based on the discussions, designed for the interested but non-expert reader and written by one author who attended all the meetings, and brought his considerable knowledge and writing skills to the project.[14] The second project focused on climate change as a threat to security, featured a two-day seminar, and resulted in a more specialized conference report.[15] Later work in this field by the Institute focused on population as a threat to security.

The Institute explored another area of conflict resolution— that which applies social psychological precepts and techniques to international conflict. During the first years, a study of selected geographical areas of ongoing conflict was undertaken and published.[16] This work was expanded by a resident social psychologist, who explored the record of third party negotiation techniques in inter- and intra-state disputes, and later focused more exclusively on Cyprus.

Public Programs

Publications formed a large part of the Institute's work.[17] While it was initially thought that the publications output would be dependent upon work produced or funded by research projects or grants, it soon became clear that, in addition, contracts with external writers could fill gaps in existing literature.

Occasional Papers were geared to academic audiences and largely resulted from Institute in-house or sponsored research. Nine titles were published, each with a press run of approximately 1,500. They were intended as the Institute's showcase publication for the academic and senior scholar community and careful attention was paid to substance, structure, editing, design and translation. Standards of excellence were set deliberately high, and it proved difficult to find suitable manuscripts. More extensive was the Working Paper series; these were works in progress, conference reports or academic studies. Working Papers were not usually translated and their format was less permanent. Thus they could be issued quickly and reprinted easily if demand outstripped supply. The press run varied according to subject matter, usually in the 900 to 1,200 range. The Institute published 44 Working Papers, along with 6 earlier Conference Reports (in 1988 Conference Reports as a separate series were amalgamated with Working Papers). Their subject matter indicates the range of Institute research and interests, and their impact was considerable amongst specialized audiences.

The Guide to Canadian Policies on Arms Control, Disarmament, Defence and Conflict Resolution, an annual volume, was undertaken to fill a gap in the existing literature. Its print run was approximately 1,500 and it became a useful and valued compendium — a reference book kept near the desks of those who needed quick access to factual information.

From 1986 onwards the Executive Director published an annual year-end review and statement. Issued in the name of the Director, the statement became an important event in the Institute's annual schedule. The media paid considerable attention to it, and speaking tours were arranged around it. While it was not a report card on the Government's performance, it drew attention to issues of international peace and security and provided a focus for public debate.

Expanding the numbers of people interested in issues of peace and security, as well as providing sound, reliable information to the interested but non-expert public, was an important preoccupation. The major innovation was a quarterly magazine *Peace and Security*. Articles were short, and the writing style non-academic. A full-colour, illustrated cover, along with inside drawings, attracted readers. The magazine provided current comment, placed international events in context, and in addition provided factual information in five short departments, including news from the Institute. The magazine was innnovative, attractive and popular; its mailing list grew from 2,000 to 8,500.

Background Papers, of which the Institute published 39 titles, were likewise intended for the interested but non-expert reader. A certain degree of knowledge was assumed, with the audience made up of journalists, teachers, students, members of NGOs and officials. Published in both English and French, and containing about 6,000 words, they had a press run of 5,000.

Factsheets were written with a high-school audience in mind, and could be inserted into the Institute's major innovation for secondary schools, "The Teachers' Handbook on Peace and Security." It was written by an Institute staff member and a high school teacher following consultation with teachers, school boards, educational organizations, provincial government officials, all of whom said that they needed factual, classroom-ready information on issues of peace and security. The Handbook focused on the concepts of foreign policy, security and international conflict, and came to be widely used throughout the country. Institute staff promoted the book through professional development days and personal contact with classroom teachers.

There was a charge for the Handbook, but it was one of the few Institute publications for which clients were asked to pay. In the early years it was thought unwise, from a marketing point of view, to charge for Institute publications. The Board revisited this question several times, but decided to stick with its policy of distributing the bulk of Institute publications without charge, citing the mandate to encourage public discussion and disseminate information. Attempts at cost recovery became an issue in the later years, as did the desire to test the market, and the sense that readers would treat more seriously products for which they paid.

From the early days of the Institute's existence, members of the Board were convinced that television was an appropriate medium for public affairs efforts. Two major problems stood in the way of such efforts: cost, and the need to express a point of view through the production of good television documentaries. A solution was found in the format worked out by the Columbia School of Journalism and the Public Broadcasting System (PBS), whereby present and former politicians, officials, and journalists are gathered together to discuss a hypothetical situation under the guidance of a moderator who sets the stage and poses the questions. The intention is to illuminate the decision-making process as well as an international issue or event. With the help of a consultant from PBS and a Canadian television documentary maker, the Institute produced two such programs as pilots, and was in the final throes of negotiating a contract with the CBC and SRC for the production and broadcast of four more when the Institute closed.

Relations with the media became an important part of the Institute's work, as the recognition grew that the Institute's research and ideas would not exercise their fullest influence on the public policy debate unless they were disseminated through the media. The Institute organized media round tables on current issues for journalists; sessions were open to the media across Canada via conference speaker phone. With few exceptions, Institute events were open to journalists, and their attendance was encouraged.

Conferences and seminars were a major part of research projects, but they also formed an important part of the Institute's day-to-day existence. In particular, it was able to provide logistic and organizational support for requests to receive visiting scholars, officials and journalists, and to attract audiences with special knowledge of the subject matter.

Both the research and public programs sections initiated joint projects with external organizations or universities. The research section advertized for commissioned research for several years and Institute staff played a major role in shaping the work and the product. Public programs staff administered one continuing joint undertaking, together with the Council for Canadian Unity's Terry Fox Centre in Ottawa, and several finite projects. These projects were subject to continuing review and evaluation, and, especially as funds became tighter in later years, decisions were taken to scale down their number and scope. While the Institute was conscious of the need to spend a certain percentage of its income externally, joint undertakings presented problems of management, and it was thought wiser to expand the grants program than to continue commissioned research obtained by advertisement and joint projects.

Grants and Awards

Initially, the grants program was both responsive and guided, and it consumed about half of the Institute's early budget. As CIIPS developed its own expertise, there was less emphasis on grants, although in percentage terms direct outside funding never fell below 37 percent of the total budget. In the early years, Board committees, and indeed the full Board, spent a large amount of time considering grant applications; by 1989 the Board had decided that it would do better to concentrate on issues of policy and strategic planning. By the creation of the Peace and Security Competitions Fund, the process was removed from both the non-grants staff and the Board, although the Fund reported once a year to the Board. External committees gave preliminary advice and final decisions were taken by the four Board and three non-Board members.

From 1985 until 1992 the Institute made 618 grants totalling $5.5 million: 244 grants were made for conferences, 170 for research projects, 314 or 51 percent were made to individuals or organizations in Ontario, 133 or 22 percent in Quebec.

The legislation's instructions to "encourage scholarship" took the form of awards and scholarships totalling $956,000 to 58 recipients, mostly graduate students, enabling them to continue work in the field. The Institute initially contracted with the Association of Universities and Colleges of Canada (AUCC) to administer the program, but later took over the role itself, and named the scholarships the Barton Awards, after the first chairman of the Board.

Information

The collection of information occasioned a good deal of debate. What to collect? Should there be a library in the traditional sense, or should information be collected and disseminated electronically? How should the library's work be made available outside Ottawa?

The guiding principle behind the collection of information was to have available at the Institute material needed by the resident scholars and staff. Books were not a high priority, but government documents, periodical literature and "grey" material were. (The latter consists of conference reports, papers and other unpublished data.) Just prior to the announcement of the Institute's demise, the collection included 1,350 books and 270 periodical titles. With the addition of government documents, publications from international bodies, newsletters, speeches and conference papers, the total number of items was approximately 12,000. Incoming literature was classified and coded for a data base which was made available electronically. Staff developed and published a bilingual thesaurus of peace and security terminology. The library was open to the public and, especially in later years, was extensively used by Ottawa-based scholars, students, and members of NGOs.

The Institute offered bookshelf grants (valued first at $1,000 and then $500) to public and later secondary school libraries for purchasing and publicizing peace and security materials. As part of its mandate to work outside the Ottawa area, library staff ran several small conferences on peace and security information materials throughout the country.

Budget

The Institute's budget did not increase from the original allocation made in the Act of Parliament, and by 1990 it began to decline in real terms. Although a number of conversations had taken place with the Minister and one formal request was put forward by the second Chairman of the Board, David Braide, for an increase in the Institute's budget, the economic climate was not conducive to a favourable hearing for such requests. Bernard Wood had replaced Geoffrey Pearson in 1989, and he and the staff engaged in trimming and cutting to stay within the budget. As Mr. Braide said to the Commons Committee looking into the closure of the Institute, "After a career in the business community in this country, I can tell you that this institute became a model of what the federal government should be supporting. It was an effective and efficient organization, quite the opposite of the stereotypical fat bureaucracy."[18]

Demise

Introducing his budget on February 25, 1992, the Minister of Finance, Don Mazankowski, announced that the government "would eliminate, consolidate, defer or privatize a total of 46 government agencies." Those to be eliminated included the Law Reform Commission, the Economic Council and the Science Council, the International Centre for Ocean Development and CIIPS. The reason for this drastic treatment, he said, was "to streamline government."[19] The accompanying budget papers explained, with reference to CIIPS, "the government has concluded that Canada can no longer afford a separate government-funded institute for this purpose, when other sources of independent foreign policy research and analysis are available in the universities and elsewhere. Moreover, other programs of support to independent research exist elsewhere in government."[20]

Thus the official explanation for the dismantling of the Institute is to be found in the assumption that, in hard times, universities and government itself must be expected to perform the functions of policy analysis and support for research that CIIPS was established to do. This explanation turned out to be something of a half truth, for in July it was announced that the Department of External Affairs would budget $2.1 million for a "co-operative security competition" to include research, publications and conferences, and that, in addition, $200,000 would be set aside each year for scholarships.[21] These were about the same amounts that the Institute had been spending. Moreover, the announcement revealed that the library and data base would be transferred to the Canadian Forces Command and Staff College in Toronto, carrying the implication that its budget too might have to be increased.

Opposition members of Parliament had been quick to point out this inconsistency when debate began on April 30 on the Bill to dissolve the six agencies, doubting that significant savings would follow, or that the cost benefits, if such there were, would offset the educational benefits of the bodies affected. They accused the government of wishing to be rid of inconvenient critics, and of attempting at the same time to win back supporters of the Reform

Party in Western Canada by appearing to counter the charge of "waste and duplication" in Ottawa. Debate on the subject was confused by lack of focus, given the fact that the Bill dealt with all six agencies, and it was made somewhat sterile by a virtual refusal on the government side of the House to examine the records of the individual agencies, or to make distinctions between them. The government contended that, in the words of the President of the Treasury Board, "this initiative is part of our commitment to respond to the clear desire of Canadians for government that is leaner, more efficient and less expensive."[22]

In the case of CIIPS, however, the interested public reacted strongly. Over 200 letters of protest were sent to Ottawa, representing organizations and individuals from universities, schools, peace groups and defence associations, including 33 from other countries.[23] As an American scholar put it: the decision would "give a powerful negative image to the world about Canada's role in this new era . . . "[24] Media comment was equally hostile to the termination of CIIPS.

Objections were based on three main grounds: the need for continuing public education, the value of impartiality, and the advantage of a focal point and clearing house for analysis and comment on subjects of such various concern. It was argued that the end of the Cold War increased the need for public education because the range of options for security policy was now much wider, and "new thinking" more necessary. Institute publications, including material for schools and teachers, reached a spectrum of readers that could not be matched by universities and governments. Moreover, these materials brought to bear a Canadian perspective on the known facts and opinions on specific issues, and an objective accounting for such facts and opinions. Universities had neither the resources nor the will to engage the interested public outside the classroom in this way, and grants for research by departments of government would be determined by the needs of such departments and not by public demand. It was also said that, through its seminars, data base and joint projects, as well as its network of advisory committees, CIIPS had become a focal point in Canada for peace and security studies and that this was a function that no other body had the resources to perform. Finally, it was feared that comparable funds for research and scholarship would not be forthcoming from official sources, a fear that was allayed, at least temporarily, by the July announcement cited above.

Conclusion

Two main questions are suggested by the account of these events. Did CIIPS perform a function that justified the expenditure of public funds, and, if so, ought it to be resurrected in one form or another? These questions apply equally to the other two organizations which CIIPS most closely resembled, the Economic Council of Canada and the Science Council of Canada. The responses may be equally applicable. Although there are obvious comparisons to be made, it would be a mistake to apply the same criteria of profit and loss to each agency. The goal of improved public understanding, and of aspiring to some general consensus about longer-term policy, was common to all three bodies, but the means of doing this and the resources available to each were different. Economists and scientists in Canada may not usually pursue the kinds of applied research of benefit to public policy which the government would prefer, and some form of stimulus may therefore be needed in order to obtain policy-relevant results. The problem is not the absence of expertise but its focus, and the object of the two Councils was to concentrate specialized knowledge and analysis on future policy directions in the form of "an ongoing Royal Commission."[25] The main purpose of CIIPS, on the other hand, was to foster, rather than to concentrate, research on public policy, and to encourage an informed public discussion rather than to recommend policy. It was to fertilize rather than to reap.

The initial report to the government on the creation of a new organization on issues of peace and security concluded that "neither the government nor the universities can provide the credibility which the public now seeks elsewhere."[26] Did CIIPS provide this credibility? To do so, it had to satisfy public expectations of independence and academic standards of objectivity. All-party support in Parliament, the requirement of such support for appointments to the Board, and a guaranteed annual income established its independence, and at no time was this challenged by Ministers or officials. Some Board members and NGOs would have preferred that the Institute assume an advocacy role on sensitive issues, like a nuclear freeze, but the fact was that Board members disagreed on the merits of specific policies. Moreover, to promote only one side of the argument on such issues would have undermined any reputation for objectivity the Institute sought to, and did, achieve.

Initial criticisms regarding grant recipients were neither sustained nor justified. From time to time members of Parliament or officials or members of the public objected to particular positions taken by Institute staff or outline in Institute studies. For instance, controversy erupted around an early study on NORAD, and later, when Bernard Wood and Mark Heller, then the Coordinator of Research, were generally supportive of Canadian action during the Gulf War. However, if Institute studies and views had not, from time to time, created controversy and criticism, it would not have been doing its job.

In addition, the Institute's publications, notably the magazine, the background papers, the annual guide and the Teachers' Handbook, came to be accepted as reliable sources of factual information and analysis that were otherwise unavailable or difficult to find. A prominent member of the NGO community concerned with these issues has pointed to a key rationale for this kind of work: "a better foreign policy . . . can be established if we have an informed public debate and if we give some . . . basic support to the information base on which that debate takes place."[27]

A mere seven years of activity is hardly enough time to trace a connection between a better informed public and government policy, even if it were possible to do so in any analytic sense. However, it may be claimed that the Canadian perspective which guided the work of CIIPS on such questions as continental defence, arms exports, peacekeeping, racial conflict, space surveillance and naval arms control did help focus opinion and policy on issues that remain important for Canada despite the ending of the of Cold War. Its termination would have led to changes in policy in any event; for example, the withdrawal of troops from Europe. But military deployments are not central to the dilemmas of security policy. Disarmament, even if moving in the right direction, remains controversial; nuclear proliferation continues; armed conflict disrupts the lives of peoples, and places heavy demands on UN peacekeeping; and new threats to security are emerging as population pressures and the misuse of resources disturb the balance of nature. CIIPS alerted the public to these challenges from the beginning, and there have been parallel, if not necessarily related, responses in Canadian policy, such as a greater emphasis on peacekeeping in defence planning, more sensitivity to the issue of arms exports, and efforts to increase circumpolar co-operation. The Cold War abounded in the crude simplicities of good and evil, freedom and tyranny, hawks and doves. The turbulence that lies ahead will be less amenable to caricature. Citizens revolt, whether they are free to or not—"a million mutinies now," as a recent study of India puts it—governments struggle to maintain order, arms accumulate and refugees flee.

The case for objective and independent analysis of Canadian and global security, aimed at the interested public and free from the constraints of political correctness and crisis management, is therefore stronger now than before. The Department of External Affairs is not, by its nature, able to accomplish this task, and recent cuts in its budget will not encourage it to try.

Whether any new body should be organized in the same way as CIIPS is an open question. Two issues in particular require consideration. Crown Corporations are as likely to be eliminated as they are to be established by governments, some for good reason. "Peace and security" is clearly a federal responsibility, but it may be that a Corporation of this kind would be better served if it were to be provided with an initial endowment rather than a parliamentary grant, and if its growth and utility were to be measured in part by its capacity to demand payment for some of its services. Secondly, it is doubtful in the light of experience whether the same organization should be charged with equal responsibilities for research and publication on the one hand, and for making grants on the other. Grants can best be administered by the existing granting councils, or by the kind of quasi-independent fund now being administered by the Department of External Affairs. Research and publication could then receive full attention from Directors and staff, and the temptation to be all things to all people would be diminished.

Appendix

Publications of CIIPS, 1986–92

The following were published by CIIPS as either a Background Paper (BP), Conference Report (CR), Factsheet (FS), Occasional Paper (OP), Points of View (PoV), or Working Paper (WP). All except Working Papers were published in both English and French and were circulated to libraries where they should be checked for availability.

East-West Relations

The CSCE and Future Security in Europe: A Report of a Conference held in Prague in December 1991, by Michael Bryans, March 1992. (WP 40).

Reform, Reintegration and Regional Security: The Role of Western Assistance in Overcoming Insecurity in Central and Eastern Europe, by Jeanne Kirk Laux, October 1991. (WP 37).

Canada and the Transformation of the East European Economies: Policy Challenges in the 1990s, by Carl McMillan, October 1990. (BP 35).

East-West Relations in Transition: Towards a New European Order. Excerpts from a Report of the Strategic Assessment Group of Experts, to the Canadian Institute for International Peace and Security, July 1990, 44 pages. (WP 27).

Superpower Rivalry in the Indian Ocean, by Paul George, February 1989, 36 pages. (WP 16).

New Dimensions in Canadian-Soviet Arctic Relations, by John Hannigan, November 1988. (BP-PoV 6).

International Security and Canadian Interests, Report of a Working Group, June 1988, 38 pages. (WP 11).

From Lenin to Gorbachev: Changing Soviet Perspectives on East-West Relations, by Paul Marantz, May 1988, 89 pages. (OP 4).

East-West Relations in the 1980s, by Adam Bromke, May 1988, 103 pages. (WP 9).

Superpower Rivalry and Soviet Policy in the Caribbean Basin, by S. Neil MacFarlane, June 1986, 70 pages. (OP 1).

East-West Relations: Values, Interests and Perceptions, by Geoffrey Pearson, March 1986. (BP-PoV 1).

Regional Conflicts and Security Issues

Democratizing Southern Africa, Herbert Adam and Kogila Moodley, June 1992, (OP 9).

Peace for Lebanon? Obstacles, Challenges, Prospects, A Report of a Research Project in Ottawa from September 1990–November 1991, by Deirdre Collings and Jill Tansley, May 1992. (WP 43).

After the Persian Gulf War. The Potential for Economic Reconstruction and Development in the Persian Gulf Region, by Mehran Nakhjavani, March 1991, 23 pages. (WP 34).

The Gulf Crisis: the Debates and the Stakes, by Bernard Wood, September 1990, 20 pages. (WP 30).

Economic Sanctions and South Africa, by Stephen Godfrey, August 1990. (BP 33).

Cyprus — Visions for the Future: A Summary of Conference and Workshop Proceedings, by François Lafrenière and Robert Mitchell, May 1990, 106 pages. (WP 21).

The Return of Vietnam to the International System, by Gérard Hervouet, December 1988, 83 pages. (OP 6).

Destabilization of the Frontline States of Southern Africa, 1980–1987, by Dan O'Meara, June 1988. (BP 20).

The War in the Gulf, by Francine Lecours, May 1988. (BP 19).

Measures for Peace in Central America: Proceedings of the Roundtable on Interim and Confidence-Building Measures in Central America, Ottawa, May 8–9 1987, by Liisa North, December 1987, 76 pages. (WP-CR5).

Peace, Development and Security in the Caribbean: Perspectives to the Year 2000: Proceedings of a Conference, Kingston, Jamaica, March 22–25, 1987, by Lloyd Searwar, August 1987, 36 pages. (WP-CR4).

Conference on Militarization in the Third World, by Paul Rogers, Michael Klare and Dan O'Meara, presented at Queen's University, Kingston, Ontario, January 1987, 83 pages. (WP 5).

Peace in Central America? by Steven Baranyi, October 1986. (BP 8).

Negotiations for Peace in Central America: Proceedings of the Roundtable on Negotiations in Central America, Ottawa, September 27–28, 1985, by Liisa North, 59 pages. (WP-CR1).

Arms Control — Nuclear

A Review of the Geneva Negotiations: 1989–1990, by David Cox, May 1990. (BP 32).

The Implications of the INF Treaty, by Jane Boulden, March 1990. (BP 31).

Nuclear Non-Proliferation: The Status and Prospects, by Jozef Goldblat, June 1989. (BP 29).

Non-Proliferation Treaty (NPT), June 1989. (FS 10).

A Review of the Geneva Negotiations 1987–1988, by David Cox, March 1989. (BP 27).

Cruise Missiles and Strategic Arms Control, by Jane Boulden, January 1989. (BP 24).

Debate about Nuclear Weapon Tests, by David Cox and Jozef Goldblat, August 1988, 86 pages (OP 5).

Has the ABM Treaty a Future? by Ronald G. Purver, February 1988. (BP 18).

Accidental Nuclear War: Reducing the Risks, by Dianne DeMille, January 1988. (BP 16).

A Review of the Geneva Negotiations on Strategic Arms Reductions, by David Cox, June 1987. (BP 13).

Who's Ahead? Examining the Nuclear Arms Balance, by Jane Boulden, March 1987. (BP 12).

The Risk of Accidental Nuclear War: Proceedings of the Conference on the Risk of Accidental Nuclear War, Vancouver, May 26–30, 1986, by Andrea Demchuk, 38 pages. (WP-CR3).

Strategic Stability and Mutual Security in the Year 2000: Getting There from Here: Proceedings of a Meeting, Erice, Italy, April 25–27, 1986, 113 pages. (WP 3).

Reviewing the Non-Proliferation Treaty, by William Epstein, March 1986. (BP 4).

A Nuclear Freeze? by David Cox, January 1986. (BP 2).

Nuclear Weapons, Counter-Force and Arms Reduction Proposals: A Guide to Information Sources and Force Calculations, October 1985, 57 pages. (WP 1).

Arms Control — Non-Nuclear

Canadian Controls on the Export of Arms and Strategic Goods, by Jean-François Rioux, August 1991. (BP 37).

Naval Arms Control, by Ron Purver, December 1991. (BP 39).

Arms Export Controls to Limit Weapons Proliferation. A Report of a Conference in Ottawa in June 1991, by Jean-François Rioux, December 1991. (WP 39).

The Soviet Concept of Reasonable Sufficiency: Conventional Arms Control in an Era of Transition, by Elaine Holoboff, October 1990, 45 pages. (WP 29).

Ballistic Missile Proliferation, by Marie-France Desjardins, September 1990. (BP 34).

The Control of Chemical and Biological Weapons: Strengthening International Verification and Compliance: Summary of a conference held in Toronto 4–5 April 1989, by Dianne DeMille, July 1990, 72 pages. (WP 25).

Compliance with Confidence Building Measures: From Helsinki to Stockholm, by Michael Holmes, February 1990. (BP 30).

Conventional Arms Control and Disarmament in Europe: Canadian Objectives, by Douglas Hamlin, January 1990, 52 pages. (WP 20).

The International Trade in Arms, by Keith Krause, March 1989. (BP 28).

Non-nuclear Powers and the Geneva Conference on Disarmament: A Study in Multilateral Arms Control, by Michael Tucker, March 1989, 62 pages. (OP 7).

Conventional Arms Control in Europe: Western Opening Positions, by John Toogood, December 1988, 34 pages. (WP 15).

Conventional Military Balance in Europe, by Roger Hill, July 1988. (BP 21).

International Trade in Arms: Problems and Prospects: A Summary of Proceedings of a Conference on International Arms Transfers, Hull, Québec, October 21–22, 1987, by Keith Krause, March 1988, 47 pages. (WP-CR6).

Arctic Arms Control: Constraints and Opportunities, by Ronald G. Purver, February 1988, 80 pages. (OP 3).

Conventional Force Balance in Europe: Understanding the Numbers, by James Moore, January 1988, 15 pages. (WP 6).

The Stockholm Agreement; An Exercise in Confidence Building, by C.A. Namiesniowski, August 1987. (BP 14).

Satellite Surveillance and Canadian Capabilities, by Ron Buckingham, September 1986. (BP 7).

Conventional Arms Control Negotiations in Europe, by John Toogood, April 1986. (BP 5).

Disarmament

The Case for a United Nations Verification Agency, Disarmament Under Effective International Control, by A. Walter Dorn, July 1990, 41 pages. (WP 26).

Closing the Gap: Disarmament and Development, the International Debate, by Steve Lee, March 1990, 38 pages. (WP 22).

Resolutions on Arms Control, Disarmament: Canada's Record at the UN, by Bernard F. Grebene, November 1989, 79 pages. (WP 19).

United Nations and Disarmament, June 1989. (FS 9).

Nuclear Weapon-Free Zones, January 1989 (FS 5).

United Nations Special Session on Disarmament 1988: Peace Proposals Since 1982, Hanna Newcombe, May 1988, 59 pages. (WP 10).

Chemical Disarmament: From the Ban on Use to a Ban on Possession, by Jozef Goldblat, February 1988. (BP 17).

Nuclear Disarmament: The Gorbachev Initiative, by John R. Walker, January 1987. (BP 11).

Nuclear Weapons and the Averting of War, by Robert W. Malcolmson, October 1986. (BP-PoV 2).

Defence

Surveillance from Space: A Strategic Opportunity for Canada, by George Lindsey, June 1992.

Modernization of Weapons and the Qualitative Problems of Arms Control, by George Lindsey, May 1992.

The Canadian Navy: Options for the Future, by Captain Robert H. Thomas, April 1992. (WP 41).

Soviet Defence Industry Reform: The Problems of Conversion in an Unconverted Economy, by Karen Ballentine, July 1991. (BP 36).

Framework for a New Canadian Defence Policy, by Roger Hill, June 1991, 90 pages. (WP 35).

The NORAD Renewal Issue, Report of the Special Panel to the Sub-Committee on External Affairs and International Trade considering the question of renewing in May 1991 the North American Aerospace Defence Agreement, March 1991, 65 pages. (WP 33).

Indian Naval Expansion, by Paul George, February 1991, 47 pages. (WP 32).

Surveillance Over Canada, by George Lindsey and Gordon Sharpe, December 1990, 81 pages. (WP 31).

Canada et sous marins. Technologie et politique, by Bernard Goulard, June 1990, 59 pages. (WP 24).

When does Deterrence Succeed and How do we Know?, by Richard Ned Lebow and Janice Gross Stein, February 1990, 90 pages. (OP 8).

The Military Use of Space, November 1989. (FS 11).

Challenges to Canadian Security in the Year 2000: A Summary of Conference Proceedings, by Jean-François Rioux, April 1989, 45 pages. (WP 17).

The Warsaw Pact (Warsaw Treaty Organization), March 1989. (FS 6).

Security: Canada and the Arctic, March 1989. (FS 7).

Sovereignty: Canada and the Arctic, March 1989. (FS 8).

Non-Offensive Defence: The Way to Achieve Common Security in Europe, by Robert Neild, January 1989. (BP 25).

Of Fireproof Houses: Canada's Security, by Geoffrey Pearson, December 1988. (BP-PoV 7).

The Cruise Missile and Cruise Missile Testing in Canada, September 1988. (FS 3).

The NATO Nuclear Planning Group, by Jocelyn Coulon, August 1988. (BP 22).

NORAD (North American Aerospace Defence Command), March 1988. (FS 1).

NATO (North Atlantic Treaty Organization), March 1988. (FS 2).

Maintaining Peace with Freedom: Nuclear Deterrence and Arms Control, by Lorne Green, March 1987. (BP-PoV 4).

La France et l'initiative de défense stratégique, by Charles-Philippe David, January 1987, 87 pages. (WP 4).

Trends in Continental Defence: A Canadian Perspective, by David Cox, December 1986, 50 pages. (OP 2).

A Second Look at No First Use, by Fen Osler Hampson, November 1986. (BP 9).

Canadian Responses to the Strategic Defense Initiative, by Gregory Wirick, October 1985. (BP 1).

Challenges to Deterrence: Doctrines, Technologies and Public Concerns: Proceedings of the Conference on Challenges to Deterrence, Ottawa, October 17–19, 1985, by Dianne DeMille, 69 pages. (WP-CR2).

Conflict Resolution — Theory and Practice

International Humanitarian Law, November 1991. (FS 17).

Civilian Aspects of Peacekeeping. A Report of a Conference in Ottawa in July 1991, by Robin Hay, October 1991. (WP 36) (BP 38).

Economic Sanctions, September 1991. (FS 16).

The Commonwealth, January 1991. (FS 15).

La Francophonie, October 1990. (FS 14).

International Law and the World Court, July 1990. (FS 13).

Humanitarian Ceasefires: An Examination of their Potential Contribution to the Resolution of Conflict, by Robin Hay, July 1990, 52 pages. (WP 28).

Climate Change, Global Security, and International Governance: A summary of a conference in Ottawa, April 1990, by Kenneth Bush, June 1990, 59 pages. (WP 23).

The United Nations and International Security, March 1990. (FS 12).

The Reduction of the Risk of War through Multilateral Means: A Summary of Conference Proceedings, by David Cox, Steve Lee, James Sutterlin, September 1989, 32 pages. (WP 18).

Canadian Attitudes and Approaches to the United Nations Security Council, by Harald von Riekhoff, February 1989. (BP 26).

Regions of Peace — Oases of Hope, by Arnold Simoni, November 1988, 18 pages. (WP 13).

Peacekeeping, October 1988. (FS 4).

Peacekeeping and Peacemaking in Cyprus, by Robert Mitchell, October 1988. (BP 23).

Managing Regional Conflict: Regimes and Third-Party Mediators (#2): Proceedings of a Workshop held in Ottawa on May 6–7, 1988, by Kenneth D. Bush and Richard Price, August 1988, 64 pages. (WP 12).

Managing Regional Conflict: Regimes and Third-Party Mediators: Proceedings of a Workshop held in Ottawa on November 19–20, 1987, by Robert Miller, May 1988, 59 pages. (WP 8).

Peacekeeping and the Management of International Conflict, by Henry Wiseman, September 1987. (BP 15).

The Debate about Peace Education, by Elizabeth Richards, December 1986. (BP 10).

A Survey of Peace Education in Canada, by Wytze Brouwer, February 1986, 71 pages (WP 2).

Miscellaneous

The Role of the Media in International Conflict: A Report of a Conference in Ottawa in September 1991, by Christopher Young, December 1991. (WP 38).

Teachers' Handbook on Peace and Security, 347 pages, June 1990.

Towards a World Space Organization, by Elisabeth Mann Borgese, November 1987. (BP-PoV 5).

Canadian Press Coverage of Arms Control and Disarmament Issues, by John R. Walker, March 1987. (BP-PoV 3).

Origins of the Canadian Institute for International Peace and Security, by Gilles Grondin, August 1986. (BP 6).

Nuclear Winter, by Leonard Bertin, March 1986. (BP 3).

Reference Works — (Published Annually)

The Guide to Canadian Policies on Arms Control, Disarmament, Defence and Conflict Resolution, 1986, 1987, 1988, 1989, 1990, 1991, 1992.

Director's Annual Statement, approximately 20 to 50 pages, January 1988, December 1988, January 1990, December 1990, January 1992.

The CIIPS Public Opinion Survey of Canadian Views on Peace and Security, January 1988, December 1988, December 1989, December 1990.

Annual Report, from 1984/85 to 91/92.

Bibliographic Reference Works

Surviving the Nuclear Age, a bibliography on nuclear weapons, arms control and disarmament for the year 1987, by Ron Purver and Jutta Paczulla, May 1990.

Peace and Security Bookshelf. An annotated bibliography of current Canadian materials for the general public. Annual issues: 1990, 1991.

Canada and International Peace and Security: a Bibliography. Annual issues: 1985–1989, 1990.

Peace and Security Thesaurus, June 1990.

Related Publications

The Institute played a role in a number of volumes published by external publishers. Listed below are works where the Institute's involvement was significant.

David Cox and Jozef Goldblat, ed., *A Comprehensive Text Ban?*, Oxford University Press, 1987.

Boyce Richardson, *Time to Change*, Summerhill Press, 1990.

Carl Jacobsen, ed., *Soviet Foreign Policy: New Dynamics, New Themes*, Macmillan, 1990.

Carl Jacobsen, ed., *Strategic Power USA-USSR*, Macmillan, 1990.

Fen Osler Hampson, Harald von Riekhoff, and John Roper, ed., *The Allies and Arms Control*, Johns Hopkins University Press, 1991.

Fen Osler Hampson and Brian S. Mandell, eds., *Managing Regional Conflict*, special issue of *International Journal*, Vol. 45, No. 2 (Spring 1990).

Norma Salem ed., *Cyprus: A Regional Conflict and its Resolution*, Macmillan, 1992.

TRADE WARS

5   The End of Trade Policy?

Michael Hart

The end of history then means not the end of worldly events but the end of the evolution of human thought about such first principles.

Francis Fukuyama

IN 1989, U.S. STATE DEPARTMENT whiz kid Francis Fukuyama wrote an arresting article entitled "The End of History."[1] He argued that much of history — using the term in its Hegelian sense — had been organized around competing political and economic ideologies; during the post-war period, this had been symbolized by the Cold War. With the end of the Cold War and the triumph of liberal democracy, we were now at the "end" of history.

Dare we draw a parallel here to the changing nature and content of trade policy? Trade policy has for centuries been organized on the basis of the measures governments use at the border to define and defend national markets and national producers. For almost fifty years trade policy and international trade negotiations have successfully sought to reduce and eliminate barriers at the border and to contain related measures within a code of conduct administered on the basis of an agreed intergovernmental regime — the GATT. Since trade policy and trade negotiations were in tune with the way in which both domestic economies and the international economy were organized, the regime worked well and underpinned a tremendous expansion in international trade and investment. As a result, a rules-based international trade order has now become a universally accepted part of both intellectual and intergovernmental discourse.

The success of the GATT regime in integrating national economies into a global economy now poses a new series of challenges that suggest the need for both a new trade policy and a new regime. Today we have a global economy, regional economies and local economies, while the role of national economies appears to be diminishing. Yet governance continues to be organized on the basis of a national polity. The result is growing conflict between national political goals and international economic reality.

The full impact and implication of the global economic changes that are driving the demand for a new paradigm are, of course, not yet fully understood. Nevertheless, there is now sufficient analysis available to enable us to distinguish some of the main characteristics of the emerging global economy, Canada's place in it and some of the policy issues that will need to be addressed globally and nationally. We can already discern an emerging agenda of new trade policy issues including some related to substance (e.g., competition policy, environmental policy, product standards, subsidies, dispute resolution and social policies) and others relating to form (e.g., global and regional agreements, various approaches to conflict resolution and the nature and potential effect of international legislation). On the assumption that governments wish to ensure that their citizens benefit from the rapid globalization of production and markets we are likely to see international economic negotiations expand well beyond their traditional confines of border and related measures and delve into areas more typically conceived of as "domestic" policy. In true Hegelian fashion, therefore, we are seeing not only the "end" of trade policy as it has been practised for the past fifty years, but also a new beginning attuned to today's changing circumstances and tomorrow's challenges.

The Waning of the Old Regime

The 1980s saw the beginning of a substantial transformation in the way the international and domestic economies function and interact with one another. Developments in communications technology and transportation facilities have erased borders and shrunk distances, producing fundamental changes in business organization and techniques and differing perceptions of the role and influence of government. The term "globalization" has been used to capture the international dimensions of this transformation. It involves the rapid and pervasive diffusion around the globe of production, consumption and investment of goods, services and capital. Concurrently, we are seeing the development of what has been called a new economy, based on revolutionary changes in the technology and organization of production and leading to the virtual disappearance of some industries, the rise of brand new ones and radical changes in employment patterns.[2]

Changes in the way the global and domestic economies now function and interact with each other are only beginning to be reflected in domestic policy developments and in international economic arrangements. Indeed, the conduct of international business has changed to the point that many of the rules and agreements in force domestically and internationally cannot adequately address the way in which international economic exchanges are organized and pursued.

Forty-five years ago, when the basic framework of international trade and economic rules was negotiated, trade in goods was the main vehicle of economic integration. In 1950, for example, the total volume of world trade represented about ten percent of world production. The bulk of this trade consisted of raw materials (62 percent); most of the rest was made up of finished products; very little trade involved parts and components. Most trade took the form of transactions between unrelated private parties organized as nationally identifiable companies. The main barriers to trade were government measures imposed at the border (tariffs and quotas) or differential treatment in taxation and regulatory requirements (e.g., commodity taxes and mixing requirements). Relatively high tariffs helped to maintain nationally segmented markets for manufactured products. Exchange rates were fixed, and maintaining a positive current account position was an important goal of government policy.

In the 1950s, most international economic activity was undertaken by large, nationally organized firms. Companies designed, engineered, manufactured, marketed and serviced a range of related products totally within the confines of the firm. They might go outside the firm for financing and advertising but for little else. Individual firms were hierarchically organized and many employees stayed with a firm for their full working lives. Employees felt themselves to be part of their company and companies felt themselves to be part of a national economy. Most firms — and their products — had a clearly identifiable national origin and foreign investment generally involved the establishment of miniature replicas of such firms. Foreign direct investment, however, represented only a small proportion of global economic activity.

Government policy — domestic and international — reflected these facts of economic life. The GATT, for example, negotiated in 1947–48, assumes trade among national economies pursued by private entrepreneurs working largely within the confines of national borders. The GATT regards conflicts that may arise between firms in one country and firms in another as involving national interests that can be resolved through intergovernmental consultation. As negotiated in 1947, it conceded the regulation of domestic economic life — competition policy, for example, or farm income stability — to be largely within the purview of national governments, provided that any overt discrimination between domestic and foreign products would only take place within the limits of the GATT-sanctioned border regime.

Business and government attitudes to international trade also reflected the prevailing economic theory that international trade flowed from comparative advantage, a relatively static condition based on national endowments of the principal factors of production: resources, capital, and labour. The trade regime, for example, was based on the concept that government policies that distorted the most efficient allocation of these factors of production were likely to lower the level of national and global welfare while the removal of such barriers was likely to raise it. Similarly, trade and investment were considered to be alternative ways of pursuing comparative advantage; the establishment of a foreign branch-plant was thought to replace production in the home country that would otherwise have been exported to the foreign market.[3]

Few of these policy-defining assumptions and characteristics are valid today. For example, the liberalization of trade did not lead to greater inter-sectoral specialization at the national level; rather, we have seen tremendous growth in intra-sectoral trade as countries have exchanged cars for cars and steel for steel, leading to much higher levels of international competition in domestic markets than anyone would have anticipated in the 1940s and 1950s. Trade in goods, while it has grown twice as fast as production and now constitutes about twenty percent of world production, has become a less important instrument of international economic integration than international investment and capital flows or exchanges of knowledge and technology. The value of world trade in goods — in real terms about five times larger than its value in

1950—is now but a fraction of the annual value of capital movements. Fully a fifth of the value of world trade now consists of
services, and a further proportion involves services imbedded in
goods.

Billions of dollars of capital now flow around the world at the
touch of a button. Capital markets operate twenty-four hours a
day. Currency markets track minute changes in relative values
looking for quick profits. The cost of debt capital is now relatively uniform around the globe, taking into account inflation and
exchange rates. The necessary institutions and skills, organized
to make this fluid, global capital market work, are hastening the
further globalization of the economy. Most major currencies now
float freely and their values are adjusted constantly and instanta-
neously. The IMF has been transformed from an instrument for
regulating currency values and balances of payments to that of
banker and economic advisor to the Third World.[4]

Regional trade agreements have become major forums for
reducing trade barriers, negotiating rules and settling disputes,
while GATT is in danger of becoming a residual negotiating forum,
providing the systemic glue that holds various regional arrangements together and consolidating the experience and experiments
of regional negotiations.

The last decade has seen the devastation, or reorganization, of
traditional industries such as steel, automobiles and shipbuilding,
and the rise of new industries such as micro-electronics, computer
software and biotechnology. Global corporations and networks
involving local and regional firms now rely on a much more
fragmented and decentralized approach to design, engineering,
production, marketing and service. They are organized much
more horizontally than their counterparts from an earlier era and
they make much greater use of expertise and resources outside the
firm. They use strategic alliances in such forms as joint production,
R & D and other ventures, licensing arrangements, contracting out
and brokering among global corporations and networks, as basic
techniques in organizing their activities. As a result, there has been
a tremendous growth in intra-corporate and intra-sectoral trade in
parts and other components, as well as an increasing reliance on
activities taking place far from corporate headquarters or ultimate
markets.

New forms of specialization have resulted in the development of strategic links between global corporations and local suppliers and distributors on a global basis. The concern with stability in corporate organizations and relationships that was an integral part of economic life in the 1950s and 1960s has been replaced by a new emphasis on fluidity and flexibility. Employees no longer experience the same symbiotic relationship with the firm, and firms no longer feel any special attachment to political entities. With the reduction and even elimination of traditional border-based barriers to trade, political frontiers now bear little relationship to economic frontiers.

Prevailing theories about economic growth and international exchange have also become much more sophisticated and varied, and have robbed governments of the moral and intellectual certitude that characterized the trade regime of the 1950s and 1960s. New ideas about dynamic comparative advantage, the international division of labour, the complementarity of international trade and investment, the role of technology, the importance of trade in services, the management and organization of production, as well as the role of government policies, have challenged the conventional theoretical foundations of trade policy and made governments less certain about the direction of future domestic and international policies and arrangements.[5]

The Demise of the Old Trade Policy

The GATT-based trade relations system was built on the basis of a series of goals and principles that had generally stood the test of time:

- **economic** — it sought to raise national and global welfare by taking advantage of the international division of labour through the reduction of barriers to international trade and investment, thus promoting efficiency, productivity and competitiveness;
- **legal** — it sought to provide clear rules and procedures for equitable and expeditious settlement of disputes on the basis of transparency, non-discrimination and due process;
- **business** — it aimed at fostering an international business climate based on predictability, stability and fairness; and

- **political** — internationally, the goal was a set of rules within which to manage stable interstate trade relations while protecting national sovereignty; domestically, the goal was a set of rules that would allow for the equitable distribution of the benefits of international trade while permitting orderly adjustment to greater international competition.

To achieve these goals, the GATT system pioneered a specific set of tools, rules and techniques; some were present from the outset — such as the techniques for negotiating tariff concessions — while others were introduced and developed over time — such as codes of procedure governing anti-dumping and countervailing duties or the procedures for settling disputes. Closely linked to GATT were a series of regional agreements based on the same principles and techniques and broadly consistent with its requirements. Collectively, these agreements constitute what has been called the GATT-based trade relations system.

This system proved a positive force in the international economy and could lay claim to many achievements. Trade was liberalized; tariffs were cut; old-fashioned discriminatory quantitative restrictions were virtually eliminated; and many potentially harmful practices were restrained. It created the conditions necessary for the pervasive economic integration of the OECD economies; its rules provided private investors with the necessary confidence to expand their horizons; and its periodic negotiating rounds maintained momentum toward increasing trade liberalization.

Its success, however, was not unqualified. The system became increasingly complex over the years as the 35 original articles became encrusted with a series of ancillary or supporting arrangements, some of which qualified or changed the original bargain or undermined progress toward the fundamental GATT objectives of freer and less discriminatory trade. It failed to deal with a number of problems, notably trade in agriculture and textiles; it was unable to prevent the rise in regionalism; and its weak constitutional base deprived it of the authority to address new problems.

GATT's system of mercantilist bargaining thus proved capable of addressing the problems of the trade relations system of the 1950s and 1960s, but seemed unsuited to the challenges the trading system faced by the mid-1980s. The biggest challenge faced during the Uruguay Round was trying to find a formula which would make it possible to expand the GATT trade relations system to a much broader agenda, more consonant with the changing nature of the international economy and the larger number of actively engaged participants.[6]

Today, the issues of government policy that are critical to trade and competitiveness are not so much those conventionally considered as trade policy as those that foster an overall economic climate. More to the point, the focus of policy has shifted from efforts to segment markets (i.e., protect existing investment) to efforts to promote interdependence (i.e., attract new investment by both domestic and foreign investors), resulting in concurrent policy rivalry and policy convergence along a broad range of government instruments from fiscal and monetary policy to subsidies and sectorally-based regulatory schemes. In effect, trade policy is becoming more domestic while domestic policies are becoming more international.

This shift in basic policy orientation involving the interdependence of domestic and foreign policies, however, is incomplete. Much of the underlying thinking is still based on the assumption that large sectors of economic life can be understood in terms of national corporations operating within national economies controlled by national governments. In the years to come, as contentious negotiations increasingly focus on sensitive domestic regulatory schemes (involving such diverse issues as environmental protection, product standards, competition policy, innovation policy, income and price support programs and cultural identity measures), governments will need to consider the most effective way to negotiate a regime consonant with a global economy dominated by global firms operating within and between national economies. Such a new regime may well require new techniques and approaches based less on concession swapping and more on rule writing. Such negotiations will bring into play very different concerns about national sovereignty. It may prove very difficult to develop the necessary consensus and political support critical to its success.

The Emergence of a New Regime

The trade policy of the future, of course, starts with and builds on the trade policy of the past. We are not going through the same kind of discontinuity of depression and war that provided the background for the current trade and payments system. There remain problems from the past that need to be resolved. Uruguay Round difficulties in addressing such issues as agriculture, subsidies and textiles and clothing indicate that there is no shortage of such problems. Nevertheless, consolidating and strengthening the existing rules will address only a small part of the challenges the global economy now faces. Further evolutionary changes in trade rules and practices will not catch up to the fundamental changes that have taken place in the conduct of international business, let alone establish a satisfactory basis for keeping up with or even anticipating further changes.

As we have seen, the new economy, together with concomitant globalization and integration, has revealed the need to address issues traditionally considered to be matters of domestic policy, with a view to reducing new barriers to the efficient allocation of resources. Trade agreements are likely to be the focus for addressing these domestic policy issues internationally, because the problems and challenges such issues may pose in intergovernmental relations frequently manifest themselves first in the context of international trade. Until governments are prepared to enter into self-executing international agreements enforced by domestic courts, trade agreements may also provide the most effective way of enforcing international rules governing such policies and of resolving international conflicts — intergovernmental or intercorporate — that may arise as a result of them.

Addressing these new issues in the context of trade agreements raises a number of general and specific questions. To what extent, for example, are governments prepared to maintain the enduring goals and principles of the old trade regime, and to what extent do existing tools and techniques need to be modified and adapted for the purpose of handling these new negotiating challenges? Can we make meaningful progress on the basis of the concession-swapping techniques of the past? To what extent are the institutional and dispute settlement procedures of the existing regime adequate? Do we have a sufficient understanding of the issues involved to begin negotiating a new generation of international agreements?

The Canada-U.S. Free Trade Agreement (FTA), the North American Free Trade Agreement (NAFTA) and the GATT Uruguay Round have all provided opportunities to gain experience relevant to the problems of greater international integration, issues such as services, investment, intellectual property and business travel.

A striking feature of the negotiations preceding these agreements was the increasing sophistication in approach. For example, negotiating rules about financial services and investment indicate the extent to which the new or expanded trade regime will need to be built gradually and incrementally. The investment text in the FTA built on earlier bilateral and OECD experience and was geared largely to international trade in goods; the early Uruguay Round commitment to limit negotiations to trade-related investment measures gradually gave way to broader considerations. The NAFTA text reflects an expanded outlook and takes greater account of the whole range of factors involved in international business, such as trade in goods and services, the transfer of technology and strategic alliances. The financial services chapter of the FTA involved very specific concessions by each side; the NAFTA chapter completely recasts these obligations and translates them into a set of generic rules to which are appended some specific exceptions and concessions.

It is also becoming evident that applying old techniques to new problems is not necessarily the best way to proceed. It seems likely that more problems than solutions resulted from the attempt to negotiate over non-tariff barriers using the mercantilist type of bargaining over procedural codes employed during the Tokyo Round. The growing abuse of the anti-dumping system, for example, and its use in reinforcing oligopolistic practices, have indicated a major conflict between trade and competition policies. Efforts to further strengthen international consensus regarding enforcement procedures are more likely to widen than narrow that gap.

Nevertheless, efforts to begin addressing the new policy issues on the basis of the principles and techniques of the old trade regime have generally been successful. The last half dozen years have demonstrated that it is possible to negotiate enforceable rules of general application for trade in services, investment and intellectual property, based on such principles as non-discrimination, transparency, due process and openness.

Emerging Challenges

The emerging issues that now need to be faced are not just matters that have grabbed the fancy of trade negotiators eager to expand their field of operations. They have become apparent as the result of intense academic analysis and debate — e.g., discussions about strategic trade policy[7] — as well as the frustrations and experience of business and governments alike in adapting to the demands of the new economy and the forces of globalization. Some of them have arisen because of conflict between competing policy fields; others reflect the much more intense level of international integration. What is clear is that the old trade policy will not be adequate to the needs of the new domestic and international economies.

One of the most difficult themes common to many of the new trade policy issues is the question raised by Robert Reich: who is "us" and who is "them?" In a denationalized, global economy, whose interests do governments promote and protect? How do governments advance national values and priorities in a denationalized economy? DeAnn Julius suggests that there are at least six different ways of determining the nationality of a firm: where it is legally established, where its headquarters is located, the dominant nationality of its shareholders, the dominant nationality of its board of directors, the dominant nationality of its work force, or the market where it does most of its business.[8] Similar difficulties are encountered in defining the nationality of technology, goods and services. Such difficulties have tremendous implications for domestic and international policy. Reich suggests that, in the radically different circumstances we now face, the principal clients of governments are workers and that policy should be increasingly focused on ensuring their welfare.

A related set of general considerations bears on the object of the game: is it to harmonize as many national rules and standards on an international basis as possible, or to provide a basis for co-ordination and convergence but not for harmonization, or to put in place a set of guidelines aimed at establishing basic minimum standards?

An important characteristic of the new trade policy is the potential for conflict between competing policy fields arising from the insistence that one set of goals and values takes precedence over another. Public policy involves choices among competing priorities. It involves compromises not only between societies, but within them. While the perceived conflict between various public policy objectives is rarely as sharp as special interests would like the public to believe, good public policy requires that issue specialists find common ground and determine the extent to which presumed conflicts are genuine or proceed from prejudices and popular fallacies. Is it realistic, for example, to insist that one set of objectives should not compromise another? In a democratic society, is it possible for a single set of issues to be given, *a priori*, absolute precedence over all other societal goals, whether it be, for example, protection of the environment or the promotion of competition?

The task is, therefore not merely to extend the old trade policy to a broader range of issues, but to reconsider the fundamental assumptions and values that will underlie the trade regime of the future. Is comparative advantage, for example, a concept that applies to nations or to firms? Can it be shaped and advanced with the help of government policy?

Most of the emerging policy issues can be grouped around five broad themes. The initial approach to each theme can take the form of identifying (1) the conflict or overlap between traditional trade policy objectives and the objectives of the domestic policy field; (2) recent examples of conflicts and problems; (3) specific problems and challenges that need to be addressed; and potential pitfalls that need to be avoided. In addition, it will be necessary to systematically analyze ways of adapting the traditional principles, concepts and techniques of trade agreements to the disparate policy fields now emerging as critical to the trade policy of the future.[9]

Maintaining and Creating Wealth — the Trade and Investment Interface

One set of issues derives from efforts by governments to maintain and attract employment and wealth-creating investment. The increased importance of foreign direct investment (FDI) in the globalization of production and markets, in the diffusion of process and product technology and in the spread of management and organization techniques, suggests that there is increased potential for conflict as governments adopt competing policies to meet national objectives.

The complementarity between trade and investment further suggests that governments have as great an interest in a well-functioning and open investment regime as they have had in an open trade regime. Experience to date, however, suggests that they do not accept this view. In many countries there remains an ambivalent attitude toward the benefits of FDI which has produced regulatory regimes that are likely to lead to conflict.[10]

Negotiating international rules on investment within the framework of trade agreements is not wholly new. The original International Trade Organization (ITO) negotiations included an investment chapter and since then there has been a variety of experience in the OECD, regional agreements and bilateral agreements. The draft Uruguay Round final text includes a chapter on trade-related investment measures. Nevertheless, there remains considerable scope for the negotiation of rules of general application attuned to the realities of today's global economy, in which FDI is one of the most important agents of integration and exchange.

Maintaining and Creating Wealth — the Trade and Innovation Interface

The principal industries of the new economy are science- and knowledge-based and their growth and success are critically dependent on innovation, both in developing new products and in adapting new technologies. The drive to innovate starts with basic research, moves through applied research and development and culminates in the successful commercialization of new products and processes. Each of these activities lends itself to direct and indirect government involvement, aimed at ensuring that the country's nationals participate in, gain access to, derive advantage from and otherwise benefit from innovation. In this area too there is a fertile field for intergovernmental rivalry and intercorporate conflict.

Policy rivalry among governments seeking to give "our" hi-tech industries an advantage over "their" competitors has given rise to a variety of discriminatory measures including direct government sponsorship and financing of research, preferential or directed government procurement, various subsidies and incentives for private sector research, anti-trust exemptions for hi-tech consortia, government-sponsorship of R & D, more favourable intellectual property protection and restricted dissemination of the results of government research. Advocates of strategic trade policy have found this area a fertile field for their prescriptions.

The challenge will be to determine whether the industries of the future — the so-called winners — should benefit from a set of policy prescriptions differing from those applied to the industries of the past and whether international rules are required to recognize this differentiation. Prominent in the approach to this set of issues will be considerations relating to national security and future competitiveness and participation.

The degree of potential for conflict suggested by these various examples and considerations indicates that in the area of innovation there is wide scope for negotiating rules of general application which would both reduce conflict and make it easier to resolve disputes once they arise.[11]

Promoting Sustainable Development — the Trade and Environment Interface

Over the last decade, concern about sustainable development has reached the top of the public policy agenda. Governments at every level are being pressured to adopt policies that will protect and improve local, regional and global environmental conditions. Again, the potential for conflicts, arising out of different priorities, values and techniques and transmitted as a result of much greater global economic integration, is intense.

In the past few years, for example, business has expressed anxiety about the use of trade restrictive measures to achieve environmental objectives; environmentalists have offered resistance to trade liberalization/economic growth policies because of their perceived negative impact on environmental objectives; trade specialists have worried about the use of trade sanctions to enforce environmental agreements; and business and labour alike have expressed concern about the impact of environmental measures on their ability to compete internationally, and about the establishment of so-called pollution havens by other governments.

A number of recent cases has illustrated the potential for conflict between trade and environmental objectives. U.S. restrictions on imports of tuna, EC restrictions on imports of furs and bans on trade in ozone-depleting chemicals have all pointed to the need for a systematic review of the approaches to these conflicts.

Such a review would examine ways of meeting domestic and international environmental objectives without undoing the benefits of an open, multilateral trade regime, and meeting domestic and international trade objectives without derailing efforts to implement stricter environmental regulations. It would consider how to avoid both the excesses of unilateralism as well as the tyranny of international consensus. It would seek to prevent the reduction of international obligations to the lowest common denominator and the imposition of the will of a few countries on the majority. Only by addressing such tough issues will it prove possible, over time, to develop the international consensus required for negotiating a set of international rules that are consistent with both trade and environmental objectives.[12]

Maintaining Democratic Control — the Trade and Competition Interface

As the denationalization and globalization of the economy spread and intensify, governments find that they are losing their ability to influence or control the conduct of business within their jurisdictions. The need to attract international investment limits the capacity of governments in smaller economies to set market-place rules and enforce basic standards of corporate behaviour. Experience has already been gained in the negotiation of product standards and there has been some progress with setting process standards. The agreements reached have aimed less at harmonization and more at the establishment of procedures for reducing or resolving conflict. Future agreements, however, may need to go substantially further. In short, maintenance of an open trade regime requires some common rules and understandings about corporate behaviour and market-place rules if governments are to avoid a race to the bottom.

While the concern with democratic control is relevant to a number of policy areas it is critical to government efforts to promote competition, particularly in the face of efforts by global firms to eradicate or limit competition. In a global, denationalized economy, who is in charge, national and local governments or global corporations? What kinds of inter-governmental co-operation are required to ensure governments' ability to maintain a healthy level of competition at the national or regional level? To what extent should governments be allowed to extend their jurisdiction extra-territorially? How do governments manage the incidental extra-territorial effect of anti-trust enforcement? To what extent should there be a convergence in competition policy standards? To what extent should governments be allowed to use competition enforcement to provide competitive advantages to "our" firms at the expense of "their" firms?

Global competition and more liberal trade and investment conditions have in some ways reduced the need for the enforcement of domestic competition policy and in other ways heightened the need for vigorous domestic competition to foster international competitiveness. The growth in intra-firm and intra-network trade has made it hard to determine the degree of competition in a particular market and has provided firms with a wider range of techniques for exerting market power.

National competition authorities have in consequence become aware over the past decade both of the complementarity and the potential conflict between trade and competition goals and policies. They have also recognized that the globalization of production and consumption threatens to erode regulatory authority. They have noted the extent to which anti-competitive trade practices are tolerated in one jurisdiction and subject to prosecution in another. They have expressed concern about the extent to which global rationalization can promote oligopoly and oligopsony. Anti-dumping legislation, for example, has evolved in many jurisdictions to the point that it is being used by firms to reinforce anticompetitive practices. The enforcement of domestic merger and acquisition policies, on the other hand, may run directly counter to national efforts to promote international competition.

Unlike many of the other new policy issues, this area has been studied thoroughly. What is missing is business and government consensus on the purposes to be served by the negotiation of integrated international trade and competition rules. For example, efforts during the Canada-U.S. free trade negotiations to consider this set of issues floundered not because the issues were not well understood but because the necessary political and business consensus was missing.[13]

Promoting Equitable Distribution — Trade and Social Policy

The disaggregation and internationalization of production have placed tremendous strains on labour. One of the by-products of the new economy is a major adjustment in the distribution of wealth. Traditional manufacturing labour — the core of organized labour — has seen its place in industrialized societies slip as its numbers have declined and its wages have stagnated. Knowledge workers in the new economy have been the main beneficiaries of these changes. The movement of unskilled and semi-skilled labour to the service sector has been painful, often involving prolonged unemployment and lower wages.

The pressures on governments to respond with labour and social support policies have been intense, raising problems of funding and policy rivalry, with governments and corporations pleading that society cannot afford some of these measures and labour and other interest groups insisting that society cannot refuse to afford them. In effect, therefore, the emergence of the new economy and its global reach have contributed to the breakdown of the old social contract while a new contract has yet to be developed.[14]

There is broad acceptance that goods, services, capital and technology are all internationally mobile, whereas labour generally is *not* mobile, with the exception of people at the top end, such as senior management and knowledge workers. Two sets of problems result from these circumstances: pressures to allow for greater mobility of labour, particularly by developing country governments, and efforts to promote and protect the interests of workers within national and local jurisdictions. These two issues manifest themselves in a variety of policy responses and conflicts, ranging from efforts to restrict trade in some products to legislation on the right to work and the right to organize.

Three sets of issues are already apparent in the conflict between labour and trade policies: the use of trade-restrictive measures to achieve social policy ends; resistance to trade and investment liberalization policies because of their perceived impact on the distribution of wealth; and resistance to social measures because of their perceived impact on competitiveness. Each set involves conflicts within and between societies, conflicts which may be reduced or eliminated on the basis of international arrangements.

As with the negotiation of international environmental agreements, agreements on social policy issues such as fair labour standards or social contracts can as easily serve protectionist ends as social requirements. In any international negotiation, finding broad consensus on the values and priorities to be attached to particular policy goals constitutes a formidable challenge and presents potential pitfalls.[15]

The Architecture of the New Regime

As the content of trade negotiations becomes broader and more complex, attention will also need to be given to the most appropriate forums for negotiation and to defining the best forms of international co-operation.[16] Challenges relating to this set of issues include:

- **Regional agreements** — The last few years have seen the mushrooming of regional economic arrangements. To what extent are they here to stay? Are more regional agreements an appropriate vehicle for the pursuit of Canadian interests? Is it inevitable that these regional arrangements be organized around the major regional economy? Are the FTA and NAFTA singular arrangements addressing unique circumstances or should Canada be prepared to extend the NAFTA to include other countries? Is the NAFTA an embryo for a Western Hemisphere trade arrangement or could it have wider application? Should Canada consider new arrangements across the Atlantic and Pacific? Do we pursue any such initiatives alone or in concert with the United States?
- **Regional/multilateral linkages** — As regional arrangements deepen and proliferate, is there a continuing role for multilateral negotiations? Are there issues for which the leading edge will or should lie in multilateral negotiations? What should be the focus of future multilateral negotiations? Do they consolidate the work of regional arrangements? Are regional arrangements building blocks of greater global co-operation? Should regional arrangements stand on their own merits or become dependent on, or subsidiary to, global arrangements?
- **Interregional linkages** — Are we heading towards a tri-regional world — Europe, the Americas and Asia — for trade and investment? Should future global economic negotiations be organized to take place between regional groupings?
- **World Trade Organization** — What role is there for a world trade organization? Can a stronger organizational base for

world trade rules lead to better rules, quicker and more equitable dispute settlement and more certain enforcement? How should such an organization be structured?

- **One agreement or various interrelated arrangements** — The GATT has now become a very complex arrangement involving various interrelated agreements. The NAFTA negotiations were conducted at a main table and through parallel negotiations on a group of ancillary issues — environment, labour markets and adjustment. Services negotiations do not include air services, which are covered by a separate set of agreements. Is it in Canada's interest to promote the integration of various international economic instruments? Are there potential trade-offs in such integration and gains to be made from it?

- **Federal/provincial rights and obligations** — The contents of international economic negotiations are reaching deeper into national economic life and involve more and more issues of provincial jurisdiction. Are we organized to address provincial issues in international negotiations? What are the best ways to ensure provincial consensus and compliance?

- **Consensus-building** — The past decade saw great strides in strengthening formal mechanisms for consulting both the provinces and private sector interests. There remains room, however, for examining the best ways to build broader consensus among the Canadian public on trade policy issues. Are there better ways to engage Canadians in discussion of the issues raised by trade negotiations? How can Canadians be made to think more positively about the interaction between the domestic and international economies?

Conclusion: The Policy Conundrum

The global economy is rapidly becoming "denationalized" but governments continue to govern on the basis of national goals and frontiers. In a world where political frontiers bear little resemblance to economic units, a major challenge will be to conceive national economic policies that are consonant with a global economy. What is now "domestic" and what is "international"? Who is "us" and who is "them"?

The "old" trade policy of the immediate post-war years succeeded in achieving a significant degree of "shallow" integration by successfully using the concession-swapping technique of mercantilist bargaining. This technique was admirably suited to the realities of international business and polity during this period. Changes in those realities, however, now call for a much deeper level of integration and the development of techniques to provide, in effect, for international legislation and dispute settlement that globalize policy to the same degree as the globalization of business.[17]

Over the past decade, Canada has made major adjustments in both the substance and form of its trade policy. In 1985, the government decided to complement its multilateral negotiating strategy with bilateral efforts. The result was the FTA and now the NAFTA. Both agreements involve deep and broad trade and investment obligations which should help Canada to become a more competitive, outward-oriented economy. Concurrently, Canada was one of the most active participants in the Uruguay Round of GATT negotiations, pushing for the development of stronger and more modern global trade rules. Intensified efforts across the Atlantic and Pacific and down to Latin America have increased Canadian awareness of challenges and opportunities in those areas of the global economy and pointed to the need for additional institutional and other forms of co-operation. In effect, Canadian trade policy now pursues a multi-tiered strategy enabling Canada to identify and pursue opportunities along a number of fronts. In the more complicated global economy of the years to come, we will find that these adjustments will serve us well. In effect, we have already witnessed the end of the old trade policy and the beginning of the new.

As the range of issues described above indicates, the international trading system must meet a formidable series of challenges if it is to adapt and respond to the demands of the new, global economy. Governments will need to develop consensus on a potentially difficult group of issues, many of which undermine traditional concepts of sovereignty. To achieve the necessary international consensus, governments will need to rely on a fresh supply of intellectual capital generated either internally or in universities and think tanks. New negotiating tools and techniques may be required, as well as more robust institutions and firmer approaches to the resolution of conflict. The next decade is in fact likely to see a major reconsideration of the design, content and techniques of the international trade regime. The OECD has already embarked on some of the necessary spadework. A successful Uruguay Round would provide a stronger, more universal base for pursuing the examination of some of these issues.

For Canadians, the need to be actively in the forefront of these developments cannot be overemphasized. Our dependence on an effectively functioning trade and payments system and the benefits we derive from it have been well demonstrated. Our need to play a constructive role has been equally well documented. But our ability to ensure that Canadian values and priorities are reflected in the evolving new regime requires that we think the issues through and make our contributions early in the process. Since we are a relatively small player, it is at that stage where we are most likely to influence the content and course of a negotiation. We need to be quick, early and creative. That will demand collective energy and imagination from the private sector, labour and the academy as well as from government.

6 Strategic Alliances

Lynn K. Mytelka

Strategic partnering is of particular importance for firms which have historically engaged in R & D only to a limited extent. This is characteristic of the Canadian enterprise sector.

DURING THE 1980s, inter-firm technological co-operation agreements emerged as an important phenomenon in the advanced industrial countries. One indicator of this is the steep rise in the number of such agreements over the period 1975–89. In biotechnology, information technology and new materials, three of the most dynamic sectors, the number of strategic partnerships rose from an annual average of 63 per year in the 1975–79 period, to 300 per year in 1980–84 and 536 per year in the 1986–89 period.[1] In contrast to the period 1975–79, during which a total of 317 inter-firm technology co-operation agreements had been concluded, by the end of the 1980s, nearly twice that number of agreements were being signed each year.

Not only were firms spontaneously engaging in inter-firm R & D collaboration but, in addition, the growing importance of partnering activity for international competitiveness led governments in Japan,[2] Europe[3] and the United States[4] to initiate and/or finance a wide variety of different programs designed to promote strategic partnerships. Among the most well-known R & D consortia are the Japanese Very Large Scale Integration (VLSI) and Fifth Generation Computer projects, the semiconductor research corporation, SEMATECH, in the United States, the European ESPRIT (Strategic Program for Research and Development on Information Technology) and EUREKA programs.

The purpose of this paper is to assess this new context and to situate Canada within it. The first section examines the changing competitive environment that led to the growth in strategic partnering activity. The second and third sections analyze partnering activity by European and Canadian firms; this activity occurs in some cases in the context of programs designed to promote it, and in other cases independently of such programs. The concluding section highlights the level of partnering activity among European firms during the 1980s — considerably higher than the comparable level for Canadian companies — the important role that government has played in the development and funding of European R & D consortia, and the way in which this has stimulated R & D activity in small and medium-sized enterprises, strengthening their linkages to clients and reinforcing their ability to remain independent. Given the contribution that networking of this sort makes to international competitiveness, this section argues for the need to undertake new initiatives to encourage greater participation by Canadian firms in strategic partnering activities during the 1990s.

Strategic Partnerships and the Changing Competitive Environment

Inter-firm technological collaborative agreements can be distinguished from more traditional forms of linkage between firms, such as joint ventures, licensing or sub-contracting arrangements, by three main characteristics. First, they are two-way relationships focused on joint knowledge production and sharing as opposed to a one-way transfer of technology. The knowledge component of strategic partnerships, moreover, may involve the development of new products, new production processes or new routines within the firm or an enhanced ability to manage inter-firm contractual relationships. Second, strategic partnerships tend to be contractual in nature with little or no equity involvement by the participants. Third, they are part of the longer-term planning activity of the firm and not just an opportunistic response to short-term financial gains.[5]

Although the focus in this paper is on strategic partnerships in research and development, these are not the only form of collaborative activity in which firms have engaged. Exhibit 6.1 provides a taxonomy that includes both older, unidirectional forms of linkages as well as some examples of the newer forms of partnering activity in R & D, production and marketing that became more prominent over the past decade. In addition, by classifying joint ventures as both two-way and more traditional one-way relationships, this taxonomy underlines the mutability of traditional relationships. Consider the joint venture. Some, but not all, strategic partnerships are joint ventures but when they do involve an equity arrangement, as, for example, in the biotechnology industry, the intention is less to exercise control than to enable the larger firm, usually a major pharmaceutical, chemical or petrochemical company, to provide the financial and marketing resources that the smaller innovative partner lacks. Similarly the emergence of some sub-contractors, as partners engaged in a dialogue with their "principals," has been documented in both the textile and clothing and the electronics industries.[6] Customer-supplier relationships have also changed considerably, as suppliers are drawn into joint research and collaboration in the design of new products for their clients, and take on additional responsibility for the manufacture of whole modules which are subsequently assembled into complete products by the customers, notably in the automobile and aircraft industries.[7]

This shift from the almost exclusive reliance on one-way linkages to the development of two-way collaborative relationships requires some explanation. The following discussion analyzes the origins of strategic partnering activity from the perspective of the firm and of the states that are promoting it.

The Firms

Recent research confirms that the economic downturn, which began in the late 1960s and accelerated during the 1970s, was due not so much to the two oil shocks of 1973 and 1979, as to a rising inflationary trend evident in agro-related products, and to the relative and absolute declines in the productivity of manufacturing industry in the United States, Canada and much of Western Europe.[8] These declining productivity levels reflected, in part, the exhaustion of the technical possibilities of certain long-standing methods of production, notably the mass production techniques associated with the manufacture of cars, textiles and clothing, synthetic fibres and electronics.[9] The changes were accompanied by recessionary conditions in many of the advanced industrial countries, whose effect was to segment markets into a complex mosaic of product niches and to slow the growth of demand for consumer durables. The result was an intensification of competitive pressures within these product markets. In this context, heightened competition from Japanese industry, where the methods of organization of

	R & D	Production	Distribution
Exhibit 6.1 Matrix of Linkages			
One-Way	licensing cross-licensing early efforts to commercialize public sector R&D (National Research Council — NRC)	sub-contracting OEB[b] (Hitachi → Goldstar) acquisition joint ventures	franchising (McDonald's) (Benetton)
Two-Way	R&D consortia (ESPRIT)[a] (SEMATECH)[a] (VISION 2000)[a] (PRECARN)[a] (VLSI project)[a] customer-supplier networks inter-firm tech- nology collaboration agreements university/industry partnerships (Carnegie Mellon's Robotics Insti- tute for Inte- grated Systems	co-production use of common components (Renault-Volvo) modularization (auto dashboards) (aircraft) joint venture (e.g., biotechnology new forms of subcontracting (e.g., in textiles and clothing and in electronics	joint marketing system-products (the wired house) standardization of interfaces

[a] Details explained in text.
[b] Original equipment manufacturer.

production differed from established practice in much of Europe and North America, stimulated the emergence of new forms of global competition in which innovation played a central role. This was reflected in the development of innovation-based competitive strategies such as closer supplier-client relationships, customization of products, total quality control and rapid throughput.

Supporting the development of these strategies is the growth of expenditures on R & D, training, software development, design, engineering, management and marketing. OECD data, for example, show an increase in the number of scientists and engineers engaged in R & D, and a rise in the share of R & D in gross domestic product (GDP) and in manufacturing value added, especially in countries such as Japan and Germany where strategies of international competitiveness, based on technological innovation and diffusion, are being pursued.[10] Even more revealing of the growing knowledge-intensity of production are OECD data for the manufacturing sector, which show that R & D expenditure has grown at three times the rate of tangible investment over the past two decades, and that the share of these non-material, knowledge-intensive investments in the GDP of the major advanced industrial countries has been steadily rising over the past ten years.[11]

Canada has not kept pace with these developments. Throughout the 1980s, it ranked second from last within the G7, and well behind smaller countries such as Belgium, Finland, Switzerland, Sweden and the Netherlands, in gross domestic expenditures on R & D as a share of GDP. In terms of the share of business enterprise R & D expenditure in gross domestic R & D expenditure, Canada is behind all of the major OECD countries and most of the smaller industrialized countries such as Finland, the Netherlands, Norway, Sweden and Switzerland. Canadian business has also lagged behind more dynamic firms in other non-material investments, notably in training and education on which "Canadian business spends far less . . . than businesses in leading competitor countries."[12] Moreover, if, as a recent business survey by the Conference Board points out, weak domestic market demand is cited as the top factor restricting R & D expenditures by Canadian firms in the early 1990s,[13] prospects for the immediate future are not reassuring.

This is particularly disquieting since, as production became more knowledge-intensive and product life cycles in dynamic knowledge-intensive industries shortened over the 1980s, firms were obliged to spend increasing amounts on R & D in order to remain at the technological frontier in their industries. Canadian firms with their weak R & D track record have therefore been at a considerable disadvantage.

To amortize the costs of R & D, companies required wider markets. Competition, thus globalized, gave impetus to an increase in mergers and acquisitions for the purpose of consolidating positions at home and penetrating markets around the world. In the European Community the number of acquisitions per year nearly tripled between 1985 and 1989, with intra-national acquisitions predominating, followed by takeovers of firms in other European countries.[14] In Canada, merger and acquisition activity at the end of the 1980s almost doubled the level of 1985, and involved a very high proportion (50 percent) of foreign takeovers of existing foreign subsidiaries. This represents evidence of the globalization of competition, which forces smaller and hence more vulnerable Canadian firms into a competitive race against giants.

Mergers and acquisitions create critical mass and provide the in-house complementary assets that a firm needs to respond to change, although they may also add to the inertia of the firm. However, the rapid pace of innovation, the segmented structure of demand and the heightened uncertainty resulting from both the erosion of frontiers between industries and the discontinuities in what were previously incremental technological trajectories,[15] gave rise to a need for flexibility. At the same time, rising costs of R & D and wider sales networks required critical mass. Strategic partnerships were one response to these contradictory pressures. During the 1980s, they became increasingly more important as a means of providing a window on a wide variety of ancillary technologies, reducing the costs, risks and uncertainties associated with knowledge production, strengthening supplier-client relations and locking-in technology users. Participation in these networks has thus become an essential component of the ability of firms to access technology and markets. This situation offers new opportunities for innovative Canadian firms for pooling technological assets and for working collaboratively with foreign partners. Yet, as we shall see in the third section, Canadian firms lag well behind their competitors.

The States

During the 1970s and 1980s, governments at all levels — municipal, regional, national and supra-national — and in countries with widely differing historical traditions of state intervention in the economy, began to promote inter-firm collaborative agreements on R & D and links between firms and research institutions. Local governments, for example, sought to foster regional development by imitating the model of Silicon Valley and Boston's Route 128. They created incubators for small firms, industrial parks next to university centres, and promoted the development of "technopolises"; the Japanese came first with Tsukuba City, followed in the 1980s by their Technopolis concept, and the French were active followers in the promotion of dozens of technopolises of which Sophia Antipolis is perhaps the best known.[16] There are a number of reasons for these developments.

First, the growing knowledge-intensity of production, the changing competitive conditions at the global level and the uncertainties associated with this process, placed in doubt the usefulness of more traditional industrial policy instruments whose objective was to set output targets and/or pick "national champions." Earlier attempts to stimulate innovation, and thus raise productivity growth through industrial policies, rarely took into account the way in which changes in non-material investment — managerial innovations, training programs and software development, as well as R & D, design and engineering — contributed to the competitive advantages of firms. As these factors increasingly shaped the competitiveness of firms during the 1980s, science and technology policies, particularly those designed to promote the more rapid development and diffusion of generic technologies, became more important.

Second, it had also become widely acknowledged that linkages amongst firms, and between firms and research institutions through which innovation and diffusion would take place, were not occurring spontaneously, and that much depended upon government policies offering the leadership and creating the incentives needed to change traditional habits and practices. International markets are therefore powerful stimuli for firms to engage in strategic partnering activity. Designing programs to promote strategic partnership at the national and, in the European Community (EC) at the regional level, and leveraging business-financed R & D expenditures through government funding of technology development and diffusion activities, have proven to be powerful instruments in stimulating innovation and diffusion. In the United States, for example, most corporate funding of university-based research complements seed money provided by the National Science Foundation (NSF), which, since 1973, has facilitated the establishment of university/industry co-operative research centres — in polymers at Case Western Reserve and The Massachusetts Institute of Technology (MIT); in robotics at Carnegie-Mellon's Robotics Institute and the University of Michigan's Center for Robotics and Integrated Manufacturing; in biotechnology at Washington University; and in microelectronics at Stanford's Center for Integrated

Systems and at the Micro-electronics Center of North Carolina created by a consortium of universities.

Third, the need to promote R & D collaboration had quite early on been recognized, by latecomers such as Japan, as a vehicle to facilitate the process of technological catch-up, thereby speeding up the process of assimilating and diffusing imported technology. In the 1960s, mastery of synthetic fibre technology was promoted in this way, as was the development of computer and semiconductor technologies through the VLSI project.[17] Since then, many of the engineering research associations set up to master imported technology have been transformed into consortia for applied research, as Japanese industry has moved closer to the technological frontier, while in other sectors new associations have been set up, for example, the textile products manufacturing system created in 1986, and the large-scale research projects on super advanced processing systems and superconductivity created in 1987.

The catalytic role of the state continues to be important in the Japanese telecommunications industry. Japan's digital switching technology was, in fact, developed in the laboratories of Nippon Telegraph and Telephone (NTT), a state-owned corporation. Subsequently it was transferred to the big four private firms — NEC, Hitachi, Toshiba and Fujitsu. These firms traditionally have done little basic research in the telecommunications field. As product cycles in the telecommunications industry shortened, the decision to privatize NTT and the weakness of Japanese universities as research institutions, coupled with the traditional lack of basic telecommunications research in the four "national champions," made the creation of R & D consortia in this sector all the more essential. Thus, a portion of the proceeds of the sale of NTT shares has gone into the creation of The Key Technology Promotion Center, and under its aegis, the Advanced Telecommunications Research Institute, a joint public-private research facility and network.

The promotion of R & D consortia in Japan has over the past two decades stimulated the creation of a host of imitators. In the United States, perhaps the most well known but now ailing program is SEMATECH, a research and development consortium composed of 14 American firms whose objective is to develop lithography techniques and other process tools for denser integrated circuits. SEMATECH, which received direct funding from the U.S. Department of Defense, marks a departure from earlier practices and is evidence of the need for all countries to play by the new rules of international competition, whereby a role for the state in promoting competitiveness through strategic partnering activity has become acknowledged. In the second and third sections we will examine several European and Canadian examples.

Strategic Partnering in Europe

Strategic partnering activity grew rapidly among European firms and between these firms and non-European partners. Some of this activity was a direct result of promotional activities undertaken by individual states or by the European Community. But much of it was not. For example, during the period 1980–89, a research team at the Centre de Recherche et des Études sur les Entreprises Multinationales (CEREM) at the Université de Paris-X, for example, recorded a total of 2169 strategic alliances in which at least one of the partners was a European firm. Their research covered four industries — biotechnology, information technology, materials and automobiles. All of these agreements lie outside the major European programs such as ESPRIT and EUREKA, which will be discussed below.

Table 6.1 graphically represents the growth of strategic partnerships by European firms over this decade. Much of this partnering activity is concentrated in information technologies, which account for 43 percent of all agreements in this data base, though alliances in biotechnology and materials grew rapidly in the latter half of the decade.

It is of particular interest to note the categories of partners that enter into strategic alliances. Data for 2076 alliances show that 23 percent involved intra-national partnering activity, 20.1 percent consisted of intra-EC partnerships, a further 6.6 percent involved EC firms in partnership with other European firms, 33.8 percent were EC-U.S. partnerships, 9.4 percent EC-Japanese partnerships, and the remaining 7.1 percent included partnerships with firms in other, notably Asian, countries.

In addition to these "spontaneously" generated alliances, during the 1980s, a wide variety of different programs designed to promote strategic partnerships was initiated in Europe. The two most important of these are the European Community's ESPRIT

Table 6.1
European Strategic Partnering Activity: 1980–89

Year	Number of Agreements
1980	24
1	77
2	75
3	112
4	165
5	252
6	284
7	293
8	395
9	439

Source: LAREA/CEREM database.

program, whose first projects were launched in 1983, and the 20-country EUREKA initiative inaugurated in 1985.

ESPRIT[18]

In 1980, aware of the difficulties facing European firms, inspired by the Japanese experience with inter-firm research consortia, and empowered by Article 235 of the Rome Treaty to promote the competitiveness of European industry, Étienne Davignon, then Commissioner of Industry in the European Community, invited Europe's 12 largest information technology firms to draw up a work program for their industry. The ESPRIT program which resulted has as its objectives (i) to promote intra-European industrial co-operation in R & D in five main information technology areas; (ii) to furnish European industry with the basic technologies that it needs to bolster its competitiveness through the 1990s; and (iii) to develop European standards.

ESPRIT I began with a pilot year in 1983 and ran until 1987. It was renewed as ESPRIT II for an additional four-year period in 1988. By 1992, a total of 561 projects were underway or had been completed. Nearly 800 firms and 500 research laboratories in universities and research institutes across the EC's 12 countries had participated in the ESPRIT program.

Both the overall objectives and the yearly work programs elaborated by the ESPRIT Secretariat result from consultations with European firms. Initially this involved only the Big Twelve companies, but increasingly small and medium-sized companies (SMEs) have been active in the various consultative groups that structure the work program and participate in the project selection process each year. In this sense the ESPRIT programme has a "user" orientation, and initiative is shared between the public and private sectors.

Despite this user orientation, project selection, financing and monitoring are organized by the ESPRIT Secretariat located within DG XIII of the European Commission in Brussels, and staffed by a combination of "Eurocrats" and persons seconded from industry and national governments on a rotational basis. The program's budget is part of the overall Community budget, and project costs are shared equally between the EC and the project's participants. For this purpose a total of 750 Mécu[19] were committed to ESPRIT I. When the ESPRIT program was renewed, the financial commitment was increased to 1600 Mécu.

ESPRIT involves open calls for R & D projects at periodic intervals. Participation in the ESPRIT program in response to these calls has been intense, with the number of projects received considerably exceeding those that have been accepted. But it has not always been so. Stimulating firms to think about partnering and inducing them to find partners and design research projects has taken time and considerable energy on the part of both the national governments and the European Commission. In the case of France, local officials have actively promoted participation in ESPRIT, and this helps to account for the very large participation by French firms and research institutes.

Under ESPRIT's rules of operation, each project must include a minimum of two firms located in at least two different EC countries. The former ensures that the projects are user-oriented rather than driven by the technology available in universities or research institutes. By the end of 1989, of the 678 participating firms 56.9 percent were SMEs.[20] In the current phase of ESPRIT, covered by the third framework program for Community R & D (1990–94), further involvement of SMEs is being encouraged by a series of 43 'exploratory actions'.

Two recent surveys provide data on the impact of the ESPRIT program on these SMEs.[21] ESPRIT, for example, assures partners of access to all research results from within their own project, and it provides for the dissemination of information across projects on a privileged basis to ESPRIT partner firms and research organizations. For many of the small and medium-sized firms, this access to research results has created a multiplier effect considerably enlarging the impact of their own R & D effort and expenditure. Among other points to emerge from these surveys is the extent to which ESPRIT has,

- enabled SMEs to increase or maintain R & D levels
- enhanced knowledge accumulation by SMEs, thereby increasing their resistance to takeovers
- enabled subsidiaries to remain active in R & D by complementing the R & D decentralization strategies of parent firms
- speeded up the process of innovation by creating a critical mass of R & D
- encouraged networking through which supplier-client linkages have been established, and
- led to the commercialization of new products and processes.

Nearly 65 percent of the projects accepted under ESPRIT I were pre-competitive.[22] ESPRIT II moved closer to the market by deliberately selecting projects for their commercial potential. In consequence the number of pre-competitive R & D projects fell to 37.1 percent.

In addition to increasing the commercial impact of ESPRIT projects, integrated project clusters were formed under ESPRIT II. These are sets of projects which share a number of partners and focus on different aspects of a related technological problem. Perhaps the best known integrated project cluster within ESPRIT is the PCTE (Portable Common Tool Environment) which has spawned over fifteen applications and extension projects, including a number of projects within the EUREKA program. Follow-up projects are another means of ensuring that work done in ESPRIT finds its way to the market. During the current phase of ESPRIT, which began in July 1991, a number of large-scale targeted projects will be launched. These are designed to promote new techniques for software development, develop flat panel display technology for telecommunications and high definition television (HDTV), strengthen European manufacturing capabilities through computer-integrated manufacturing technologies, and develop new design and manufacturing technologies for standard integrated circuits and for ASICs (application-specific integrated circuits). As was the case with the shift away from pre-competitive R & D and towards more market-oriented projects, the development of large-scale, targeted projects in ESPRIT owes much to the demonstration effect exercised by the EUREKA program.

EUREKA[23]

Initiated by President François Mitterand of France as a response to the American Strategic Defense Initiative, EUREKA now includes 20 member countries[24] from across Europe, plus the European Community, represented by the Commission. From the Hanover ministerial meeting in November 1985 to the Rome meeting in June 1990, nearly 400 projects were approved. A year later, a further 112 projects received the EUREKA label at The Hague.[25] Within six years, EUREKA had 500 ongoing projects. However, firms and research institutions had already been stimulated to engage in trans-European partnering activity through the ESPRIT program.

Like ESPRIT, EUREKA is intended to stimulate cross-border R & D collaboration as a means of strengthening the competitiveness of European industry. Beyond that, the contrasts with ESPRIT are striking. EUREKA's projects were from the outset more market-oriented than those of ESPRIT. Nonetheless, and as in the case of ESPRIT I, many of these were long-term projects, and this has delayed the realization of marketable results.

EUREKA pursues a "bottom up" approach with respect to the selection of themes for research. Unlike ESPRIT, it defines no preselected themes under which prospective consortia must place themselves. Instead, participants have full responsibility for defining the scope of their collaboration. The result is that EUREKA tends to be even less focused than ESPRIT. To compensate, EUREKA has from the outset favoured large, longer-term, targeted projects. Twenty percent of EUREKA's projects fall into this category and they accounted for 36 percent of the total funds expended through the EUREKA program from 1985–90. The largest and best known of these projects are HDTV (EU95), designed to develop a new high definition television system at a cost of 625 Mécu over 66 months, and JESSI (EU127), the Joint European Submicron Silicon

Initiative, aimed at moving the European semiconductor industry rapidly to the technological frontier at a cost of 550 Mécu over 96 months.

EUREKA also has a number of umbrella projects. These are groups of related projects covering "well-defined technology areas which governments and industries consider to be of strategic importance for the competitive position of Europe."[26] Umbrellas, however, have become the subject of considerable debate within EUREKA, because of the tendency for such projects to be organized from above rather than being generated from below. The exception is FAMOS, the EUREKA umbrella project in robotics. Over the period 1985–90, a total of 29 projects involving different applications of robot technology to manufacturing components for robotics used in manufacturing and related software, were approved for a total of 291 Mécu. Because of its many industrial partners, FAMOS (flexible manufacturing projects) is a market-driven umbrella. More recent umbrellas such as EUROCARE and EUROENVIRON, both of which have environmental focuses, were set up mainly by government and research bodies and are still looking for industry partners.

EUREKA's 20 member-states finance the EUREKA program, including its secretariat in Brussels. Unlike the role of the EC Commission in ESPRIT, EUREKA is a flexible, decentralized network in which this small secretariat plays no operational role. Instead, it serves as a support unit whose main responsibilities are to gather and distribute information on projects, facilitate the search for partners through its EUROBASE service, and promote the EUREKA concept. It is the national project co-ordinators who are the principal operational units and constitute the sole interlocutors with project partners. It is they who advise and assist in the preparation, organization, selection and financing of projects. The mechanisms through which the latter two tasks are performed differ from country to country. National project co-ordinators and their staff are also responsible for project monitoring, although there is a tendency to minimize such monitoring activities within EUREKA. National project co-ordinators are in personal touch with each other and they meet several times a year.

Unlike ESPRIT, EUREKA does not receive organized project calls. Interested firms and research organizations, moving at their own pace, find partners, prepare a proposal, negotiate a co-operation agreement amongst themselves and organize the financing of their project. Once the consortium is in place, each of the participants submits the proposal to its national project coordinating body. Acceptance or rejection takes place at this level, and decisions on project financing are reached. Although EUREKA project funding falls below ESPRIT's 50 percent of eligible costs, the number of large projects in EUREKA boosted the total cost of the 386 projects approved between 1985 and June 1990 to 7533 Mécu.

Because of its "bottom up" approach, EUREKA initially had more problems in attracting SMEs than ESPRIT. Roughly 30 percent of the EUREKA projects have SME participation as compared with over 50 percent in ESPRIT. The relatively low participation rate of SMEs in EUREKA was particularly noticeable in France, where only 19.5 percent of the industrial participants were SMEs as compared with 23.8 percent in Germany, 27.6 percent in the UK and over 35 percent in smaller countries like Norway, Switzerland and the Netherlands. In 1990, therefore, the French government shifted responsibility for EUREKA from IFRAMER, a public sector marine research institute, to ANVAR (Agence nationale pour la valorisation de la recherche), the National Agency to promote Research, which has regional antennae throughout France and which normally provides financial support to the SME sector. Within ANVAR, a fund to aid European Technological Partnerships was set up to subsidize an SME's search for partners and the definition phase of its participation in a trans-European R & D project. Other countries have also begun to recognize the need to provide additional financial support for SMEs and have created special funds for this purpose.

In contrast to ESPRIT, EUREKA has opened its projects to a few non-European participants. Canadian participants are, for example, involved in four EUREKA projects—EU5, dealing with membranes for micro-filtration, EU20, in informatics, EU226, a laser project, and EU417, a marine-related environment project.[27] An Argentine firm, VILMAX, with 30 years of experience in organic dyestuffs has joined with IBF Biotechnics, a subsidiary of the French firm Rhône Poulenc, Smithkline Biologicals and the University of Patras in EU384, a project designed to study dyes and dye absorbents for purification of biologicals.

Strategic Partnering in Canada

There is no overall source of data on partnering activity by Canadian firms. Most earlier data bases, such as that developed by Michael Geringer[28] for Investment Canada, do not distinguish strategic partnerships from joint ventures, and generally do not focus on partnerships involving a joint knowledge-creation or sharing function. Data from such data bases does not therefore permit us to estimate the growth or extent of strategic partnering activity by Canadian firms.

Data collected through interviews by a team at CREDIT in Montreal does make the relevant distinctions for 128 Canadian firms, of which 36 are in electronics, 36 in advanced materials, 36 in biotechnology and 20 in transportation equipment other than automobiles. From these data it is possible to draw some comparisons with European partnering activity. Of these 128 firms, 83 were established before 1980 but only 43 percent of these had engaged in any collaborative R & D prior to the 1980s.[29] A closer examination of the Canadian electronics firms in their survey confirms the late start of Canadian firms in partnering activity. Thus Niosi and Bergeron found that 64 percent of the alliances concluded by these firms were started in 1988 or later.[30] This contrasts with the earlier start of European firms, even those from the smaller European countries, in partnering activity. Between 1980 and 1985, for example, Dutch firms were involved in 51 alliances outside European programs and in 10 ESPRIT projects. Non-EC European firms were also more intensively engaged in partnering before than were Canadian firms. From 1980 to 1985, for example, Swedish firms were involved in 18 alliances and this figure had risen to 33 by 1987.[31]

Table 6.2 summarizes data drawn from the LAREA-CEREM data base and from ESPRIT and EUREKA project documentation on the direction and extensiveness of the partnering activity of firms from Canada and four small European countries. Of these four, only the Netherlands was a member of the European Community. Its firms were therefore able to participate in both ESPRIT I and ESPRIT II. The latter was opened to firms from Switzerland, Sweden and Norway along with other European Free Trade Association (EFTA) countries. For comparative purposes Table 6.2 presents data only for ESPRIT II.

Table 6.2
Participation in Strategic Partnerships:
Netherlands, Sweden, Switzerland, Norway and Canada
(figures are in number of alliances)

Country	(1) Intra-Nat'l	(2) with EC	(3) with US	(4) with Japan	(5) with other Europe	(6) Total[a]	(7) Esprit II[b]	(8) Eureka[c]
Netherlands	8	75	40	13	12	154	111	117
Sweden	11	52	6	1	5	77	16	83[e]
Switzerland	–	32	17	3	3	56	11	60[f]
Norway	1	9	2	1	–	13	13	72[g]
Canada	–	42	2	2	2	48[h]	–	5[i]

Notes:

[a]The total includes a small number of agreements with "other" principally Asian countries.

[b]Only figures for ESPRIT II are used since Swedish, Swiss and Norwegian firms were not eligible for participation in ESPRIT I.

[c]The EUREKA totals are as of June 25, 1991, when 470 projects were underway.

[d] This includes 137 different firms of which 45 were SMEs.

[e]76 firms of which 28 were SMEs.

[f]58 firms of which 37 were SMEs.

[g]66 firms of which 26 were SMEs.

[h]These included, inter alia, Massey Ferguson, DAP, Allelix, Biomega, Connaught, Mitel, Telecom Canada and Northern Telecom.

[i]As of December 1990 the firms included Zenon Inc., Jentec, LNO, DMR Ltd., and Seastar Limited.

Source: LAREA/CEREM database for non-European program data, EUREKA: 1991a, and Commission of the European Communities, ESPRIT Annual Report, 1990/91.

Since the data in columns 1–6 are drawn from the LAREA/CEREM database, which covers only alliances in which at least one European firm is a partner, intra-national alliances involving Canadian firms are excluded. It may, however, be possible to generalize from the experience of Canadian electronics firms, for which other Canadian companies were the most frequent partners chosen by firms in the sample. This was the case for 16 (47 percent) of the companies; another 18 percent (6 cases) had created alliances in the EC; two were mostly looking to the U.S. and another two had sought partners mostly in Japan and Korea."[32] From this table it is clear that, in terms of independently initiated strategic partnering activity, Canadian firms lag well behind firms from countries whose economies are only half the size of ours! When we add to these the data from Columns 7 and 8, the gap is even greater.

In the latter half of the 1980s, late by Japanese and European standards, private-public sector partnerships such as VISION 2000 and private sector initiatives such as PRECARN Associates were launched in Canada. A brief discussion of each of these however, suggests that they alone cannot overcome the weakness in Canadian partnering activity.

PRECARN Associates[33]

PRECARN Associates is a non-profit organization incorporated in Canada in 1987. Its membership includes 34 Canadian-based corporations ranging from natural resource sector companies, such as Alcan, Falconbridge, Inco, Noranda, Petro-Canada and Shell, to energy producers, such as B.C. Hydro, Hydro-Québec, Ontario Hydro and TransAlta Utilities Corporation, and to high-tech firms, amongst which are Asea-Brown Boveri, Bell Northern Research, CAE Electronics, Hatch Associates, Hewlett Packard, MPR Teltech and Spar Aerospace. In contrast to all of the other programs discussed here, the initiative to set up PRECARN came from the private sector and it is managed by that sector.

PRECARN Associates engages in precompetitive R & D in the field of intelligent systems technologies, ranging from the simplest expert systems to the development and application of autonomous robotic devices. This sector was chosen because of the considerable corporate and university expertise that already existed in Canada, and the double need to avoid wasteful duplication and create critical mass, so as to ensure that the expertise will result in a competitive Canadian position in this field.

All PRECARN members make an annual payment to the Corporation of $25,000. Of this amount, $100 is a membership fee and $24,900 is a contribution to the research and development program undertaken by PRECARN. This latter amount is eligible for Canadian government investment tax credits. In addition, members cover the costs associated with their own participation on the Board of Directors, on committees and at briefing sessions and workshops. They also make significant additional contributions of a project-specific nature, such as covering the salaries of researchers participating in joint projects as well as overhead and equipment costs for these projects. In total, PRECARN and its membership have committed about $12 million for the first five projects, and a further $6 million in cash and in-kind support for the administration and feasibility study program.

In addition to its membership fees, about 10 percent of PRE-CARN's administrative costs during its first three years were borne by a grant from the National Research Council of Canada (NRC). Grants from the NRC, the Federal Department of Industry, Science and Technology Canada — through its Strategic Alliance Program — and provincial governments currently contribute roughly $20 million for project support.

The project cycle in PRECARN begins with a call for research proposals. These are reviewed by PRECARN's Technical Advisory Committee, composed of representatives from industry (70 percent) and from universities (30 percent), which decides whether to support a feasibility study. These studies may take up to 6 months and may receive up to $100,000 in support from PRECARN. "On average, the participants match PRECARN's support through in-kind support."

> The Technical Committee reviews the results of feasibility studies and recommends some for long-term research support (four to five years). This Committee also reviews technical progress of the research, while the Exploitation Committee monitors the research for exploitable results and helps in the dissemination of all results.[34]

Ownership of the intellectual property resulting from research undertaken in a PRECARN project has not been an issue. With regard to the four ongoing projects, PRECARN Associates own the intellectual property in two of them and the industrial participants own it in the other two. However, all members of PRECARN, whether they participate in a particular project or not, have access to the resulting technology. Companies which were members of PRECARN in the year in which a particular project started are assured of royalty-free licence rights to any intellectual property arising from that research. Members joining PRECARN in the second year of a project pay 25 percent of the third party royalty rate, those joining in the third year of a project pay 50 percent, in the fourth year 75 percent and thereafter 100 percent of the third party royalty rate. All members of PRECARN also receive regular briefings and reports on the progress of research in each PRECARN project.

In addition to managing joint research projects, PRECARN has created an Institute for Robotics and Intelligent Systems (IRIS), which is itself a network of researchers from 18 universities across Canada. The Institute has received a grant of $23.8 million over four years from the federal government's Centres of Excellence program. All PRECARN members have preferential access to the results of the IRIS research network. "If the university owning the results wishes to issue an exclusive licence, PRECARN has a right of first refusal on behalf of its membership. If a non-exclusive licence is issued, PRECARN members pay 50 percent of the third party royalty rates." PRECARN pays special attention to bringing together both users and producers of new technology. Therefore, while the research projects are of a longer-term nature, they focus upon identified needs and applications within the Canadian economy and they involve the parties who can apply the research results to those needs.

All PRECARN proposals must involve at least two PRECARN members, as well as university researchers, and should normally include both a producer and a consumer of the contemplated technology. The four projects currently underway all meet these conditions.

In the five years since its incorporation, PRECARN has competed for and won $23.8 million over four years to support 22 university-based research projects in the IRIS network. These projects involve computational perception, knowledge-based systems and intelligent robotic systems. Eleven feasibility studies for joint R & D have been approved for support, of which eight had been completed by 1992, two were underway and one had been abandoned.

Following the eight completed feasibility studies, six research projects have been approved. Four of these six are currently underway. The first began in July 1990 and the remaining three started up during 1991. Funding is being negotiated for a fifth but the sixth has so far not been able to find sufficient private sector support. The total cost of the four projects underway is $33.8 million over five years. These projects involve 14 PRECARN members, 4 universities and 2 government agencies.

VISION 2000[35]

As was the case with ESPRIT and EUREKA, the initiative to form VISION 2000 came from the public sector. As happened with ESPRIT, there was immediate involvement of the private sector through attendance of chief executive officers (CEOs) from Canada's leading communications companies at meetings organized by the Department of Communications (DOC) and Industry, Science and Technology Canada (ISTC). The objective of these meetings was not merely to involve the private sector in the design of a program, but rather to convince the private sector that it should fund and manage the program.

> Vision 2000 is a private-public sector partnership designed to enhance the competitiveness of the Canadian communications industry. Its primary objective is to facilitate strategic alliances in advanced personal communications. The principal goals of Vision 2000 are to foster collaboration in research and development, to accelerate innovation in communications and information technology, and to introduce new products and services to domestic and world markets.

VISION 2000 is thus a market-driven program whose membership comes overwhelmingly from the business community.

Both the management and financing of VISION 2000 differ from those of the programs we have discussed thus far. Inaugurated in 1989, it initially went through two difficult years, during which the Business Plan and the Research and Development Framework were developed and the first President resigned. This left the Department of Communications to manage the program, initiate the process of identifying and promoting the formation of R & D consortia, and broker the first series of projects announced in May 1991. DOC was aided by an executive committee composed of representatives from private and public sector corporations and from the department. Since then, the secretariat of VISION 2000 Inc, a private sector company supported by its membership fees, has assumed responsibility for managing and financing the initiative. Unlike the European Community programs and EUREKA, there is no direct public financing of VISION 2000 Inc., but public sector support for VISION 2000 projects does come through the involvement of public sector research laboratories as partners, and through a variety of government programs that fund R & D and strategic partnering activity, such as the Microelectronics and Systems Development Program and the Strategic Technologies Program.

Alongside the VISION 2000 Inc. secretariat is a VISION 2000 program office within the Department of Communications. In the initiation of VISION 2000 this office had played an important role, but its functions have since been reduced to the collection and dissemination of information, partner brokering and promotional efforts for VISION 2000 Inc. The brokering function is especially important in the Canadian context, where a culture of co-operation among firms is not well developed, and where a neutral arbiter in negotiations is needed to help firms overcome their fear that project ideas will be appropriated by rivals and to induce them to work together. The ability of the VISION 2000 program office to play such a role has been seriously limited by a lack of financial leverage, and by weak government support for the idea that the state should play a catalytic role in partnering activity.

The project cycle in VISION 2000 begins when a Canadian company, research institute, university or government agency responds to VISION 2000's Request for Expression of Interest, whether or not that firm or institute is a member of VISION 2000 Inc. While the initial approach must include a presentation of a project concept that fits within the scope of VISION 2000's activities, it does not need to specify who the collaborators might be. Usually, after discussion with the initiator, the Project Review Committee nominated by the Board of Directors of VISION 2000 Inc. will attempt to form a project consortium brokering for both partners, and providing funding. In this, the committees are assisted by the VISION 2000 program office in DOC.

The Project Review Committee plays a central management role within VISION 2000 Inc. that combines elements of the roles played by the ESPRIT Secretariat and EUREKA's National project co-ordinators. Its terms of reference, for example, include the following responsibilities: (1) to review project concepts and full proposals with a view to verifying that projects are innovative, proactive and, where appropriate, use leading-edge technologies, and that the project is potentially marketable and has business viability; (2) to make recommendations to the Directors regarding the support required. This might include assistance in setting up a strategic partnership, help in planning a project, representation to government authorities for an experimental license, allocation of spectrum or support for a policy decision, co-funding of a feasibility study, and identifying and soliciting sources of funding; (3) to look for an overall "mix" of projects with national, regional and inter-regional aspects; and (4) to provide opportunities for participation by small and medium-sized companies; (5) to suggest potential new members who may be invited to join consortia and VISION 2000.

Among its 40 members, VISION 2000 includes Canada's major telecommunications and information technology companies, Northern Telecom, MPR Teltech, UNITEL, IBM, Ericsson Communications, Gandalf Technologies, Rogers Cantel Inc., Bell Canada and Mitel; two federal government Ministries—DOC and ISTC—the Ministère de Communications du Quebec, two post-secondary institutions—Sheridan College of Applied Arts and Technology and the University of Victoria's Faculty of Engineering—and several government research laboratories. The composition of VISION 2000's membership, with its predominance of private sector companies, resembles PRECARN Associates rather than EUREKA, whose members are national governments.

Although universities are key participants in some of VISION 2000's ongoing projects, few are members of the corporation. VISION 2000 Inc. includes few small companies among its membership, although efforts are being made to include SMEs among project partners. VISION 2000 does, however, accept membership of foreign-based multinational corporations, provided that the research they undertake as part of the VISION 2000 initiative is done in Canada.

As to what VISION 2000 has accomplished, despite its growing pains, it now has a new private sector Chairman and President, and has launched fifteen R & D projects with a combined value of almost $30 million. The projects involve 44 different partners of which 22 are private companies, 11 are universities and 11 are public sector bodies including laboratories of the Department of Communications Canada and Transport Canada, the City of Calgary, the Montreal Museum of Fine Arts and the Canadian Automation Research Centre, to name only a few. The projects are focused on satellite, cellular, and radio communications technologies. Of the $30 million in project costs, only $7.7 million comes from the Department of Communications through the participation of its various laboratories. The remainder is provided by Vision 2000 membership subscriptions, partner finance in cash and in kind, and grants from a variety of government programs.

Whither Canada?

During the 1980s, as competition became more innovation-based, strategic partnering in R & D emerged as an important means of accessing both technology and markets. Partnering stimulated SMEs to engage in research and development, and enabled larger firms to gain a window on a wide range of ancillary technologies, thereby reducing the costs, risks and uncertainties of knowledge production. It increased marketability by building in required interfaces between products in the course of their development, and it strengthened the supplier-client linkages that assure market access for products whose very design incorporates the user's needs.

Strategic partnering activity of this sort is of particular importance for firms which historically have engaged in R & D only to a limited extent, and which thus require both encouragement and support to do so. This is characteristic of the Canadian enterprise sector, which not only lags behind the comparable sectors of both larger and many smaller OECD member countries with regard to R & D expenditures, but has spontaneously engaged in far fewer strategic partnerships than European firms, even those from considerably smaller European countries such as the Netherlands and Sweden.

As ESPRIT and EUREKA demonstrate, high rates of participation in strategic partnering activity, especially by SMEs, have required a catalyst. In Europe, that role has been played by states and quasi-states such as the EC. These bodies have consciously set out to strengthen the technological capabilities of the SME sector and to encourage larger firms to pool resources in longer-term risky projects by engaging in promotional activities, taking an active role in brokering partnerships, and leveraging R & D spending through direct financial assistance. In contrast, Canadian governments, for the most part, have tended to remain behind the scenes, financing projects when approached, but initiating few activities to encourage reluctant or uncertain Canadian firms to engage in strategic partnerships with each other or with firms abroad. The result is evident in the slower start-up of Canadian consortiums and the far smaller number of firms that they touch. Thus, between 1983 and 1990, while over 2000 European firms joined 401 EUREKA and 561 ESPRIT projects, PRECARN initiated six research projects involving 14 firms and VISION 2000 launched 15 R & D projects involving 22 companies.

Strategic partnerships do not produce results overnight. First, as the example of PRECARN illustrates, a minimum of three years is required to stimulate the formation of inter-firm partnerships, secure financing for the definitional phase, undertake the necessary feasibility studies and organize the financing for the research phase. Second, in both EUREKA and ESPRIT, projects normally required a minimum of two years to bring an innovative product or process to the prototype stage,and yet another year before it is fully marketable. A minimum of 5–6 years would be needed before positive results could be expected from the partnering activity, even if a significant number of Canadian firms were to get involved immediately.

Two avenues for involvement have appeared in the 1990s. Of critical importance is the recent European initiative to open still further to non-European firms both the EUREKA and a number of EC programs, such as those in biotechnology and in technologies that are environmentally sound. The coincidence between European interests and Canadian expertise in these areas creates a host of new opportunities for exploitation by Canadian firms. But from where will the stimulation and support for such activities come? Similarly, within the context of market liberalization in the Southern Cone Common Market (MERCOSUR), the Andean Group and the North American Free Trade Agreement, Latin American firms are currently looking for technology partners. Canadian firms could also play an active role here. But, as in the European case, an institutional mechanism is required to organize and to facilitate such partnering activity. Once again, it is a question of leadership. From whence will it come and will it come soon enough?

THE ROAD FROM RIO

7

The Road from Rio

David Runnalls

We owe the world to be frank about what we have achieved here in Rio. Progress in many fields, too little progress in most fields, and no progress at all in some fields.[1]

THE 1972 UNITED NATIONS CONFERENCE on the Human Environment marked the emergence of the environment as an issue on the international agenda. Canada played an important role in the Stockholm Conference. It provided the Secretary-General, Maurice Strong, who was released from his job as President of the Canadian International Development Agency (CIDA) at the request of UN Secretary General U Thant. It fielded a strong delegation, and it offered to host one of the follow-up conferences. This later became the United Nations Conference on Human Settlements, held in Vancouver in 1976.

The Stockholm Conference had a number of achievements to its credit, including a Declaration, a broad and all-encompassing action plan of 109 items and an agreement for follow-up conferences on more specific sectors such as human settlements. It also created a new institution, the United Nations Environment Program (UNEP) and a fund to support it. UNEP became the first major United Nations agency to be located in a developing country (Nairobi, Kenya).

After Stockholm the environment became a staple item on the agendas of international conferences. It also became *de rigeur* for governments and international agencies to set up institutions or units to deal with the environment (Canada had jumped the gun by establishing Environment Canada in 1971). Soon, well over 100 countries had established some kind of environmental watchdog. These were armed with the usual panoply of weapons: environmental impact assessments, pollution control regulations, permits and the like. Additionally, the environmental NGO (non-governmental organizations) movement, established in North America in the late nineteenth century (we forget that the

Sierra Club is over 100 years old), broadened its areas of concern and spread throughout much of the world.

When UNEP came to commemorate the tenth anniversary of the Stockholm Conference, it was clear that the global environment had continued to deteriorate at an alarming rate, in spite of all of these achievements. It was also clear from the debates in the tenth anniversary session of UNEP's Governing Council that environment and development were still being viewed as opposing concepts. Geoffrey Bruce, Canada's Permanent Representative to UNEP, therefore proposed the creation of a global commission to examine the state of the world's environment and the relationship between environment and development.

The World Commission on Environment and Development (the Brundtland Commission) was in existence for a little less than three years. Its final report[2] documented the accumulating evidence of planetary decline in startling terms: the annual loss of an area the size of Saudi Arabia to the march of the deserts, the loss of over 17 million hectares of tropical forests per year, the destruction of the earth's ozone shield by chlorofluorocarbons (CFCs) and halons, and the possibility of a warming of the earth's climate over the next fifty years, greater than that experienced over the previous 10,000 years.

Despite some progress in slowing population growth in some countries, the world's inhabitants will inevitably come to number around 10 billion people — roughly twice the present number, with all the claims on resources implied by a number of that size.

The Commission reminds us that this unprecedented growth in human numbers is being accompanied by equally unprecedented increases in industrial production. It has grown more than fiftyfold over the last century. An astonishing 80 percent of this growth has occurred since 1950. Fossil fuel use (principally oil and coal) has grown by more than thirtyfold in the last hundred years. A full three quarters of this increase has come since 1950.

The Commission pointed out that a five to tenfold expansion will be needed in the world economy to meet the minimum needs and aspirations of the 10 billion people who will be on the planet by the middle of the next century. Economic growth on this scale with current patterns of resource and energy use is clearly at odds with the environmental analysis described above. The growth of fossil fuel consumption implied by a fivefold increase in energy consumption would by itself be enough to trigger climate change of an unprecedented magnitude. The earth's economy and its ecology are now so closely interlocked that policies in one area which ignore the other are bound to fail.

As the Commission's report was published in 1987, scientific evidence was building that the deterioration of the earth's ozone shield was even greater than had previously been thought. Scientists were also beginning to uncover more information about the possible extent of global warming. Against this background, Canada hosted the Toronto Conference on the Changing Atmosphere in 1988. The Conference, a sober gathering of more than 300 scientists and policymakers, began its declaration with the following rather alarming statement:

> Humanity is conducting an unintended, uncontrolled, globally pervasive experiment whose consequences could be second only to a global nuclear war. The Earth's atmosphere is being changed at an unprecedented rate by pollutants resulting from human activities, inefficient and wasteful fossil fuel use and the effects of rapid population growth in many regions. These changes represent a major threat to international security and are already having harmful consequences over many parts of the globe.[3]

The Conference called for urgent measures to reduce emissions of carbon dioxide (CO_2), the principal greenhouse gas, by 20 percent by the year 2005, and for the strengthening of the Montreal Protocol on substances that deplete the ozone layer. Although CO_2 is the main ingredient in global warming, the chemicals which destroy the ozone layer are also potent greenhouse gases.

The Toronto Economic Summit brought global environmental issues to the attention of the G-7 leaders for the first time. As host of the meeting, Brian Mulroney lobbied to place environment and sustainable development on the agenda. He was aided and abetted by Chancellor Kohl, who was under considerable pressure from the German "greens" to take action on tropical deforestation. The Paris Summit in 1989 continued the practice, with environmental issues dominating the communiqué at the expense of the traditional economic concerns.

The Brundtland Commission had recommended that a world conference be held five years after the release of its report to assess progress on the implementation of its recommendations for more sustainable paths to development. Urged on by the Paris

Summit, the United Nations General Assembly began debate on the resolution authorizing the conference and setting its agenda in the winter of 1989.

Unfortunately the New York debates were dominated by the same divisions which had appeared at Stockholm and at the tenth anniversary discussions of the UNEP Governing Council. Instead of the "win-win" agenda of sustainable development produced by the Brundtland Commission, the General Assembly recommended a conference on environment *and* development with an agenda which would inevitably come down to environment *versus* development. The agenda was an uneasy blend of the concerns of the developed countries with climate change, the loss of biological diversity and tropical deforestation and those of the Third World with financial transfers, trade, debt, technology transfer and poverty alleviation.

The Road to Rio

A decision was made at the outset to proceed with all of the global environmental issues raised by the World Commission. A negotiating process was set up under the auspices of the World Meteorological Organization (WMO) and UNEP to produce an agreement on climate change. UNEP took the lead on a convention to protect the remainder of the world's biological diversity. Although neither of these processes were under the direction of Strong's Secretariat, each was intended to develop a convention for signature in Rio.

Fearing that this process would relegate the world's forests to carbon sinks in a climate change convention or to a protocol in a biological diversity convention, Canada and a number of other countries attempted to initiate a similar process leading to a global forestry convention.

As the official Conference Preparatory Committee began to wrestle with the issues, Strong made a deliberate decision to up the ante. As a member of the Brundtland Commission, he subscribed to the the principle espoused by that body that the integration of the environment into all decisions could only be accomplished at the top. He therefore persuaded the UN that at least a portion of the Rio Conference should be a Summit. This rather daring move served to elevate the preparations for UNCED to a much higher level in national capitals and to stimulate media interest in the conference. The disadvantages emerged only later when the United States threatened that President Bush would refuse to attend unless it had its own way on a number of critical issues.

The preparatory process proved long and arduous. Much of the often acrimonious debate centered around the clash of the two agendas. Developing countries were suspicious that many of the issues on the agenda would become the subject of deals worked out between relatively few countries. They therefore insisted that the Preparatory Committee be open to all members of the UN and that no more than two sub-committees of the Prepcom be allowed to meet simultaneously. While this helped to ensure that countries with small delegations could participate in all decisions, it led to a number of marathon sessions with well over 100 countries participating. The Conference Prepcom met four times, for at least four weeks at a time, beginning in August 1990 and concluding in April 1992, (the gruelling final session, dubbed the New York marathon, lasted six weeks).

The parallel processes lasted just as long. The climate change convention was not finished until May 9. Biodiversity came even closer to the wire with a final version on May 22, barely a month before the Earth Summit. The negotiations on both conventions were wracked by North-South disputes and by what many viewed as the intransigence of the United States.

Canada played a prominent role in all of these negotiations. The Canadian delegation to the Preparatory Committee was very ably led by John Bell of the Department of External Affairs. Elizabeth Dowdeswell of Environment Canada (and now the Executive Director of UNEP) chaired the critical committee in the climate change negotiating process while Arthur Campeau, the Prime Minister's sherpa to UNCED, was one of the crucial figures in the final negotiation of the biodiversity agreement.

In his previous stint as Secretary-General of the Stockholm Conference, Strong had demonstrated his belief in the importance of non-governmental groups. NGOs were present at Stockholm in unprecedented numbers. In addition, thousands of young people thronged to the three alternative conference sites, despite the fact that the Lod Airport massacre a few weeks earlier limited their access to the official deliberations. In one memorable clip from the CBC "Nature of Things" program about Stockholm, a rather younger looking Strong is seen on a makeshift stage on an abandoned airport runway, proclaiming to a substantial number of long-haired, partially dressed 1960s types, that he felt more comfortable with them than with the government delegates downtown.

Strong and his Secretariat determined to take this NGO involvement one step further with UNCED. Here they would be involved in the Preparatory process itself. With the assistance of CIDA and a number of the other bilateral aid agencies, substantial numbers of non-governmental groups from developed and developing countries participated in the preparation of many of the conference documents and attended the Prepcom meetings and the negotiating sessions for the conventions. And they made their weight felt. They formed regional climate action networks. They lobbied delegations. They participated in the drafting of agreements, particularly during the hectic final session of the Prepcom in New York in April 1992. They produced lively, often irreverent newspapers for the climate change sessions and the Prepcoms. Not only did these papers serve to enliven some of the debates, they often served the official delegates as substitutes for reporting telexes to their home bases.

The preparation of Canada's positions and even the conduct of the Canadian delegations at the meetings were surprisingly open. The Canadian Preparatory Committee for UNCED (CPCU) brought together church groups, environmental groups, development NGOs, indigenous groups and organizations representing women. It prepared positions, sent some of its members as part of the Canadian delegations and played a role in the development of the Canadian national report for UNCED and of specific Canadian positions on individual issues. John Bell responded to these initiatives by incorporating the NGOs into the main delegation, instead of following the usual practice of tolerating them as observers.

At the End of the Road to Rio: The Earth Summit

After all of this agonizing preparation, was UNCED a success or a failure? In Prime Minister Brundtland's own words, "We owe the world to be frank about what we have achieved here in Rio. Progress in many fields, too little progress in most fields, and no progress at all in some fields."[4] What constitutes progress?

First, the Conference was attended by 105 Heads of State, including Canada's Prime Minister. Each of them made a speech, the length of which seemed in inverse proportion to the size of his (unfortunately, almost always *his*) country. One of the most unlikely exceptions to this rule was the six-minute speech delivered by Fidel Castro. On the whole, most of their speeches demonstrated a surprising grasp of the importance of integrating environment into economic decisions. And, despite the epidemic of creative bookkeeping which characterized their speeches, most developed country leaders seemed to accept the need for new and additional financial resources to help developing countries achieve sustainable development.

Most of these speeches were of course written by bureaucrats. And the fact that they were given by the Head of Government caused economic departments to speak to environment and natural resource management departments civilly about things they had not discussed before. What the Green Plan failed to accomplish occurred because of the need to write a speech for Brian Mulroney.

Second, more than 8,000 journalists turned up in Rio. Despite the recession in the newspaper industry, the morning press conference given by Jean Charest was full of Canadian journalists. Most journalists showed a greater degree of knowledge and sophistication about these issues than many knowledgeable observers had expected.

For two weeks, the entire world's media were full of stories about environment and development. Although it is impossible to assess the long-term effects of this kind of blanket coverage, it must have some influence on public attitudes.

Third, more than 15,000 people were involved in the NGO activities at Rio. Some 1,400 participated in the official conference itself, continuing their lobbying and drafting activities. More than 30 countries included NGOs as members of delegations. Continuing its habit of openness, Canada included a number of NGOs on the official delegation and many others attended the delegation meetings in the Intercontinental Hotel. Some non-governmental groups attempted to influence their governments through the 8,000 journalists present in Rio. Others confined themselves to the NGO site in downtown Rio, more than one hour's drive away from *Riocentro* where the governments were meeting. There they convened a series of scientific and technical meetings, had a good time and wrote treaties of their own. As Chapter 8 in this volume points out, Canadians were central to this process.

Although many of these treaties themselves have little value, the process of their preparation may turn out to be one of the most significant legacies of Rio. The idea of direct citizen involvement in UN affairs has long been a fond dream of the World Federalists and the special role of NGOs is cited in the Charter. But Rio represents the first occasion on which these groups have seriously tried to forge agreements among themselves to replace the official deliberations. Many of the more prominent NGOs have vowed to continue this process well after Rio. The existence of computer networks may well ensure that these links grow stronger, particularly if the official follow-up activities to Rio deliver less than expected. Future international conferences are likely to see the NGO presence strengthened, perhaps finally emerging as a potent independent sector.

Fourth, the conventions on climate change and biodiversity, although far from perfect, are a start. A total of 153 governments signed each of the conventions. Fifty must move on to ratify the climate change convention before it comes into force and thirty must ratify the biodiversity convention. Although the targets and timetables for curbing CO_2 emissions were removed from the convention at the last minute to satisfy American objections, there is hope that the Clinton Administration will agree to their addition when the parties to the convention first meet. This may serve to place a good deal of pressure on both Europe and Canada. Although both were supportive of the targets and timetables being included in the convention, some observers suspect that this support was offered in the full knowledge that the United States would veto their inclusion in the treaty. Given the interdepartmental bickering in Ottawa and the unwillingness of the provincial energy ministers to endorse a national CO_2 strategy, Canada might, in the end, fail to stand firm on this question.

There is also hope that the United States will agree to sign the biodiversity convention when the signatories come together. Under pressure from the biotechnology industry, Mr. Bush was the only Head of State who refused to sign the treaty. The Americans objected to what they perceived as unfair intrusions into their patent rights and a provision which could require them to compensate developing countries should genetic material collected in a country prove to be the basis of a successful commercial product.

Many of the other outputs from Rio proved to be less valuable. The Rio Declaration is a genuine disappointment. Conceived originally as a ringing endorsement of sustainable development, it is now an uncomfortable compromise between "the right to development" and traditional environmental concerns. Many feel that it is actually a step backward.

Agenda 21, the central action "plan" of the Conference remains a vast and inaccessible document. Its 700-odd pages contain schemes for dealing with everything from toxic waste to safe drinking water, from international trade to Antarctic conservation. In the words of the Canadian delegation reporting telex: "There is no critical centre or first key steps to Agenda 21. Every one of the 130 plus program areas is presented as equally important. This makes it very hard to summarize Agenda 21, and potentially very easy to ignore. The immediate challenge now after Rio will be for governments to identify their priorities for implementation — and for the NGOs that have followed this process closely to do the same . . . " Its budget is as daunting as its length. The annual cost is predicted to rise to $600 billion by the turn of the millenium, with one quarter of this to come from the developed countries.

In spite of the comprehensive nature of Agenda 21, many feel that the document and the conference as a whole ducked the two key issues underlying the world's environmental deterioration. An informal arrangement between the Vatican and conservative Muslim and Catholic countries kept the discussion of population to a minimum. And the United States led the charge by the rich countries to prevent meaningful debate on the need for the developed world to radically change its consumption habits. It will be interesting to see whether these issues can also be evaded by the 1994 UN Conference on Population.

Throughout the UNCED process, it was clear that developing countries would insist on a substantial transfer of new financial resources as a condition for buying into the North's agenda. If the $125 billion set out by the Secretariat was always unrealistic, expectations were still high. Meeting for the last time as a group in May 1992, the Brundtland Commission estimated that at least

$10 billion in new and additional resources would need to be put on the table for the Earth Summit to be a success.

Although Rio was never intended as a "pledging conference," there was some reason to hope that new resources would become available. A meeting of so-called "eminent persons," convened in Tokyo by former Japanese Prime Minister Takeshita, was supposed to be the key to unlocking new resources. Leaks to the Japanese press predicted a huge jump in the Japanese aid budget for the environment, perhaps to as much as $10 billion a year — the amount that was being collected by the surcharge imposed to pay for the Japanese share of the Gulf War costs. Rumours from Brussels and Bonn also seemed to herald the possibility of major new contributions from Europe.

In the end, the Conference delivered little. In Maurice Strong's words, "never have the rich felt so poor," and they showed it. When the developing countries tried to revive the old chestnut about devoting 0.7 percent of gross national product (GNP) to development assistance, the North resisted. The final section of Agenda 21 contains only an opaque reference to the need to reach 0.7 percent by the year 2000 (it was first proposed in 1964). Only the Heads of State of France and Spain pledged to join the select group (the Scandinavian countries and the Dutch are the only current members) who have reached that total. Chancellor Kohl promised to achieve the target as well, but his remarks indicated that Germany expected at least some of its contributions to Eastern Europe to be included. Hindered by the absence from the delegation of both the Minister responsible for CIDA and the President of that agency, Canada appeared muddled on the issue, with the result that the Prime Minister did not refer to it in his address at all.

Industrialized countries were also unwilling to talk seriously about either debt or trade — two other sources of new and additional resources that the Third World counted on. The recent recovery in many of the large Latin American debtors and the survival of the Northern banking system has reduced the sense of urgency surrounding the issue in international discussions. Although Agenda 21 contains the obligatory references to freer trade being a key to sustainable development, and most of the Heads of Government made reference to the need for success in the Uruguay Round, the trade issue was left to the GATT to sort out.

The Politics of Rio and the Canadian Position

The United States took the lead at the Stockholm Conference in 1972. It fielded a large and influential delegation, took positive positions and brought money to the table. The United States also dominated Rio and its preparations, but as a negative force. The American delegation to the Preparatory Committee had taken a hard line on the question of financial resources and was resistant to many of the proposals of the UNCED Secretariat. The U.S. delegation to the climate negotiations openly exercised a veto in the discussion of targets and timetables for CO_2 reduction when they threatened that President Bush would not go to Rio unless the U.S. was happy with the convention. They took a similarly hard line on the biodiversity convention.

The opening days of Rio were taken up with the news that the United States would not sign the biodiversity convention and were marked by American efforts to persuade the other countries in the Organization for Economic Cooperation and Development (OECD) to abstain as well. These attempts failed, in large part because of a pledge by Prime Minister Mulroney on June 1 that Canada would sign the convention. When William Reilly, Administrator of the Environmental Protection Agency (EPA) and the head of the U.S. delegation, cabled the President with a proposal for a process that would allow him to sign the convention, the memo was leaked to the Press by officials from the Vice-President's office. After this incident, the G-7 Ministers of the Environment, meeting for only the second time outside a G-7 summit, spent most of their meeting trying to find ways to prevent Reilly from becoming even more isolated.

This desire not to isolate the U.S. also extended to the climate change discussions. A number of countries, led by Austria and Germany, campaigned to have the goal of stabilizing CO_2 emissions at 1990 levels by the year 2000 enshrined in a declaration that countries would sign at the same time as they signed the convention. These were the targets and timetables removed earlier at American insistence. They correspond to official European Community (EC) policy and to that of Canada. Yet Canada and others resisted the attempt, arguing that ensuring U.S. co-operation on the existing rather toothless convention was preferable to isolating the President on both biodiversity and climate change.

Many observers expected that the traditional American leadership role would be taken up at least in part by Japan. The Japanese had been sending signals to indicate that Rio would be the occasion when they would come out of the diplomatic closet and assume the political role to which their economic strength entitled them. Their delegation was large and extremely well prepared but they were never able to make their mark on the Conference. Part of this was due to the absence of their Prime Minister, who was detained in Tokyo for the conclusion of the very impassioned debate in the Diet on a provision permitting Japanese peacekeepers to join the UN group in Cambodia. But they were also constrained by the desire not to embarrass President Bush by making a large financial and diplomatic contribution. There were strong rumours that Washington had indicated to Tokyo that if Japan upstaged the President in Rio, it could encourage more Japan-bashing in the election campaign. Finally, the glacial process of Japanese decision-making made it difficult for the delegation to make even relatively quick decisions. For instance, they were clearly caught flat-footed when Canada and other developed countries decided to sign the biodiversity convention. It took Japan almost a week to indicate its willingness to go along. As a result, even when Japan announced its rather substantial contribution to increased environmental aid, it came as an anti-climax, given the expectations that had been built up.

In the absence of Japanese leadership, many hoped for some direction from the European Community, in general, and Germany, in particular. Led by the Dutch, the Community had been one of the most effective participants in the Prepcoms. By the time of Rio however, the leadership had passed to Portugal, which proved woefully inadequate to the task. And the Germans seemed strangely quiescent. Despite their bold domestic moves on climate change (German policy is to *reduce* their CO_2 emissions by 25 percent by the year 2005) and on packaging legislation, they were also worried about isolating the United States. Chancellor Kohl, in political and economic trouble at home and in need of an international success, was to be the host of the G-7 Summit in Munich, barely three weeks after Rio. He wanted U.S. concessions on the GATT negotiations and support for some further initiatives in Eastern Europe.

In some ways, then, Maurice Strong achieved what he set out to do. But the transformation of the environment into a major political issue, made it just one of the pieces on the chess board of the world's leaders. And they bargained with it as they did with the other pawns.

This left leadership in the Conference to the middle powers and the Group of 77 developing nations. As Clyde Sanger illustrates in Chapter 8, the G-77 demonstrated more coherence and effectiveness than it had in a very long time. In fact, most of the discussions on the more controversial items took place around G-77 drafts and not drafts from the other groups. Along with the rising importance of the NGOs, this renaissance of the group of developing countries, which continued through the subsequent Jakarta Summit of non-aligned nations, could be one of the more important long-term outcomes of Rio.

Where did all of this leave Canada? The Canadian delegation had come to the Conference with a number of key issues. The first to emerge, and perhaps the most risky, was the Prime Minister's announcement that Canada would resist U.S. pressure and ratify the biodiversity convention. As Elizabeth May of the Sierra Club, no friend of the government, put it: "Let's face it, Canada saved the biodiversity treaty."[5]

Perhaps the most urgent issue transposed to Rio from the domestic agenda was the issue of high seas fishing. Originally oceans issues had been only a marginal issue on the developed country agenda of climate change, deforestation and biodiversity. But as the "northern cod" dispute gathered steam in Canada, diplomats determined to use the oceans chapter of Agenda 21 as a vehicle for extracting concessions from the European Community on the question of fish stocks that lie across boundaries. They succeeded so well and so early, that Canada could barely contain the announcement of a conference on high seas fishing until the arrival in Rio of John Crosbie. His chief rival, Newfoundland Premier Clyde Wells, was left with little to do upon his arrival, other than to shuttle to one or two technical meetings on the subject.

The second domestic issue which was carried from Ottawa was less successfully implanted. Canada had been one of the main advocates of a convention on forests. This fell victim, early in the preparatory process, to a furious onslaught from a number of the tropical wood producing countries, led by Malaysia. They feared further incursions into their own domestic sovereignty, often by Northern environmental groups, which such a convention might bring. In addition to this concern, the forest issue became a symbol of the Southern resentment against the overall rich country approach to the issues at Rio. The Third World felt strongly that the developed countries had caused most of the world's environmental problems and that nevertheless they were being asked to curb their own development and put their natural resources under international control to help solve these problems. Their desire to single out the forest discussions could only have been strengthened when George Bush declared that his chief goal at Rio was to make progress on the forestry issue.

As a result, the Canadian delegation came back with a poor set of agreed forest principles and no agreement to proceed towards an eventual convention. Even these principles were only agreed upon after a series of gruelling all-night sessions skillfully chaired by Klaus Toepfer, the German Environment Minister.

Canada had also been an advocate of a Rio Charter. This was to be a short, eloquent moral and ethical commitment to sustainable development. What emerged in the Rio Declaration is vastly less. In an effort to salvage the situation, the Prime Minister announced Canada's support for the development of a suitable Charter to coincide with the 40th anniversary of the United Nations in 1995. Although this proposal received a good deal of acclaim from other delegations, it is not clear where it will go after Rio.[6]

On the three key "cross-cutting" issues of technology transfer, post-Rio institutions and finance for Agenda 21, the Canadian positions were less impressive. Technology transfer, which many developing countries regard as the key to their future sustainable development, can be a problem for Canada, a huge net technology importer. In the preparations for UNCED, many developing countries had called for technology to be transferred to them on preferential and concessional terms. While it is not clear what that phrase actually means, it could be interpreted as giving the newly industrialized countries of the Asia Pacific region a competitive advantage over other technology importers such as Canada. Canada therefore kept an almost invisible profile on one of the critical issues facing the Conference.

The only significant initiative announced by Canada in this area was a change in the mandate and Board of Directors of the internationally acclaimed International Development Research Centre (IDRC). Saved at the last minute from the budget axe which claimed such bodies as the Canadian Institute for International Peace and Security (CIIPS) (see Chapter 4), IDRC's Board will have UN and World Bank nominees added to it and the federal government's annual $115 million contribution to its operating expenses guaranteed. In fact, the Prime Minister seems to have underwritten the Centre's basic budget for ten years when he stated that ". . . over the next ten years, Canada's contribution to this agency alone will exceed $ 1 billion."[7] This could well turn out to be the most cost-effective initiative launched by Canada in Rio.

On institutions, Canada followed the crowd in endorsing the composition and mandate of the Commission on Sustainable Development. Canada did press hard and successfully for the inclusion of NGOs in the operation of the Commission and for its members to be at a high level in government. It was the only country to include NGOs in its delegation to the General Assembly discussions of the Commission. But at the end of the day, the follow-up to a Conference whose purpose was to integrate the environment and economics at the Head of State level will lie in the hands of a group of Environment Ministers (or, perhaps, UN diplomats) reporting to that graveyard of good intentions, the Economic and Social Council.

It was on the critical issue of finance that Canada had perhaps the least to offer. Given the budgetary situation of the government, it is perhaps not surprising that the delegation left Ottawa with little in its strongbox. The Prime Minister was therefore stuck with a number of re-announceables. He promised to maintain Canada's level of ODA for forestry assistance at $115 million. He promised to maintain IDRC's budget at the same level. He announced, for at least the second time, that Canada would contribute $25 million to the World Bank's Global Environmental Facility (far less than our usual proportional contribution to such a fund), and that Canada would provide "our fair share"[8] when the facility was replenished. Curiously, he also chose Rio as the venue for announcing a $50 million contribution for famine relief in Southern Africa. Finally, in contrast to his policy of writing off Canadian official debt in most of the rest of the world, he announced that Canada would exchange its $145 million official debt in Latin America for sustainable development projects.

Canada also achieved its goals with the two conventions. The rescue of the biodiversity convention began with the Prime Minister's speech before Rio. Although official policy on climate change was to stabilize CO_2 emissions at 1990 levels by the year 2000, there was continuing strong resistance from the Department of Energy, Mines and Resources, the fossil fuel industry and some of the provincial governments. There cannot have been much grief in Ottawa when the Americans succeeded in killing the targets.

The Road from Rio

What do Bob Hope and Dorothy Lamour do on the way back from the Earth Summit? That is a critical question given the meagre accomplishments of the delegations.

Canada faces a number of critical choices as it plans its follow-up activities. Canadian politicians have now mastered the rhetoric of sustainable development. But environment and economics remain divorced in our national and provincial institutions. Perhaps the greatest challenge for the country will be the reform of its own mechanisms for decision-making, so that economic decisions are not taken before their environmental implications have been assessed. The recent report of the Ontario Round Table on the Environment and the Economy[9] provides a number of suggestions for doing this. One of the most interesting is a requirement that each provincial budget should be assessed for its environmental implications and that the analysis should be tabled simultaneously with the budget. The Round Table also calls for sustainability analyses of all decisions before they go to Cabinet and for each department of government to prepare its own sustainability strategy and to report on its implementation. Most of these recommendations were contained in the Canadian response to the Brundtland Commission in 1987[10] and little has been done to implement them.

Much was made in Rio and after of the government's weak financial situation and its inability to contribute to global efforts toward sustainable development. There is clearly little "new" money around. But there is plenty of existing money tied up in ecologically damaging subsidies. Canadian agriculture annually receives up to $10 billion in subsidies which encourage unsustainable forms of agriculture.[11] They encourage wetland drainage and overcultivation of marginal soils and discourage crop diversification. Subsidies to energy megaprojects such as Hibernia and the heavy oil upgrader contribute to global warming and exceed by a factor of 50 or more the monies spent on more environmentally benign forms of energy.[12] The rest of the economy is also shot through with economically and environmentally damaging subsidies and tax breaks. Elimination of these would free up substantial sums for sustainable development without increasing either the deficit or the tax burden. It would have the added advantage of removing a force for unsustainable development from the economy. Needless to say, the politics of removing subsidies in an election year are distinctly unpromising.

But unsustainable development can be expensive. Studies prepared for the German Ministry of the Environment place the annual cost of environmental damage at more than 100 billion Deutsche Marks per year. Ernst von Weizsäcker, the distinguished German scholar, puts the figure even higher — as high as 10 percent of GNP.

Another major challenge lies in Jean Charest's desire to continue in an election year with the open process begun with the Summit preparations. In November 1992, he convened a meeting of the Rio stakeholders under the Chair of the National Round Table on the Environment and the Economy to plan for a *projet de société*. In his testimony to the House of Commons Environment Committee he described it as an effort to "facilitate the development of a broadly shared vision of what sustainability means in Canada as well as identify the key policy, institutional and personal changes that are necessary."[13] Some feel that this is simply a way of getting the federal government off the hook of fulfilling its commitments in Rio. Charest and others seem to feel that this wide open consultative process is not only the new way to take environmental decisions but that the development of just such a *projet de société* might be critical to rekindling a sense of purpose in the country as a whole.

This is a high risk operation. Most of the stakeholders are hostile to the government. Most of them share no more than a common commitment to Rio. And the agenda is vague. But the enthusiasm of the Rio group still remained, at least in the first two meetings.

Much of Agenda 21 relates to matters which are largely or entirely under provincial jurisdiction. Obtaining provincial agreement to their implementation will involve the development of new techniques of federal/provincial co-operation. This is perhaps best illustrated by the issue of climate change. Canada's position on climate change was arrived at only after tremendous battles between the two Ottawa Departments concerned — Environment and Energy, Mines and Resources. And there is no indication that these battles have concluded even now.

After several meetings of the federal/provincial councils of Ministers of the Environment and Ministers of Energy, no credible national instruments for achieving stabilization are yet in place. It is easy to see why. Any national climate change policy necessitates a national *energy* policy. This may or may not mean carbon taxes; it certainly is likely to mean more regulation of the energy industry. Not only is such a strategy anathema to the western provinces, but it is also difficult for a conservative government to justify. It has been opposed tooth and nail by the fossil fuel industry, already crippled by low exploration rates, diminishing (or disappearing) profits and massive layoffs.

Other Agenda 21 items are likely to be less disruptive, but will nonetheless place some strain on federal/provincial relations. For example, if the federal government withdraws from forestry altogether, as the Charlottetown Accord stated it would, the negotiation of an international agreement on forestry and its domestic implementation could prove very difficult.

There is a very real suspicion on the part of many provinces that the federal government will use its treaty-making power in the environmental field to continue to encroach on their turf. Just as the government's room for manoeuvre on domestic economic issues is limited by the trend toward globalization, so are its options on domestic environmental policy limited by the internationalizing of environmental problems. As more and more environmental issues are dealt with by convention, Canada's range of domestic choices will be constrained. These international initiatives will continue to be negotiated by the federal government, but the provinces will continue to be responsible for implementation. This will place additional burdens on the federal/provincial structures and will require a fundamental re-examination of the way in which Canada formulates its environmental foreign policy.

In previous international conferences, Canada has been able to separate its domestic policy from its international commitments. But as the realization dawns that environmental policy and economic policy are completely interlinked, a country's national policies may determine how much influence it can exert on a number of international environmental issues. This is perhaps most obvious in the case of forestry.

Canada will continue to press for an international agreement on forests. Canada has traditionally enjoyed an excellent international reputation for its environmental policy. But the furore over the Newfoundland seal hunt, the sale of furs from animals caught in leg hold traps and the James Bay controversies are tarnishing the country's reputation abroad. The forest industry is worried that it might well become the next target of the wrath of European consumers, who have already been effective in their boycott of tropical timber. It is therefore anxious for a legally binding convention which, among other things, would somehow "certify" timber harvested sustainably.

The failure of the Rio efforts illustrates the need for some sort of fact-finding, consensus-building exercise, similar to the role played by the Intergovernmental Panel on Climate Change in the development of the climate convention. An independent commission on forestry and development has been proposed by a number of NGOs and concerned experts. It could provide the timber producing states with some room for manoeuvre so that they can eventually return to the negotiating table.

Canada will need to take positions on the refinancing of the Global Environmental Facility and on the tenth replenishment of IDA, the World Bank's soft loan window. Rio called for the creation of an "Earth Increment" to be added to IDA to help implement Agenda 21. As mentioned earlier, developing countries will be looking for new and additional resources as part of the price for going along with the Northern agenda. The need for "new" environmental money and the recent cuts in CIDA's budget could reinforce the tendency to divert funds from the agency's traditional concern with the poorest of the poor toward the seven or eight developing countries which produce the most greenhouse gases, have the largest forest cover and the greatest amount of biological diversity. Canada will also need to take advantage of the opportunities created by the decision in Rio to convene an international conference on high seas fishing.

In his speech prior to Rio, the Prime Minister offered Canadian support for a post-Uruguay GATT Round with environment as a focal point. It is now accepted that trade agreements must be far more environmentally acceptable than they have been in the past. The NAFTA is perhaps the first proof of that. Can trade agreements in general, and the GATT in particular, be reformed to support sustainable development? Can unilateral actions by one country in support of its environmental goals (or protectionism dressed in more fashionable green clothing) be replaced by a multilateral rules-based system that is more environmentally sensitive and fairer toward a small and open economy such as Canada?

Some of these questions may be resolved in the further development of the environmental "side agreements" which President Clinton has insisted on in the NAFTA. The proposed North American Commission on the Environment could provide an interesting vehicle for incorporating environmental considerations into trade disputes. If the NAFTA is successfully concluded, it will then raise the question of how to include environmental considerations as other countries seek to become members of the agreement. But the broader questions will need to be resolved in the context of the conclusion of the Uruguay Round, the future of the proposed Multilateral Trade Organization, or a future "green round" of the GATT. Here Canada has promised to take a leading role.

Shifting to more sustainable forms of development can also make good economic sense. Environmental industries are the fastest growing sector of both the U.S. and Canadian economies, and the sector is now larger than aerospace. The OECD market for products, technologies, processes and services within the environmental industry was estimated to be $255 billion in 1992. In Canada, the industry is growing at rates far in excess of GDP, as high as 21 percent in some segments.

In conclusion, therefore, it is fair to say that Rio was both a success and a failure. It did focus the attention of world leaders on a set of problems that will only grow worse over the remainder of the millenium. It did produce some useful international agreements. But it fell well short of the major shifts in policy and financial transfers, recommended by Maurice Strong and the Brundtland Commission to move the world toward more sustainable forms of development. The next time the international community attempts to deal with these issues, the choices will be even harder.

8   Environment and Development

Clyde Sanger

The environment is not going to be saved by environmentalists. Environmentalists do not hold the levers of economic power.

Maurice Strong, UNCED Secretary-General

It is high time that we abandon the colonial heritage whereby developing countries are relegated to the function of mere plantation economies.

President Suharto of Indonesia,
at Rio Summit, June 1992

THE PITY IS THAT, for 20 years or more, it has not been a matter of the environment *and* development; rather, it has been the environment *versus* development. And, despite the best efforts of Gro Harlem Brundtland and her commissioners in 1984–87, this was almost as true at the Earth Summit in Rio, in June 1992, as it had been at the Stockholm Conference on the Human Environment in 1972. Others beside the Brundtland Commission made an effort in the 1980s to integrate environmental concerns into development planning, and these included the Canadian International Development Agency (CIDA). The gap was indeed narrowing, at least between environmentalists and development agencies in the North and in the multilateral organizations; but the South-North chasm remained through all the preparations for the Rio summit. The governments of the poorer nations, either bitter at being neglected or else gaining self-confidence, stood their ground. For once, they had a strong hand of cards to play against the rich nations: if you want co-operation on the environment, they said, then you must produce the funds, change the trade rules, forgive the remaining debt. Acknowledgement of this difference of stance was made at the outset of preparations for Rio by giving the conference an awkward tandem title, the United Nations Conference on the Environment and Development (or UNCED). It particularly reflected the gap between the attitudes of northern activists (whether in government or outside) and the swiftly industrializing countries of Asia. Their two agendas scarcely overlapped. The big gain came among non-governmental organizations (NGOs), North and South: they gained credibility and greater influence with their own governments, and they built important links — and commitments — between regions.

This chapter is divided into three sections. The first sketches the international scene during the twenty-year journey from Stockholm to Rio. The second focuses on Canadian policies, and what changes took place in the pre-Rio period. The third section looks at the Rio Conference, and how Canada came out of it.

The World Scene: Stockholm to Rio

It is worth recalling the main theme of the Founex panel, a group of 27 scientists and development experts who met in Switzerland just before the Stockholm conference. Gamani Corea of Sri Lanka and the United Nations Conference on Trade and Development (UNCTAD) chaired the group, which was mostly from the Third World. In a shortish document they managed to find a balance between environment and development, and clothed it in language acceptable in the South. Here are two key paragraphs:

> In both the towns and countryside [of developing countries] not merely the 'quality of life' but life itself is endangered by poor water, housing, sanitation and nutrition, by sickness and disease and by natural disasters. These are problems, no less than those of industrial pollution, that clamor for attention in the context of the concern with human environment. They are problems that affect the greater mass of mankind.
>
> It is evident that, in large measure, the kind of environmental problems that are of importance in developing countries are those that can be overcome by the process of development itself . . . For these reasons, concern for environment must not and need not detract from the commitment of the world community — developing and more industrialised countries alike — to the overriding task of development of the developing regions of the world.[1]

This was penned, of course, in days before holes were spotted in the ozone layer or the alarm was sounded about global warming. The symbol of northern concern about the environment was then the factory smokestack spewing sulphur dioxide, a symbol that the Brazilians argued was really an index of development. To their credit, the Founex panel then reeled off a formidable list of ills that might result from development. They took, for example, the development of river-basins and quickly listed water-borne diseases, sedimentation of reservoirs, drying up of downstream fisheries, salination, waterlogging — not forgetting the displacement of population and the possible loss of mineral resources, wildlife areas and historic sites.

The prime emphasis at Stockholm, however, as laid down by the industrialized countries, was on pollution control. This is not to say that, among the 26 Principles that are the meat of the Stockholm Declaration, there is no call for an increased transfer of resources or for fairer trade with stable prices (Principles 9 and 10) and no plea for "rational planning" to reconcile "any conflict between the needs of development and the need to protect and improve the environment" (Principle 13). But a good deal of time was spent debating the wording of Principles 21 and 22, which deal with the responsibility of states to prevent pollution slopping over to their neighbours and, if it does, to compensate them (a Principle forgotten in the wake of Chernobyl). In the Stockholm Action Plan there are no fewer than 25 recommendations on "Identification and control of pollutants of broad international significance."

By 1980 a convergence was evident. In a single month the environmentalists — principally the International Union for the Conservation of Nature and Natural Resources (IUCN) — had drawn up the World Conservation Strategy (WCS), and the large multilateral banks (representing economic development) had responded in kind. The Strategy, launched in 30 national capitals in March 1980, pinpointed as a prime obstacle to conservation the attitude that treated development and conservation as separate issues, and began using a word that Brundtland made more familiar — "sustainable." A main objective of the WCS was "to ensure the sustainable use of species and ecosystems."

Moving onto this common ground, seven multilateral banks (the World Bank and six regional ones), the UN Development Programme, the UN Environment Programme and the Organization of American States all signed a "Declaration of environmental policies and procedures relating to economic development." In the preamble they declared themselves "convinced that in the long run environmental protection and economic and social development are not only compatible but interdependent and mutually reinforcing." Granted that they inserted the weasel words "in the long run," the declaration nevertheless contains a strong commitment to integrate "appropriate environmental measures in the design and implementation of economic development activities." And they moved away from Stockholm's emphasis on pollution control to a more basic concern with resource management.

Now, of course, these are just words and good intentions. Activities are not always so reassuring. An outstanding report published in 1992 was the independent review of the Sardar Sarovar Projects on the Narmada river in Gujarat state, India. After tribal people had vigorously protested against the building of a dam that would submerge the homes of 100,000 people (not to mention the digging of the world's largest irrigation canal system that will affect 140,000 farmers), the World Bank called on a predominantly Canadian team to assess the resettlement arrangements and the general environmental impact. The Bank had contributed U.S. $450 million to the project and was on the verge of adding a further $350 million. The report, signed by Tom Berger (of Mackenzie valley fame) and Bradford Morse, was critical of the way so little consideration had been given to many ecological aspects: safeguards against malaria and water-borne diseases, the effect on downstream fisheries, sedimentation and poor planning for reafforestation. Their toughest words were saved for the resettlement mess:

> The [World] Bank and India both failed to carry out adequate assessments of the Sardar Sarovar Projects . . . There was virtually no basis in 1985 on which to determine what the impacts were that would have to be ameliorated. This led to an inadequate understanding of the nature and scale of resettlement. This inadequate understanding was compounded by a failure to consult the people potentially to be affected. Failure to consult the people has resulted in opposition to the Projects [which] has created great obstacles to successful implementation.[2]

When the Canadian House of Commons Sub-Committee on International Financial Institutions held a special session on the Sardar Sarovar dam project in November 1992, the director of the Lokayan research centre, Dr. Smitu Kothari, told MPs:

No other project has so challenged the World Bank and, unfortunately, exposed its real face. I say 'unfortunately' because over the last seven years we have been closely interacting with senior staff of the World Bank, and we had thought at one time that it was possible to create a process whereby the World Bank would reform itself significantly, not in rhetoric but in practice; and we found that indeed this is not the case.[3]

Sea Lawyers and Brundtland

Another landmark in the twenty years came in December 1982, when 119 countries — Canada prominently among them — signed the United Nations Convention on the Law of the Sea. In several ways it sought to marry issues of the environment with those of economic development. It declared all the oceans beyond the limits of national jurisdiction "the common heritage of mankind" and left to national management (and enlightened self-interest?) the exploitation of fisheries and mineral resources within a 200-mile economic zone. It brought new concepts into pollution control, creating a category of "port state" with the powers of an environmental policeman. It did its best to regulate, with a fairly loose rein, the anticipated industry of mining manganese nodules from the seabed. But, ten years later, the process of ratifying the Convention is stalled, a few signatures short of the 60 that will bring it into force, because of the Reagan-Thatcher opposition to Part XI, the seabed mining section of the Convention. In 1992 Canada rejected the tactic of gathering enough other middle powers to complete the ratification process, and instead acquiesced in a British move to have the Secretary-General canvass member states about possible changes to Part XI. It would be surprising if anything other than further delay results from this consultation. In the meantime, states implement those parts of the Convention that suit them (the essence of customary law), and one may be sure that respect for its pollution controls are not a priority for maritime nations.

The call to the faithful to support "sustainable development" was enshrined in the Brundtland Report (1987). The primary task given to the World Commission on Environment and Development was "to propose long-term environmental strategies for achieving sustainable development by the year 2000." Mrs. Brundtland herself wrote that, when the Commission's terms of reference were first being discussed, "there were those who wanted its considerations to be limited to 'environmental issues' only. This would have been a grave mistake." The report goes on to speak of "interlocking crises—an environmental crisis, a development crisis, an energy crisis. These are not separate crises. They are all one." The Brundtland Report achieved its effect by showing the bright as well as the dark side of the coin, and by credibly linking economic growth with increasing equity:

> This Commission believes that people can build a future that is more prosperous, more just and more secure. Our report, *Our Common Future*, is not a prediction of ever increasing environmental decay, poverty and hardship in an ever more polluted world among ever decreasing resources. We see instead the possibility for a new era of economic growth, one that must be based on policies that sustain and expand the environmental resource base. And we believe such growth to be absolutely essential to relieve the great poverty that is deepening in much of the developing world.[4]

This vision is clouded today. Brundtland's prescription of an annual 3 percent economic growth rate is unfulfilled. The determined cheerfulness did not last to Rio. But her report inspired the adoption by CIDA of its overarching policy of Sustainable Development, standing upon five pillars (economic, political, environmental, social and cultural), according to the architect-president, Marcel Massé. It also inspired the creation of the International Institute for Sustainable Development, based in Winnipeg.

By 1992, the World Bank was securely onside, indeed echoing many of the points made by the Founex panel two decades earlier. Its *World Development Report 1992* was devoted to the environment, and it breezily spoke of "win-win links" between environment and development: more emphasis on agricultural extension, sanitation, clean water, female education and population programs. It also urged "open trade and investment policies," which presumably included the removal by rich countries of non-tariff barriers to the products of poorer countries. "Win-win links" also meant removing distortionary policies—particularly subsidies for energy, chemical inputs and for logging. And among five environmental priorities for good development, the Bank placed concern about atmospheric change last—after clean water, reducing air pollution and wastes and after a concern for land and habitat.

In 20 years, the big agencies had reached a common line. From this vantage point, there was solid reason for Maurice Strong, back at the centre again as Secretary-General of UNCED, to think that a convergence of environment and development had really occurred, and the crossing point was marked "sustainable development" and maybe even "Rio."

Sowing Seeds in CIDA

When Maurice Strong left the presidency of CIDA in 1971 to organize the Stockholm Conference (and then went on to become the first executive director of the UN Environment Programme in Nairobi), one might have expected Canada's development agency to move into the forefront of environmental initiatives. Certainly Canada was helpful, in the preparations for Stockholm, to smaller countries struggling to draft national environmental reports (just as the National Film Board helped several nations make good documentaries for the 1976 UN Human Settlements Conference). But CIDA itself was surprisingly slow to show a full degree of environmental awareness. In fact, it took a push from outside to build any momentum. For in 1978 the London-based institute which Barbara Ward founded, the International Institute for Environment and Development, mounted a six-country comparative study of the environmental performance of bilateral aid agencies. The Canadian study was done by the North-South Institute (mainly by Roger Ehrhardt) and Dalhousie University's Institute for Resource and Environmental Studies (then headed by Arthur Hanson). CIDA, putting its best face on a poor situation, asked the researchers to use their interviews to increase the awareness of some 90 agency staff to whom they planned to talk — and also to set out recommendations and guidelines.

The researchers found only modest achievements. Someone had written a 21-page environmental section into the 1976 Sectoral Guidelines, but

> there is no strong Agency commitment to incorporate environmental concerns in regular program planning and project activities; there is no systematic assessment of the environmental consequences at the project proposal stage; there is little feedback

into CIDA on the environmental effects of projects because of inadequate monitoring and evaluation procedures; and there is too little commitment to training programs in developing countries.[5]

It was, in fact, a low baseline from which to start. There were plenty of reasons then for a poor performance. CIDA staff were under pressure to move faster on projects, because they had accumulated undisbursed funds that were equivalent to more than one year's appropriations. Nor could they confidently go outside the Agency for much help. In the registry of 3,000 specialists in the talent bank of consultants kept by the Human Resources Division, there were only 60 people who had claimed any specific environmental interest.[6] Rural development projects, which could bring training in resource management, involved high local costs in labour, and Canada's "tied aid" policy discouraged such projects. In big, multi-donor projects like the Mahaweli Dam in Sri Lanka it was much easier for CIDA staff to leave environmental questions to the more prominent donors or to the host government. Anyway, sectoral guidelines were not directives, but merely recommendations.

The study made many recommendations. It set out to show the importance of building environmental considerations into each of the four main stages of a "project cycle" — from identification through approval to implementation and evaluation — and pointed out that there was plenty of time, since the four stages were often spread over seven years. It also argued that the country program reviews of some 35 priority countries, each done about every five years, and the regional program reviews, done annually, should contain annexes focusing on major natural resource and environmental issues. And it emphasized the need for institution building in those countries.

The response was lukewarm. Only a few country programs, such as Indonesia, paid real attention to an environmental assessment (CIDA's current concern was to reorganize on a "country focus" basis.) But by the later 1980s it bore fruit: an overall environmental strategy in 1986, and an environmental division soon afterwards. In the latest (1992) restructuring, there are two environment units: one in the Policy Branch, the other in Professional Services, where specialists give advice on every project. For in 1992, under Bill C-13, it became a requirement, domestically in Canada and also abroad, to subject every development project proposal to environmental assessment. CIDA is drafting its own regulations to fit the legislation, and its specialists in the environment unit will now have to "sign off" projects.

Just how large CIDA's environmental program has been is a matter of definition. In a document prepared for the Rio summit, *Our Common Agenda: CIDA and environmental sustainability 1986–1991*, the statement is made: "Since 1986, CIDA has invested $1.3 billion in projects that meet the objectives of Agenda 21." Well yes, but . . . the Rio summit's plan of action, Agenda 21, gives wide scope to those claiming to have undertaken valid work; for, in essence, it is the framework of a plan to save the planet. On the other hand, CIDA's "corporate memory," asked in November 1992 to list bilateral projects coded "environment," flung out 13 pages with a total budget of $693.3 million. Even there, the term embraces such a broad range of projects that one is reminded of earlier days when CIDA was criticized for giving too little support to agricultural production (3 percent of bilateral expenditures, by one count) and responded by listing all funds disbursed for roads and railways as being in support of agriculture. For it does not seem likely that a 10-year project on the highway between Cameroon's two main cities, Douala and Yaoundé, is in any strict sense environmental. (In comparison, the World Bank's *Annual Report 1992* mentions only 24 projects in Africa and in East and South Asia as having environmental components.) But, obviously, many projects on CIDA's list have as their first objective an improved natural and human environment: a prime example is the Agency's support of activities in the Sahel region aimed at stabilizing the plant cover, restoring the food balance to make the area self-sufficient, and developing renewable energy sources such as solar power. By November 1992, more than $192 million had been disbursed separately in one decade to the four Sahelian countries — Mali, Niger, Burkina Faso and Senegal — and another $31 million to the region as a whole.

The February 1992 federal budget, unlike that of 1989, did not make a direct cut in Official Development Assistance, but it inserted an ominous innovation. A year earlier, the Finance Minister had said the increase in net ODA cash would be "capped" at 3 percent. In 1992 the increase was halved (to $40 million, making a total of $2.73 billion), for ODA was now placed inside the International Assistance "envelope," out of which is also taken multilateral debt reduction, concessional funds to mix with Export Development Corporation loans, and imputed foreign students' costs.

From its founding in 1970, the International Development Research Centre (IDRC) had been in the forefront for Canada in supporting research in harmony with the local environment. For example, its best-funded division, Agriculture, Food and Nutrition Sciences, focused research work on staple foods (sorghum, millet, cassava) rather than export crops. The forestry program concentrated on stemming desertification (e.g., shelterbelts of casuarina trees facing Egypt's western desert) and on social forestry, while John Bene led the way in setting up the International Council for Research in Agro-Forestry (ICRAF) in Nairobi. Large changes and staff reductions were heralded with the replacement of Ivan Head in the President's office by Keith Bezanson; and the February 1992 federal budget signalled considerable loss of independence in announcing that IDRC would become "a departmental corporation." The Centre would have been tied more closely to Treasury Board rules and to Canada's own economic planning by becoming subject to the Financial Administration Act. Fortunately, the scheme was dropped after negotiations, while IDRC strengthened its links with the United Nations through a new arrangement for nominating members to its international Board of Governors.

During the same period some major Canadian NGOs which had built reputations on relief work and development projects were displaying greater environmental concern. CARE Canada was putting its most publicized efforts in 1992 into famine relief in Somalia, but its work in agroforestry, particularly in Haiti and South America, has become an important part of its activities.[7] In July 1992 CARE Canada set up its own six-person environmental unit. The Aga Khan Foundation's rural development project in northern Pakistan, and USC Canada's leadership in the "Seeds for Survival" project, building up regional seed banks around Ethiopian farming communities, are other praiseworthy examples.

The Business of Dollars at Rio

Maurice Strong took on a pushing and shunting task at Rio that proved impossible to maintain. He has, no doubt at all, a respect and admiration for the activism of environmentalists. But, as the quotation at the head of this chapter indicates, he turned to other constituencies for the leverage to put the world on a course toward sustainable development — to the circles of big business and governments. He seems to have counted heavily on the efforts of the Business Council for Sustainable Development (BCSD), on to which his Swiss friend Stephan Schmidheiny recruited 48 top executives of banks and multinational corporations, to influence the U.S. and Japanese and European governments, so that they would provide the resources — $75 billion a year — for the implementation of Agenda 21. In turn, this Northern largesse would persuade governments in the South to support, for example, a Forestry Convention.

The plan did not work. There were too many uncouplings and discontinuities. For a start, it is doubtful whether the heads of Shell and Dupont and Mitsubishi share a view of sustainable development which involves lowering consumption patterns in the North. Then, it became clear that, in an election year held in depression times, President Bush would be hard to shift in any worthwhile direction. At the same time, the Japanese leadership (on whom Strong pinned hopes), having made their country the largest aid giver among the Development Assistance Committee (DAC) group, shied away from the role of rallying governments behind large-scale financing of Agenda 21. There is little evidence that the BCSD positively influenced (or really sought to influence) the governments of the North. A Greenpeace campaigner wrote bitterly of the baleful vision of business leaders "linking environmental protection to profitability, through a system in which all of nature is priced and patented . . . And in Rio, UNCED came close to adopting this vision of free market environmentalism as its own."[8]

Two crucial subjects that were soft-pedalled at Rio were the twin needs to change consumption patterns (mostly in the North) and to reduce the rate of population increase (mainly in the least developed countries, where the rate in 1991 was 2.8 percent). True, these chapters appear as Chapters 4 and 5 in Agenda 21, but they received all too little discussion at UNCED. Why? Various reasons for silence on population (called "Demographic dynamics" in official texts) were given, such as Papal disapproval and the fact that programs had been agreed upon at PrepCom meetings and "no discussion was necessary at Rio." The other subject was certainly raised at the summit round table by the Western spokesperson,

Chancellor Franz Vrantitzky of Austria, who asked: "Have we really accepted, as a basis for future decisions, that current patterns of consumption and production are unsustainable?" For those who remembered Mr. Bush's statement that the quality of life in the West was not for debate, the question hung in the air. It was underlined by an item in a UNEP study released in December 1992, predicting that by early next century there could be one billion cars in the world, almost twice as many as there are today.

Canadian officials worked hard to provide finance for development, chairing the Finance working group in the four lengthy Preparatory Commmittee (PrepCom) meetings, where all negotiations were supposed to be concluded. When the issue dragged its way through UNCED and only some $7 billion of new resources were pledged, Canada appeared comparatively generous. It had in recent months offered some $115 million for forest management in developing countries; the cancellation of the ODA debt to Latin America at a cost of $145 million; a further $50 million in humanitarian aid to Africa, and promises to help replenish the Global Environment Facility (see below) and to contribute to an Earth Increment if it were added to the next replenishment of the World Bank's "soft loan window," the International Development Association. But Canada would not commit itself to a date (the year 2000 was being promoted) for achieving the ODA target of 0.7 percent of GNP, to which it first agreed two decades ago.

Developing countries were, in any case, not so interested in new aid flows as in debt reduction, transfer of technology and trade. Dawood Ghaznavi, head of the Worldwide Fund for Nature in Pakistan, has said: "The fact that trade was largely left out of the financing discussions is the most regrettable thing that happened at UNCED."[9] The forests were, at least symbolically, the battleground for argument on responsibilities for environmental protection. Prime Minister Mahathir Mohamad of Malaysia, criticized for its heavy logging in Borneo, turned on the United States for refusing to accept a timetable for reducing its carbon emissions while calling for the preservation of carbon-absorbing forests in Asia and Latin America. It would be fair, he said, to have a convention on forests only after a "worthwhile" convention on industrial emissions had been reached.[10] After you, Alphonse. But these, and other arguments with the North, served one useful purpose: they revived some of the lost coherence among the Group of 77, and this was further reinforced at the spirited conference of the Non-Aligned Movement in Indonesia.

Treaty-Making NGOs

A major redeeming feature of the Rio summit was provided by non-governmental organizations. Canadian NGOs were in the forefront of the networks that were built during the PrepCom meetings and at Rio, and the Canadian government was far more open than at previous UN conferences to the idea of allowing NGOs to be active players in the policy-making process. During the two-year period over which the four PrepComs stretched, Canadian NGOs with differing concerns had come closer together through the Environment and Development working group set up by the Canadian Council for International Cooperation (CCIC), and they in turn had made firm links with Southern networks forged by, among others, Martin Khor of Malaysia. As an example, these partners met in February 1992 at the IDRC headquarters in Ottawa, and together went to PrepCom IV in New York, where they pressed for the issues that governments were tending to duck: trade and debt reduction, and the acceptance that consumption patterns in the North were simply not sustainable.

At Rio the 300 or more Canadian NGO representatives were strategically placed. A few, like Jeanine Ferretti of Pollution Probe, were part of the Canadian delegation and later praised the ease of access to Environment Minister Jean Charest, as well as the Canadian leadership in half a dozen areas, including the biodiversity convention, overfishing and forestry. But from her viewpoint the general picture was depressing. She wrote: "It was clear to those of us watching from the bleachers that there was greater emphasis placed on protecting the status quo than the environment."[11] Meanwhile, Johannah Bernstein, who had been the national co-ordinator for the Canadian Participatory Committee for UNCED (a coalition of social movements and NGOs), went on to use her lawyer's skill at precise wording as principal author of the daily *Earth Summit Bulletin*, which chronicled and discreetly commented on the tangled minutiae of the delegations' work; and David Runnalls not only wrote a punchy daily commentary as Issues Editor of the official *Earth Summit Times*, but was a prime source of comment for the 70 Canadian media covering Rio.

However, one hopes the most durable work came from the treaty-making efforts of the International NGO Forum, of which Peter Padbury of CCIC was one of three co-ordinators. The idea of NGO representatives sitting down to draft treaties of their own arose from their frustration at watching the official delegates spend weeks during the PrepComs becoming mired in fixed positions and losing sight of both broader horizons and the urgency of action as they sank in their own mud. There were critics among NGOs of the decision to spend a majority of time and effort on this process: drafting treaties, they said, was a distraction from the real task of NGOs, that is, influencing governments; or else it was simply aping the behaviour of officials. But others have spoken almost lyrically. Tim Draimin, CCIC member of the official delegation, has written that the treaty writers — and about 3,500 people took part in one way or another — were aiming to be "inventors and builders of the sustainable society." Sophia Murphy of CCIC, who facilitated the treaty co-ordinators' work, writes that the step was taken with "the clear determination to move NGOs from their traditonal role as a critical voice to hammering out the likely nature of an alternative program."[12] She adds that they were planned as "open and living documents", inviting additions from later adherents.

Some 39 NGO treaties were agreed upon and signed at Rio, and Canadians co-ordinated seven of them. They covered the gamut of concerns at the Forum: women, education, sustainable agriculture, debt, trade, energy, militarism, population, consumption patterns. They have been translated into the summit's four languages — Portuguese, Spanish, English and French — and NGO groups in many countries are seeking ways to work points from them into national and international policies. They have been used this summer for popular education in 60 Dutch cities. Swedes claim their government's debt policies have already been altered, while there are plans to use the women's and the population treaties in UN world conferences in coming years. NGOs wanted some central point of information, but no elaborate superstructure. The organizers were given a one-year mandate to distribute the treaties and to plan later co-ordination. They resolved to keep networks alive through regional groupings or devices like phone or fax "trees." The challenge for Canadian NGOs is to compile a national sustainability plan with input from these treaties; for, in Draimin's words, "Rio was mostly about the environment, partly about development and certainly not about sustainability, which is an extraordinarily subversive concept."

The Global Environment Facility

The Rio summit prompted changes in the Global Environment Facility (GEF) that may make it more acceptable in the South. Originally proposed by France and Germany, the GEF was launched in May 1991 as a three-year experiment to provide developing countries with funds to explore ways of protecting the global environment, and to transfer technologies that are benign to the environment. Its scope was strictly limited. The facility had U.S. $1.2 billion to allocate among three problem areas: the largest part for reduction of global warming, less for the conservation of biodiversity and less still for the protection of international waters; it also had $200 million provided under the Montreal Protocol to help developing countries phase out the use of CFCs and other ozone-destroying substances.

Southern countries have had a major problem with the governance of the GEF. While the scientific work it would fund falls under the supervision of the UN Environment Programme, and the technical assistance side is in the hands of the UN Development Programme, the World Bank runs its administration and is responsible for the investment projects. Moreover, it seemed obvious that the World Bank was positioning itself to become, through the GEF, the funding mechanism for the two Conventions to be signed at Rio, on Climate Change and Biodiversity, and for support of work under Agenda 21. The World Bank's record on environmental issues was speckled at best, and its lack of transparency and its system of donor control raised further worries.

In April 1992, in good time for Rio, agreement on restructuring the GEF was reached at a Participants' Meeting; that is, a meeting of those countries that had contributed funds — 25 at the time of its launching, including nine developing countries. The GEF was thrown open to universal membership, with no entry fee; and they proposed that it should be governed by a Participants' Assembly with countries grouped into some 25 constituencies and the designated representative of each group being rotated — a compromise between the systems of the UN General Assembly and the World Bank. They also agreed to broaden the scope of its financing to include land degradation issues (desertification and reforestation), an addition devised to attract African support. This restructuring had some desired effects: the GEF was accepted as the interim financing mechanism for both Conventions, at least until other permanent arrangements are made. However, the Rio conference made clear, in the Finance chapter of Agenda 21, that new resources might pass through many channels, including the multilateral development banks, the UN specialized agencies, bilateral donors and private direct investment. So, as Andrew Clark writes, "the World Bank did not fulfil its ambition to be the main channel of any new and additional funds at UNCED."[13]

The question, in any case, remains whether the GEF, even if restructured and provided with perhaps double its present funds for the 1994–96 period, is not simply marginal to the main efforts to achieve sustainable development. The consumption patterns of the North and the poverty of the South are surely the main cause of global environmental problems, and neither is addressed by work funded by the GEF. In fact, "to the extent that it is perceived as the major source of Green funding for developing countries it deflects attention from the real environmental needs of the South."[14]

9

Toward Sustainable Development in Canada's Arctic: Policies and International Relations

Nigel Bankes, Terry Fenge and Sarah Kalff

Cleaning up past mistakes is urgently required, but is an insufficient policy response to Arctic environmental problems.

THE INTERNATIONAL ENVIRONMENTAL AGENDA for 1992 was dominated by the global concerns of the Rio Conference. The issues addressed were global warming, biodiversity and deforestation. Bilateral and regional concerns received relatively little attention.

How did the Arctic fare in this context? What are Canada's Arctic concerns? What impact, if any, do the events at Rio have on regional initiatives involving the eight Arctic circumpolar states: Canada, Denmark (Greenland), Finland, Iceland, Norway, Sweden, the United States, and Russia? Are these regional initiatives compatible with and complementary to the way in which global issues were dealt with at the Rio Conference?

This chapter begins with preliminary comments on the value to Canada of a multi-faceted approach to Arctic international relations, an approach that makes use of bilateral dialogue, regional or multilateral agreements, and global initiatives. Second, we identify in a general way some of the leading features or principles of the Rio Conference and agreements common to national Arctic environmental policy or to circumpolar regional initiatives in which Canada is participating or to both these areas of activity. Third, we look at Canada's Arctic Environmental Strategy. At the regional level, we discuss the Arctic Environmental Protection Strategy, agreed to by the eight Arctic nations in 1991. Following this, we discuss four of the products of the Rio process, the Bio-Diversity Convention, the Climate Change Convention, the Rio Declaration, and Agenda 21. We then look at a current initiative that may hold much for the Canadian and circumpolar North: the proposed Arctic Council. Finally, the chapter examines the complementarity of global and regional initiatives, and looks towards the negotiation of an Arctic Sustainable Development Treaty.

Which Approach Works Best: Bilateral, Regional or Global?

The globalization of environmental issues at Rio was not new. At least since the Stockholm Conference of 1972,[1] there has been a growing appreciation that environmental problems facing us are not confined to local or bilateral issues between states or even regions, but are in fact truly global in their impact. In comparison, our bilateral and regional approach to issues of the circumpolar North may seem parochial, but this emphasis is justified for several reasons.

First, and obviously, not every environmental problem requires a global solution, even if the problem is of global interest. For example, the protection and management of migratory species such as barren ground caribou, polar bear and bowhead whales are best resolved by the migratory states concerned.[2] If the migratory states are unable to deal with the issues, it may be argued that additional states should be involved, on the grounds that migratory states owe stewardship obligations to the rest of the world. But it should be recognized that the addition of other players will often complicate efforts and therefore should be avoided.

Second, even though environmental or resource management problems may be global in scope, it may still be possible to achieve significant regional results without encountering serious "free-rider" problems. For example, the problem of toxics in the food chain is undoubtedly a global issue, but many of the toxics in the Canadian Arctic are thought to originate from land-based pollution in the former Soviet Union and Eastern Europe. This is a critical issue for Canada, and also for Greenlanders, Alaskans, and other circumpolar communities. It is an issue on which progress needs to be made, and can be made through bilateral and regional agreements without waiting upon the sometimes glacial progress of global initiatives.

Finally, global problems may pose particular concerns that are shared by countries within a region, and consequently there may be good reason for wishing to co-operate on the development of regional adaptive and mitigative measures and on research. This might be the case even though avoidance measures on a bilateral or regional scale might be unsuitable because of the free-rider problem. A current example is posed by the problem of global warming. Although there are significant scientific uncertainties associated with global warming, all agree that the amount and rate of warming will be greater in the high latitudes.[3] This awareness ought to give rise to research and policy questions specifically regional in scope, such as: whether Arctic ecosystems or particular components thereof will be able to adapt to an enhanced rate of change? What are the consequences of global warming for permafrost and Arctic construction methods? What will be the likely successor vegetation and ground cover in tundra areas? What will be the consequences for northern shipping and resource development projects?

Questions such as these have driven regional research and management initiatives in the last few years. Canada has an additional reason for wishing to participate in regional initiatives. Historically, Canadian Arctic policy has focused on our relationship with the United States — our most powerful neighbour.[4] This has been reflected not only in security agreements but also in environmental and navigational concerns related to the status of the Northwest Passage and the risk of pollution from Arctic shipping. More recently, there has been a growing appreciation that multilateral or regional initiatives may assist in redressing the power imbalance between Canada and the United States.[5] Canada's experience with the Arctic Waters Pollution Prevention Act[6] is a case in point. The most vociferous opponent of this legislation was undoubtedly the United States, which feared its provisions affecting security and shipping interests. Nevertheless, by working through the multilateral forum of the United Nations Third Law of the Sea Conference,[7] Canada was able to gain international acceptance for a special Arctic clause in the treaty. Remaining differences over navigation were dealt with in a bilateral agreement,[8] designed to ensure that the special case of the Arctic could not readily be replicated in other parts of the world.

Common Themes

Apart from the foregoing considerations, certain global environmental problems, such as toxics and global warming, represent for the circumpolar states a group of shared themes. The first of these is the concept of sustainability, popularized in recent times by the Brundtland Commission, and appropriated, used and abused by every conceivable organized interest.[9] Sustainable development will prove to be a very demanding objective in the Arctic, perhaps more so than in any other region of the globe. In part, this is related to the ecological fragility and sensitivity of the Arctic and to the fact that it is a "hinterland." It is also due to the limited range of economic development options available to the small, isolated communities that typify the northern circumpolar world.

A second theme relates to the situation of the indigenous peoples of the area. Again, this is a theme that looms large in the Brundtland Report, which adamantly insisted that environmental issues could not be divorced from their social and political context. True sustainability, it was argued, could only be achieved in tandem with social justice and intra-generational, as well as inter-generational, equity. One vehicle for attaining social justice as well as improving the management of natural resources in the Arctic will be found in the recognition of the political rights, special skills, and knowledge of indigenous peoples. This is an especially strong theme in the Arctic Environmental Protection Strategy, but it is also echoed in Canadian policy and the Rio instruments. That this should emerge as a theme in the Arctic is not surprising. It would hardly be an exaggeration to suggest that Arctic regional initiatives of the last few years have been NGO-led, and that the torch was originally lit by the Inuit Circumpolar Conference (ICC), supported by NGOs such as the Canadian Institute of International Affairs and the Canadian Arctic Resources Committee.

Canadian Arctic Environmental Policy: Early Days

The federal government's first major policy pronouncement on environmental issues in the Arctic came in 1973, when Jean Chrétien, then Minister of Indian Affairs and Northern Development, proposed a "balancing" of developmental and environmental interests.[10] Legislation and regulations to achieve this balancing included the Territorial Lands Act, the Northern Inland Waters Act, the Arctic Waters Pollution Prevention Act, and the Offshore Ocean

Dumping Control Act. Beginning in the early 1970s, national parks and conservation areas were proposed in the Arctic as a further element in the balance and as a counterpoint to projected oil and gas development in the Beaufort Sea, the Mackenzie valley, and the high Arctic regions.

Also, in 1973, the federal government announced that it would negotiate land claim agreements with aboriginal peoples who had not ceded their aboriginal title to land through treaties, and whose title to land had not been superseded by law. Inuit, Dene, and Métis resident in the Northwest Territories and Yukon, and Inuit in northern Quebec were the first aboriginal peoples to begin negotiations with government. Inuit and Cree residents of northern Quebec settled their land claim in 1975. Inuvialuit of the Beaufort Sea region did likewise in 1984. Ratification of the Nunavut Treaty, and of the land claim agreement negotiated by the Council for Yukon Indians, is expected soon.

Environmental protection and management of Crown-owned natural resources are dealt with at some length in these agreements.[11] Many implementation problems loom, and it remains to be seen whether government will provide sufficient funding to resource management institutions established through the agreements. Nevertheless, land claim settlements may well be useful vehicles for implementing principles of sustainable development in the North. Brevity precludes developing this argument further. However, to illustrate the point, it might be noted that the environmental assessment and review of Hydro Québec's proposed Great Whale hydroelectric project is taking place because of — and perhaps solely because of — requirements in the James Bay and Northern Quebec Agreement.[12] The utility of land claim agreements as a means of implementing sustainable development policies and programs in the Canadian Arctic is a theme yet to be fully explored by academics and decision-makers.

The Green Plan and the Arctic Environmental Strategy

There is an environmental policy and plan for the nation as a whole, the federal government's Green Plan, released in 1990, which includes sections of particular relevance to the Arctic.[13] For example, commitments in this Plan to complete the national park system will require action in the Arctic, for this region is under-represented in the system. The Green Plan adumbrates a new environmental strategy for the North, formally released by the Department of Indian Affairs and Northern Development in 1991. This Arctic Environmental Strategy (AES) put forward the following goal and objectives:

Goal

To preserve and enhance the integrity, health, bio-diversity and productivity of our Arctic ecosystems for the benefit of present and future generations.

Objectives

1. To ensure the health and well-being of Arctic ecosystems;
2. To provide for the protection and enhancement of environmental quality and sustainable utilization of resources, including their use by indigenous peoples;
3. To ensure that indigenous peoples' perspectives, values and practices are fully accommodated in the planning, development, conservation and protection of the Arctic region;
4. To ensure better decision-making through integration of local, national and international interests as part of new legal, constitutional and co-operative arrangements; and
5. To develop international agreements and arrangements to use, conserve and manage resources and protect the circumpolar Arctic environment.[14]

The AES recognizes the need for broad scope and a systematic approach, and identifies four programs to focus on key environmental challenges in the North: contaminants, waste, water, and the integration of the environment and the economy. In each case the AES identifies an objective and a work plan.

The objective on contaminants is "to reduce and where possible eliminate contaminants" in the food chain. This is to be achieved through the identification of sources and transportation, the assessment of contaminant levels and their effects, the provision of health advice, and the establishment of international controls. Unsafe, hazardous, and unsightly waste is to be eliminated through the identification, assessment, and clean up of hazardous sites and the support of local waste management strategies. Distant Early Warning (DEW) line sites are specifically identified for clean-up. Enhancing water resource management is to be achieved through increased research. The all-important objective of integrating the environment and economy emphasizes the need to integrate traditional ecological knowledge and values with modern science, and to generate new economic development opportunities. The objective is to be achieved through a work plan that emphasizes community-based resource management and environmental action plans.

The AES acknowledges the importance of the international context to achieve its goals and objectives. The ministerial message accompanying the AES emphasizes that it "requires intensive negotiations and co-operation with circumpolar nations . . . ," while the document itself recognizes that the Arctic is a hinterland. More specifically, the objectives of the AES emphasize the need to integrate local, national and international interests, and the need to develop international agreements and arrangements. The work plan on contaminants envisages international controls. It is therefore rather puzzling that the section of the paper entitled "A Circumpolar View and Common Concern" is tagged on awkwardly to the report, almost in the form of an appendix.

The AES has been criticized by Keith,[15] who believes it to be demonstrably inadequate. In his view, the socio-cultural dimension is missing from the goals and objectives of the AES. He observes: "From a human ecological perspective Arctic ecosystems have existed in adaptive and resilient relations with the region's subsistence societies, and ecosystem characteristics are, in part, an expression of that interdependence." This omission is reflected, he says, in a failure to give explicit support to subsistence cultures and economies, and to the importance of aboriginal knowledge of the Arctic. Keith is also critical of the treatment of the four "key environmental challenges." He points out that the work plan on contaminants, with its emphasis on assessment and research, is unlikely to achieve the objective of reduction and "where possible" elimination of contaminants. At a more general level, however, Keith calls into question the selection of only four issues which is hardly, he says, what one might expect of a comprehensive approach. Other issues thought to merit attention include conservation areas, marine policy, species protection, and restoration and rehabilitation.

The Regional Context:
The Arctic Environmental Protection Strategy

Until recently, regional Arctic initiatives were few and far between. Arctic states attempted to resolve problems on a bilateral basis such as, for example, the 1983 Canada/Denmark/Greenland Marine Environmental Co-operation Agreement. Academics from time to time have urged governments to develop a vision of the Arctic Ocean as a regional sea, but there seems to have been considerable reluctance to conceptualize the Arctic in these terms. The only regional international agreement is apparently the Polar Bear Convention, concluded in 1973 by Canada, Denmark, Norway, the United States, and the Soviet Union.[16]

Recently, however, Canada has been an active participant in, and enthusiastic supporter of, what has become known as the Rovaniemi or Finnish initiative, an initiative of the government of Finland that brought together officials of the eight Arctic countries in September 1989 to discuss co-operative measures to protect the Arctic environment. This meeting resulted in the adoption of an Arctic Environmental Protection Strategy (AEPS) signed on June 14, 1991.[17] The Strategy has no formal legal status, but it might provide the basis for binding norms in the future.

In outline, the document bears some resemblance to the Canadian strategy paper. Both begin with a statement of objectives and principles and then identify "problems and priorities" or, in the case of Canada's AES, "key environmental challenges." Existing international mechanisms for dealing with these priorities are then identified, as well as necessary further action. In addition to problems and priorities, however, the Strategy identifies the need for further action in areas of Arctic monitoring and assessment, emergency response and conservation of Arctic flora and fauna.

The AEPS statement of Objectives and Principles, although lengthy, is set out in Exhibit 9.1.

Despite its length, this statement seems preferable to its Canadian (AES) counterpart for at least two reasons. First, it emphasizes interdependence and the effects of activities upon ecosystems. It therefore recognizes the dynamism of the natural and human environment, and firmly grounds its usage of the term "sustainable utilization" in the broad context of the ecosystem. Second, the strategy is more specific in its reference to the importance of indigenous peoples. Not only are their cultural needs, values, and

Exhibit 9.1

The Arctic Environmental Protection Strategy

Objectives

i) To protect the Arctic ecosystem including humans;

ii) To provide for the protection, enhancement and restoration of environmental quality and the sustainable utilization of natural resources, including their use by local populations and indigenous peoples in the Arctic;

iii) To recognize and, to the extent possible, seek to accommodate the traditional and cultural needs, values and practices of the indigenous peoples as determined by themselves, related to the protection of the Arctic environment;

iv) To review regularly the state of the Arctic environment;

v) To identify, reduce, and, as a final goal, eliminate pollution.

Principles

The Strategy and its implementation by the eight Arctic countries will be guided by the following principles:

i) Management, planning and development activities shall provide for the conservation, sustainable utilization and protection of Arctic ecosystems and natural resources for the benefit and enjoyment of present and future generations, including indigenous peoples;

ii) Use and management of natural resources shall be based on an approach which considers the value and interdependent nature of ecosystem components;

iii) Management, planning and development activities which may significantly affect the Arctic ecosystems shall:

a) be based on informed assessments of their possible impacts on the Arctic environment, including cumulative impacts;

b) provide for the maintenance of the region's ecological systems and bio-diversity;

c) respect the Arctic's significance for and influence on the global climate;

d) be compatible with the sustainable utilization of Arctic ecosystems;

e) take into account the results of scientific investigations and the traditional knowledge of indigenous peoples . . .

vii) Consideration of the health, social, economic and cultural needs and values of indigenous peoples shall be incorporated into management, planning and development activities;

viii) Development of a network of protected areas shall be encouraged and promoted with due regard for the needs of indigenous peoples;

ix) International co-operation to protect the Arctic environment shall be supported and promoted;

x) Mutual co-operation in fulfilling national and international responsibilities in the Arctic consistent with this Strategy, including the use, transfer and/or trade, of the most effective and appropriate technology to protect the environment, shall be promoted and developed.

Source: See note 14.

practices to be recognized (but only to the extent possible) and incorporated into management, planning, and development activities, but it is also recognized that their traditional knowledge has an important role to play in assessing development activities.

Although there are some similarities in the national and regional identification of problem areas, there are significant differences in the complete lists. The regional strategy identifies six problem areas: (1) persistent organic contaminants (e.g., PCBs, DDT); (2) oil pollution (especially in relation to what are called in the report "marginal ice zones"); (3) heavy metals (e.g., cadmium, lead, arsenic, methyl mercury and nickel); (4) noise (especially in relation to marine mammals); (5) radioactivity (from both atmospheric tests — long-since banned by Arctic powers — and the Chernobyl incident); and finally (6) acidification.

The regional strategy is more comprehensive than the AES, and for the most part contains a more specific analysis of the problems and the steps required to deal with them. One could anticipate this in relation, for example, to the steps required to strengthen international agreements such as the Economic Commission for Europe's (ECE) Long Range Transfrontier Air Pollution (LRTAP) Convention,[18] but it is more surprising in relation to issues such as noise. In fact, the complete failure of the Canadian strategy to deal with this seems, in retrospect, to be quite remarkable. Noise is a major issue for Inuit hunters. They have concerns about low-level flying and about helicopter-based mineral exploration activity and its effect on caribou, yet their views continue to be doubted or dismissed by scientists. Concerns are at least equally great with regard to the effect of noise on marine mammals. Indeed, these concerns formed the core of Inuit opposition to Petro-Canada's Arctic Pilot Project in the early 1980s.[19]

The Global Context: Rio and the Arctic

Although the oxymoronic quality of this sub-heading may well conjure up visions of winter escapes for frozen northerners, our intent is to examine whether Canada's Arctic concerns and priorities are reflected in the various documents and agreements emanating from the Rio Conference on Environment and Development, particularly in: the Bio-Diversity Convention,[20] the Climate Change Convention,[21] the Rio Declaration on Environment and Development,[22] and Agenda 21.[23] In doing so we shall focus on the extent to which the Rio instruments reflect an interest in the need for and importance of regional initiatives, and the extent to which they recognize the special role of aboriginal peoples.

The Bio-Diversity Convention

The main concerns of the Bio-Diversity Treaty are with the twin problems of preservation of diversity and the exploitation of genetic resources. Much of the Treaty is therefore taken up with terms of access to genetic resources and the associated problems of the ownership of intellectual property and technology transfer. Nevertheless, given the emphasis that the Convention places on *in-situ* conservation (Art. 8), we can expect it to provide further impetus to Canada's Green Plan commitment to meet the Brundtland Commission's recommendation that each state set aside 12 percent of its land mass under some protected area status. In the North, progress on this commitment can be expected provided that governments co-operate with aboriginal peoples on shared management of sites though the vehicle of land claims agreements.[24]

The Bio-Diversity Agreement, although championed by Canada, contains no reference to the special or unique situation of the Arctic, polar regions, or Arctic ecosystems. Instead, special consideration is reserved for developing countries, especially Art. 20(7): "those that are most environmentally vulnerable, such as those with arid and semi-arid zones, coastal and mountainous areas."

Unlike other global agreements (notably UNCLOS III), the Bio Diversity Agreement provides little encouragement for regional initiatives. It issues a general call for co-operation between states on matters of mutual interest (Art. 5) and on education (Art. 13), but is short on specifics. However, in the context of impact assessment, the Convention does require each contracting party, by Art. 14(1)(c) to:

> (c) Promote, on the basis of reciprocity, notification, exchange of information and consultation on activities under their jurisdiction or control which are likely to significantly affect adversely the biological diversity of other States or areas beyond the limits of national jurisdiction, by encouraging the conclusion of bilateral, regional or multilateral arrangements, as appropriate.

The Agreement is of particular interest where it deals with the special position of indigenous peoples. The role of such peoples is dealt with in various articles, including those on *in-situ* conservation, exchange of information (Art. 17), and technical and scientific co-operation (Art. 18(4)). Art. 8(j) on *in-situ* conservation is probably the most far-reaching. It commits the contracting parties to:

> (j) Subject to its national legislation, respect, preserve and maintain knowledge, innovations and practices of indigenous and local communities embodying traditional lifestyles relevant for the conservation and sustainable use of biological diversity and promote their wider application with the approval and involvement of the holders of such knowledge, innovations and practices and encourage the equitable sharing of the benefits arising from the utilization of such knowledge, innovations and practices; . . .

On the whole one has to conclude that while the Bio-Diversity Agreement seems consistent with Canadian Arctic policy, it has little to add, and fails to come to terms with many of the most pressing issues facing the Arctic.

The Climate Change Convention

There remain significant uncertainties as to both the degree and origins of global warming. Nevertheless, as mentioned earlier, there is a clear consensus that if global warming occurs, its effects will be magnified in high latitudes. Some of the consequences of warming can be readily stated. For example, ice cover will decrease and there will be, over time, a melting of permafrost giving rise to a range of construction problems in the Arctic. Much more difficult to predict, however, are the consequences of warming on particular species or the Arctic ecosystem as a whole. For example, will mammals such as the polar bear be capable of adapting to what may be relatively rapid changes in ice-cover, and how will biologically important polynias of the high Arctic be affected?

If one believes in the intrinsic worth of all beings or sentient beings, these questions are important in and of themselves, but they are of much more pressing concern to the aboriginal inhabitants of the Arctic. To them, the continued viability of their culture, economy and way of life depends upon the availability of country food, which in turn depends upon the resilience and adaptability of the Arctic ecosystems in the face of potentially unprecedented rates of change.

The relationship between global warming and risks to food supply is recognized in the key objective of the Framework Convention on Climate Change opened for signature in Rio in June 1992. The "ultimate objective" of the Convention is expressed to be the stabilization of greenhouse gas concentrations "at a level that would prevent dangerous anthropogenic interference with the climate system." This level is to be achieved in a time-frame "sufficient to allow ecosystems to adapt naturally to climate change, to ensure that food production is not threatened and to enable economic development to proceed in a sustainable manner." This is an important objective, but it remains to be seen whether the states party to the Convention achieve it.

Much of the Convention addresses the needs of developing countries. Committed as we are to the principle of intra-generational equity in the context of ecologically sustainable development, that treatment seems to us to be entirely appropriate, as does the listing at various points in the Convention of specially vulnerable developing countries, including small island countries, countries liable to drought and desertification and energy producing land-locked countries.

Less understandable, however, is the total failure to mention the special position of high latitude countries. In textual terms, this can be readily explained, since references to the special needs of particular regions occur in the context of an article dealing with developing countries. Such a context, of course, excludes the northern high latitude countries that, with other developed countries, have produced "the largest share of historical and current global emissions of greenhouse gases . . . " But that, surely, is only part of the story. Of equal importance must be the prominence given to Arctic concerns by the respective high latitude states. Here there is little evidence that the Arctic is an important motivating issue in the development of domestic greenhouse policy. In other words, far from the Arctic serving to define Canadian greenhouse policy because of its vulnerability, due to the rate of warming in the high latitudes, it may very well end up being used as the miner's canary.

In conclusion, despite the obvious risks to the Canadian Arctic of unchecked global warming, there is little that one can point to in the Convention that addresses the needs of the polar regions. True, the objective provides an appropriate goal, but the commitments fall short. Finally, although there is provision in the Convention for a conference of the parties and other institutionalized forms of co-operation, including measures for co-ordinating research, the emphasis is very much on global issues, rather than regional concerns. This is perhaps entirely appropriate in a global convention dealing with global problems, but the emphasis does point to the need, as mentioned at the outset, for other fora to focus on regional measures.

The Rio Declaration on Environment and Development

The Rio Declaration has been criticized as a weak document that, despite its claims, does not improve upon the Stockholm Declaration of 1972. At a technical level this is well illustrated by the adoption of Principle 2, which does little more than reiterate the much-worn Principle 21 of the Stockholm Conference.[25] That principle has always been problematic because it embodies a tension incapable of providing guidance in concrete situations. The failure to improve upon the language of Principle 21 is a measure of how little has been achieved in the last 20 years in defining the relationship between development and the environment. Perhaps more telling, however, is the boldness of the anthropocentricism underlying the first Rio principle:

> Human beings are at the centre of concerns for sustainable development. They are entitled to a healthy and productive life in harmony with nature.

That stands in stark contrast to the sentiment underlying to the Bio-Diversity Convention, to the effect that the contracting parties are:

> Conscious of the intrinsic value of biological diversity and of the ecological, genetic, social, economic, scientific, educational, cultural, recreational and aesthetic values and its components.

As befits the title, however, the Rio principles are certainly broad-ranging. They cover many policy areas, from trade, poverty and population through to war and peace. There are principles dealing with the special contributions of women and youth, and there are provisions articulating the precautionary principle and urging states to make progress with the topics of liability and compensation for harm.

The references to peace and to the inherent destructiveness of warfare strike several responsive chords. Not only do they recall the extensive discussion of this issue in the Brundtland report, but, in the present context, they also recall the long-standing position of the Canadian Inuit and Inuit Circumpolar Conference, which is that the Arctic should be established as a demilitarized zone. This does not however reflect contemporary Canadian policy, which has tended to be driven by the security interests of the United States.

The themes of citizen involvement and of the special role of indigenous peoples also find specific treatment:

> Indigenous peoples and their communities, and other local communities have a vital role in environmental management and development because of their knowledge and traditional practices. States should recognize and support their identity, culture and interests and enable their effective participation in the achievement of sustainable development.

Agenda 21

Agenda 21, an extraordinary grab bag of statements, initiatives, exhortations, and commitments agreed to in Rio, is meant to provide a blueprint for the acceleration of the adoption of sustainable development policies throughout the world. The range and scope of this non-binding agreement is impressive. But as in the Bio-Diversity Convention, no mention is made of the special needs and issues of the polar regions or their ecosystems. The sheer comprehensiveness of the agreement does ensure, however, that many polar issues are dealt with indirectly. For example, the chapter devoted to bio-diversity speaks indirectly to renewable resource harvesting, an important economic and cultural activity in the Arctic, when it calls for:

15.5 Governments at the appropriate levels, consistent with national policies and practices, with the co-operation of the relevant United Nations bodies and, as appropriate, intergovernmental organizations and with the support of indigenous people and their communities, . . . should, as appropriate:
(d) Take effective economic, social and other appropriate incentive measures to encourage the conservation of biological diversity and the sustainable use of biological resources . . .

And, importantly for the northern circumpolar world, Chapter 26 of Agenda 21 recognizes the need to strengthen the role of indigenous peoples and their communities. National governments are called on to include indigenous peoples and their knowledge of the environment in national decision-making. The agreement also advocates regional co-operation on issues linking sustainable development and indigenous peoples. More specifically, Agenda 21 recommends that:

26.6 Governments, in full partnership with indigenous people and their communities should, where appropriate:
(b) Co-operate at the regional level, where appropriate, to address common indigenous issues with a view to recognizing and strengthening their participation in sustainable development.

Despite the indirect and generally weak support of Agenda 21 for regional co-operation, the agreement may encourage changes in the way Arctic regions are managed.

Regional Institutional Initiatives: The Arctic Council

Whatever the substantive strengths and weaknesses of the Rovaniemi initiatives and AEPS in particular, it is clear that they are but "weakly institutionalized." This has led non-governmental commentators to renew their proposals for establishing a forum, an Arctic Council, within which on-going co-operation might be institutionalized.[26] At the end of 1992, there were signs that this initiative was receiving the support of the Canadian government and other Arctic nations, but the government of the United States has yet to come out in favour of it.

Background

The idea for some form of institutional regional co-operation in the Arctic is not new. Professor Donat Pharand traces its history back to a proposal by Professor Maxwell Cohen in 1971.[27] The idea remained dormant until, in 1988, a working group of the National Capital Branch of the Canadian Institute of International Affairs recommended the creation of an Arctic Basin Council. This proposal was subsequently taken up by non-governmental organizations that constituted themselves into an Arctic Council Panel.[28]

The Arctic Council Panel Proposal

The panel suggested that an Arctic Council should be established by a non-binding agreement and should be characterized by what the authors termed "laminated co-operation." By using this term, the Panel intended to capture and build upon the regional economic links that are being promoted in the Northern Forum between regional governments. Four structures for the Council were discussed: a plenary, bicameral, compact and tripartite delegation.

The Panel urged that the agenda of the Arctic Council be left open: "No international Arctic matter should in principle be barred from discussion or negotiation in council." In taking this position the Panel was cognizant of the fact that Arctic states wished military and peace and disarmament questions to be dealt with in non-Arctic fora. It would seem that the agenda of the Council, if established, will be dominated by environmental, social, and economic affairs. A key measure of the success of an Arctic Council will be its responsiveness to the needs and aspirations of the indigenous peoples of the region.

> The challenge in creating an Arctic Council is therefore not to construct yet another conventional means of inter-governmental co-operation, this time for the north circumpolar region. It is to devise a central Arctic institution that innovates in giving new voice to those most heavily affected by decisions currently made by politicians and officials far removed from the consequences of their acts. Not business as usual, but boldness and generosity

of purpose are called for as we begin to create a new instrument for comprehensive collaboration in the circumpolar Arctic.[29]

Conclusion

What can we usefully conclude? First, that there is a degree of complementarity between regional and national initiatives. Both the regional Arctic Environmental Protection Strategy and Canada's Arctic Environmental Strategy identify many of the same concerns, although the regional strategy is clearly more comprehensive. However, complementarities are not always well developed at the national level. For example, the AES identifies as a major concern the full integration of the environment and the economy. This is perceived primarily, if not entirely, as a domestic rather than a regional issue.

Second, there are obvious points of contact between global and regional concerns. For example, the Bio-Diversity Convention places an emphasis on *in-situ* conservation that complements Canada's commitment to protect 12 percent of its landmass. However, none of the multilateral instruments coming out of the Rio process deal specifically with Arctic issues. In general this is not entirely surprising, but the omission is particularly noteworthy in relation to the problem of global warming. Given the vulnerability of the region it might have merited specific attention.

Third, each of the national, regional and global instruments that we have considered here evidences a concern for the participation of aboriginal peoples and yet, especially at the global level, much of this is, for the time being, simply rhetoric. On this issue the Arctic offers the potential for significant innovation and perhaps the opportunity to develop a model of local and regional sustainable development for use by the rest of the world. The development of the Home Rule Government in Greenland, the North Slope Borough in Alaska, and the Nunavut Territory in Canada, all represent political successes that will better equip northerners, particularly aboriginal northerners, to deal with environmental and development issues.

Finally, one cannot escape the conclusion that Canada's environmental plans and programs for implementation in its North, the regional agreements between Arctic states and the global initiatives do not fully take account of the ramifications of the collapse of the Soviet Union. Old certainties that froze the northern circumpolar world into mutually suspicious camps now have no meaning. As a result of this geopolitical earthquake, accurate information on the environmental and public health impacts in the circumpolar North of military and industrial development in the former Soviet Union is becoming available. The environmental legacy that Russia and other Eurasian states have inherited from the Soviet Union is quite appalling.

Certainly a massive environmental clean-up task faces not only Russia but also other Arctic nations, as the long-term environmental bills of the Cold War become due. Are national environmental plans and programs, and the main regional instrument — the Arctic Environmental Protection Strategy — sufficient responses to the problems at hand? The answer is probably no. Yet, ironically, at a time when the magnitude of environmental problems in the circumpolar North is, at last, becoming widely appreciated, the Canadian government has drastically cut the level of funding it provides to implement its Green Plan and Arctic Environmental Strategy.

The response to recent environmental revelations in the circumpolar Arctic by the eight Arctic states reflects not the language and principles of sustainable development, but the old approach of environmental protection divorced from on-going economic development needs and realities. This is puzzling, given recent global initiatives and agreements which glue together these themes, and the striking similarities and parallels between problems of developing nations and those of the Arctic portions of the northern circumpolar states. Cleaning up past mistakes is urgently required, but it is an insufficient policy response to Arctic environmental problems.

Aboriginal leaders from the Inuit Circumpolar Conference, the Nordic Saami Council and Russia have called for further economic development in their homelands, but only development that is culturally and environmentally sustainable. Certainly economic development is needed in these regions, which currently suffer from very high rates of unemployment. But how is this to be provided? What rules, regulations, and norms will guide resource development in the circumpolar North? While the clean-up of past environmental errors continues, how can we ensure that history does not repeat itself? Here is a big ticket item for the Arctic

Council—developing the case for a new legal regime in the circumpolar North to implement principles of sustainable economic development. The Council should, in fact, develop and promote the concept of an Arctic Sustainable Development Treaty.

The principles of the various Rio instruments need to be woven into the AEPS. This document then needs to be given teeth by making it an enforceable agreement. That it may happen is not an unrealistic hope. Environmental groups in the United States and Canada are now exploring how best to achieve this goal. Northern aboriginal peoples have for long favoured this approach, and the new administration in Washington seems to have a genuine interest not only in environmental matters, but also in polar regions. The Arctic Council could take up this matter and put it on the agendas of the Arctic states. Such a treaty would equip the circumpolar North and residents of this far-flung region to face the next century with greater confidence.

NEW AGENDAS
FOR GLOBAL CHANGE

10 The Era of Living Less Dangerously: Diminishing International Threats to Human Life and Health

Mark W. Zacher

. . . it would be difficult to claim that the lives and health of most people today are more seriously threatened by foreigners or foreign events than they were in the past.

WHILE OUR NEWSPAPERS AND MAGAZINES dramatize disasters and violence around the world, the fact is that overall foreign threats to the lives and health of most peoples are less serious today than they were in the past. Certain threats are less acute than they used to be because of scientific and technological developments, but, what is equally important is that states are co-operating more to manage existing threats. Such an evaluation may seem out of place to some, given the nature of modern military technology, the growing AIDS pandemic, and the emergence of various international environmental problems. However, it would be difficult to claim that the lives and health of most people today are more seriously threatened by foreigners or foreign events than they were in the past.

Over recent centuries and even over several millennia, millions of people died regularly or were physically debilitated from the international transmission of diseases. The spread of traditional diseases has largely been brought under control, and while AIDS is a frightening pandemic, international epidemics of the past were much more serious by comparison. Of course, a failure to find a medical antidote to AIDS over the next several decades could alter this picture.

The international military environment from one perspective appears very frightening as a result of the emergence of nuclear weapons with their vast destructive power, but from another perspective it is far less frightening than before. The nuclear powers and their allies have been very reluctant to engage in any military adventurism that would risk nuclear war, and this has meant that since 1945 we have not had a nuclear war or a great power military clash. Also, we have witnessed a growing body of explicit and implicit international co-operation to prevent and control international violence. While it would be foolhardy to expect an end to wars, it is quite possible that we are crossing a historical threshhold with regard to the magnitude and frequency of international military conflict.

While the traditional major foreign threats to our lives and health—namely, the spread of diseases and military combat—appear to be receding, a new set of threats has emerged that generally goes under the rubric of the environmental crisis. Basically it comprises negative side effects of modern industrial activities. Environmental problems have not, to date at least, involved extensive threats to life and health (certainly not approaching in scope the traditional threats from war and disease), and the more life and health have been threatened, the stronger the international response has been. It is, of course, possible that civilian nuclear activities and the buildup of greenhouse gases (global warming) could threaten lives and health more than we can anticipate at the moment, but they are unlikely to have catastrophic effects. If population growth, which results from progress in medical science, is viewed as an environmental problem, then this dimension of the environmental crisis could have some major long-run impacts on life and health. But these impacts are likely to be long-run, and of course it is extremely difficult to project how they might threaten life and health in different parts of the world.

Many people do not want to admit that real progress has occurred in the world, since they do not want to appear naive or to encourage complacency in dealing with the very real problems that exist. Such an attitude, however, undermines a recognition of what has been accomplished and what the real nature of existing problems are. The reality of our present era is not that this is "the best of all possible worlds," but that at least certain forms of progress have definitely occurred. Some of the most important types of international progress concern the most elementary of all values—people's concerns to protect their lives and health from external threats. States increasingly view such threats as *common enemies* and have joined together in controlling them.

In this chapter, some of the progress that has occurred in reducing threats from military weaponry, the environmental side effects of industrial activity, and the spread of diseases will be explored. The conclusion of the chapter will reflect on the meaning of some of these developments and how Canada might contribute to the control of existing problems and threats.

Threats from Military Technology

In recent centuries there has been a dramatic increase in the destructive capability of military weaponry that has led to less frequent, but more destructive, wars. However, until our present era, the growing destructiveness of weaponry did not have an important impact on the acceptability of war as an instrument of policy. In the words of Hans J. Morgenthau, war was "a perfectly legitimate instrument of national policy."[1] Many people were horrified by World War I, as they had been by the Thirty Years' War and the Napoleonic Wars, but few realistic statesmen thought that the world might be at a turning point in military security relations. The advent of the nuclear age in August 1945 *may* have changed this traditional perspective.

In thinking about the growing perception of a common enemy in the military sphere, it is desirable to look at both historical developments and some observations by scholars. Two of the most important facts in evaluating the impact of nuclear weapons are that since the end of World War II they have never been used and there has never been a war between the great powers that possess them. A half century is certainly not long enough to judge definitively that a new era is upon us, but it is long enough to conclude that the new weaponry has created some very strong constraints. Of great import to the development of a regime for the prevention of nuclear war were the decisions of the United States not to use nuclear weapons in the Korean and Vietnam wars and the cautious and conciliatory behaviour of both the United States and the Soviet Union in the Cuban missile crisis. These examples of prudential diplomacy were followed by the gradual evolution of explicit and implicit accords to reduce (if not eliminate) the likelihood of a nuclear war between the West and the Soviet bloc. Of particular note were the hot-line agreement, SALT I and II, the recently concluded START agreements, and the Bush-Gorbachev initiatives to remove nuclear weapons from surface ships. In addition, implicit diplomatic rules developed that reduced the probability of direct East-West confrontations and wars. In a sense what developed was not just a nuclear war prevention regime but a great power war prevention regime because of the fear that a great power war could escalate into a nuclear war.[2]

Academic students of international relations have generally been conservative in their judgments as to whether there have been or are likely to be any important transformations in global politics, since many predictions in recent centuries have proven to be wrong. Also, there are few greater sins in the academic community than naiveté. Still, international relations scholars have moved gradually and fitfully toward the conclusion that the common enemy of nuclear war has brought about a qualitative change in security relations. The result has been "a critical intellectual breakthrough" in the general study of international relations.[3] The intellectual breakthrough started almost as soon as the bomb was dropped in 1945. The following year one of the most important postwar strategic analysts, Bernard Brodie, concluded in *The Absolute Weapon* that the atomic bomb was useful basically just for deterrence — and not for fighting. However, in the following years when the Cold War was at its height, few academics ventured to predict a basic transformation in security politics. It took the Cuban missile crisis, the development (albeit in fits and starts) of détente starting in the late 1960s, the lengthening period without great power war, and finally the revolution in the Soviet bloc, to consolidate thinking that something fundamentally different had emerged on the global political scene.

The key thing about the advent of nuclear weapons is that they have provided states with the capability of wreaking phenomenal *mutual* destruction on one another's populations and economies. In reflecting on some of the literature on the nuclear revolution, Robert Jervis has commented that "what is signficant about nuclear weapons is not 'overkill' but 'mutual kill'."[4] A similar observation is made by Kal Holsti in his recent study of war since 1648: "An actor cannot use such weapons in the Clausewitzian instrumental sense of war . . . To say that any political value is worth national self-immolation and probably the destruction of modern civilization makes no sense." With regard to their impact on postwar international relations he notes that there "have been numerous

Soviet-American crises, any one of which would probably have led to war in earlier eras." Then, in an observation relevant to the common enemy theme of this article, Holsti states that "The greatest threat to the security of the modern industrial state is not a particular adversary but nuclear war and perhaps even some forms of conventional war."[5]

In case the above comments on the impact of the nuclear revolution are unconvincing, it is valuable to look at the views of several scholars who have been associated with archetypal realist or neorealist perspectives on international relations. Kenneth Waltz has written that, because of the explosive power of modern weaponry and the robustness of major powers' second strike capabilities, "The absolute quality of nuclear weapons sharply sets a nuclear world off from a conventional one." In fact, he sees great power wars that start at the conventional level as every bit as dangerous as those that start with the use of nuclear weapons, because of the likelihood of escalation. He concludes that "although the possibility of war remains, nuclear weapons have drastically reduced the probability of its being fought by the states that have them...waging war has more and more become the privilege of poor and weak states."[6] Even John Mearsheimer (albeit in one of his less pessimistic moods) states that nuclear weapons "seem to be in almost everybody's bad book but the fact is that they are a powerful force for peace. Deterrence is most likely to hold when the costs and risks of going to war are unambiguously stark."[7] It is simply impossible to escape the fact that the technological revolution in military weaponry since 1945 has created a political revolution in international relations.

One issue that the above analysis ignores is the influence of the revolution in military technology on war between those states that are not linked intimately at the military and economic levels with the nuclear great powers — namely, the large number of Asian, African, and Latin American states. Nuclear weapons are certainly not the common enemy of developing countries that they are to the states in the northern industrial world, but they have had and will have an impact on their security relations. They have had a stabilizing effect on India's relations with Pakistan and China, since all are aware that a military conflict could escalate to the nuclear level. It is almost inevitable that another ten or more Third World states will acquire nuclear weapons in the coming decades, and this will probably encourage prudential behaviour on the part of the new nuclear states. Of great significance is that both the Northern powers and most Southern states are very concerned about the possibility of nuclear war and attempts at nuclear blackmail in the Third World. Apart from the fact that Third World nuclear states are likely to fear the effects of nuclear exchanges between one another, they will also probably be reluctant to use nuclear weapons because of the sanctions that developed states might exert against them. Because of the importance for the Third World countries of their economic ties with industrial states, the developed world will be able to exert considerable influence over the security policies of Third World states. There are certainly a good number of Third World conflicts that would not engender strong First World involvement, but nuclear adventurism and the possibility of a nuclear war would provoke strong reactions. Although the Gulf War of 1990–91 cannot be taken as typical of future Third World conflicts, one conclusion that can be drawn from that war and its aftermath is that there is a broad concern about discouraging the acquisition and use of nuclear weapons by revisionist states.[8]

In the terminology of Emanuel Adler, the world seems to be evolving from "a season of general stability" to "a season of common security."[9] This particularly applies to security relations among great powers and, more generally, Northern developed states. While the emergence of a new international security system can be attributed to a variety of factors, its ultimate cause is the common enemy of nuclear weaponry. While the present situation could be overturned by a new revolution in military technology, this does not appear likely. We could well be in the midst of a fundamental transformation in global politics.

Threats of Environmental Damage

International ecological or environmental problems, which are products of modern industrial civilization, do not involve solely threats and damage to human life and health. In fact, many "environmental problems" do not have a strong impact on life and health. Such environmental issues are primarily concerned with quality of life considerations and future economic productivity.

Until the 1960s the traditional environmental movement was concerned with the preservation of wilderness areas. The birth of the modern environmental movement can perhaps be dated at the publication of Rachel Carson's *Silent Spring* in 1962. It focused on the impact of chemical pesticides on the natural habitat and humans, and it touched on health questions. The decade from the publication of Carson's book to the 1972 United Nations Conference on the Human Environment saw an explosion of peoples' concern with pollution. In both the 1960s and the decades that have followed, health has been only one concern of environmentalists (aesthetics and future economic productivity being others), but it has often been issues of health and human survival that have provided the impetus for international environmental action.

Before dealing with marine and air pollution separately, it is useful to focus on one important source of pollution that can appear in water and in the air — namely, radioactive substances. It is precisely because of their impact on health that they have provoked so much international action. With regard to preventing the poisoning of the marine environment, there are some general restrictions on the shipment of nuclear material and the disposal of radioactive waste in law of the sea treaties and customary international law, and more specific ones in the 1972 Ocean Dumping Convention. (The latter does not ban discharges of weak concentrations of radioactive substances.) There are also several important conventions dating back to the early 1960s and 1970s that impose liability for damages on operators of nuclear ships and ships carrying nuclear material. While many important states have not ratified the conventions, these instruments do encourage strict safety standards, since it would be difficult for states to escape liability in the case of a major polluting incident.

The centrepiece of the regime for radioactive air pollution is the 1963 Nuclear Test Ban Treaty that bans atmospheric tests. Scientific tests concerning the spread of strontium-90 had an important impact on the conclusion of this accord and on compliance with it. There are also extensive controls related to nuclear power facilities. The International Atomic Energy Agency has conducted an active program of formulating safety standards and encouraging compliance. In 1979, an international treaty concerned with ensuring the safety of nuclear material during transport was signed.

And six months after the Chernobyl accident in 1986, states formulated two conventions regarding information to other states on the occurrence of accidents and offers of assistance to states that are faced with a nuclear accident. In 1989, the World Association of Nuclear Operators was created, and one important purpose of this body was sharing information on safety matters. Many of the conventions have not been widely ratified, but there has been a strong network of *de facto* rules and consultative arrangements that have developed to prevent radioactive pollution.[10]

The two decades since the 1972 Stockholm Conference have seen a growth in the number of regulations and conventions concerning the discharge of chemicals and minerals that might have a negative effect on the health of inhabitants of foreign countries. There was first the 1972 Ocean Dumping Convention that forbids using the oceans as a garbage dump for a wide range of industrial wastes. Then came the 1973 Convention on the Prevention of Pollution from Ships, which dealt mainly with intentional discharges of oil and other substances but also covered some aspects of accidental spills. The prevention of accidental spills from oil and chemical tankers is largely regulated by the Convention on Safety of Life at Sea and other treaties formulated by the International Maritime Organization. While the regulation of oil discharges is motivated mainly by a concern for the marine environment, the controls on chemical spills flow mainly from a concern for human health. There has also developed a large body of regulations concerning the shipment of other dangerous substances. At first the regulations were largely regional, but in 1989 a global conference accepted the Convention on the Control of Transboundary Movements of Hazardous Wastes and Their Disposal. The Bhopal chemical spill (with 3,000 killed) in 1984, the Rhine River chemical spill in Switzerland in 1986, and the Chernobyl nuclear incident in 1986 gave an impetus to international negotiations on the regulation of international movements of hazardous substances, even though these disasters originated from industrial plants. There have been plenty of criticisms of the international regulations concerning marine and land pollution (for example, the failure of the 1989 treaty to forbid the shipment of waste from developed to developing countries), but there is no doubt that significant progress has occurred. As knowledge improves concerning the nature of pollutants and the efficacy of existing regulations, new conventions will be formulated to assure that the industrial activities of countries do not poison the populations of other states. While there are certainly weaknesses in international pollution-control regimes, there is a clear momentum in the direction of stronger international pollution controls on sea and land.[11]

Air pollution has been one of the most interesting areas of regulatory activity over the past fifteen years. In the late 1970s, the issue on which most states focused was acid rain, that is to say, the deposit of sulphur dioxide and nitrogen oxides as a result of the burning of fossil fuels. The most publicized effects of acid rain are the deaths of forests and fish in lakes, but it does have some negative health effects in the form of respiratory diseases. Essential components of the international regulatory process have been the 1979 Convention on Long-Range Transboundary Air Pollution and the three protocols that have committed states to particular control strategies. While most real regulatory activity has been, formally or informally, at the regional level, there have been positive (albeit still quite limited) movements on a broad international scale. In fact, the quite modest progress can be attributed in large measure to the fact that human health is not regarded as a central aspect of the acid rain problem.

Perhaps the major environmental issue that, more than any other, has posed questions about health is the depletion of the ozone layer. Its effects are spread more evenly over the globe than any other form of environmental damage. The ozone problem arises from the depletion of the ozone layer in the stratosphere as a result of the release of chlorofluorocarbons (CFCs) which are used for aerosols, refrigerants, and insulation. The negative effects of ozone depletion that capture attention are skin cancer and eye cataracts. While there is some variation in the depletion of the ozone layer above different parts of the earth, the depletion has occurred and is occurring everywhere. Of some importance is the fact that CFCs in the atmosphere have an impact for up to 80 years after they are released so that even if people stopped using them immediately, the effects of past usage would last for many decades. The first findings concerning ozone depletion were announced in the mid-1970s, but it was not until the discovery of an ozone hole over the Antarctic in 1985 that real impetus was given to an international political process aimed at solving the problem. A framework convention was accepted in 1985, and this was followed by protocols in 1987, 1989, and 1992, in which states accepted obligations to phase out the use of CFCs. They also accepted the creation of a fund to facilitate the phasing out of CFCs by developing countries. It is precisely because the depletion of the ozone layer is regarded so broadly as a common enemy of humankind's health that co-operation has progressed so rapidly.

Probably the most important international environmental problem of coming decades (and perhaps the next century) is global warming. Industrial activities have increased the release of certain gases (carbon dioxide, methane, nitrous oxide, and CFCs) into the upper atmosphere, and the thickening of the gaseous layer has created a greenhouse effect by reducing the release of radiation from the earth's surface. The scientific consensus at the moment is that the temperatures on the planet will go up by an average of 1.5 to 3 degrees Celsius over the coming century if major action is not taken to reduce the emission of greenhouse gases. It is projected that the increases in temperature will cause a rise in sea level of perhaps a metre and will alter patterns of rainfall in the world. However, there is still a great deal of uncertainty as to the nature of the impacts. If large coastal areas (for example, the Nile delta and the coastal region of Bangladesh) are inundated by the sea and desertification occurs in some areas, human health is bound to be affected, but both the health and economic costs are difficult to judge at this point. Two things that are clear are that the effects on countries will vary considerably and that human survival and health are likely to be affected much less than economic well-being. Also, the remedial costs are likely to be huge in comparison to those occasioned by other problems. Therefore both the status of global warming as a common enemy and the willingess of states to co-operate to reverse it are likely to be of more modest dimensions than has been the case with other international environmental problems — at least until our understanding of the costs becomes much greater. Even so, the 1992 United Nations Conference on the Environment and Development did formulate a framework convention for global warming, and therefore international co-operation on the management of this huge problem has begun.[12]

The threats to human life from the externalities of economic "progress" are not as direct as the threats from warfare and disease, but they should not be underestimated both as menaces to survival and health and as a force that is shaping the nature of global politics and governance. On this issue Lynton Caldwell has written:

> ... the environmental movement, becoming world wide in incidence, is a manifestation of a major historical change of state, or discontinuity. . . . It marks the end of that half-millennium of exuberant, exploitive expansion of (chiefly) western society that we have called modern times . . . the threats to future life exemplified by global climate change, ozone depletion, toxic contamination, and environmentally catalyzed disease represent a backlash of nature against the improvident optimism of human ingenuity.[13]

In other words, the environmental crisis represents the fact that modern science and technology have created common enemies that humankind must now combat with new technological, and social and economic strategies.

Threats from the International Transmission of Diseases

While war is often regarded as the major foreign threat to the physical survival and well-being of citizens of particular states, diseases transmitted from foreign lands have claimed many more lives. However, the international spread of diseases was not a major policy issue until very recently, largely because people were often unaware of the foreign source of diseases and because there was so little that political authorities could do to stem the spread. Early examples of major regional and possibly intercontinental pandemics were those in the first and second centuries when the Roman and Han dynasties were stricken by the spread of devastating diseases which seriously weakened the two empires. William MacNeill has asserted that the diseases were probably transmitted across the Eurasian landmass.[14] The devastating Justinian plague of the sixth century wreaked havoc throughout much of the eastern Mediterranean. (Plague or bubonic plague is a specific disease caused by bites from fleas living in infected rats or by contact with infected persons.) Within Europe there were plague pandemics that swept from country to country and killed hundreds of thousands (and occasionally millions) of people. The Black Death (a popular term for the plague) in the fourteenth century killed between a quarter and three quarters of the population in vast areas. The development of transoceanic shipping, starting in the fifteenth century, had major effects on the spread of diseases. The African slave trade introduced a number of infections into the New World, but much greater disasters resulted from Europeans' introduction of smallpox, measles and other illnesses into the Western Hemisphere. Between 1500 and 1650 the native population of what became Latin America fell from 50 to 4 million, and this was largely a product of disease. Over the past four centuries many diseases have been spread among Asian countries and from Asia to Europe. The international spread of diseases was often associated with religious pilgrimages.

The diseases that most people associate with international pandemics are plague, cholera, yellow fever and smallpox. Without modern medicines both plague and cholera kill most people that contract them very quickly. Plague was at the root of the Justinian epidemic and the Black Death and ebbed and flowed over the centuries. Cholera was endemic in parts of India for centuries, and on four occasions during the nineteenth century it spread across all continents. Millions of people died from these outbreaks of cholera. Yellow fever also spread to many areas of the world in the nineteenth century with the worst effects being felt in the Western Hemisphere, but it was fatal for a much smaller percentage of the population that contracted it. As with yellow fever, a small percentage of the people that contracted smallpox died from it, but very large numbers of people were infected by smallpox. People often do not think of influenza in the same way that they think of the foregoing diseases, but it has often spread across many countries and claimed large numbers of lives. The pandemic in 1918–19 killed 20–21 million people. The two diseases that have caused more deaths than any others in recent centuries have been malaria and tuberculosis. While they are not generally associated with foreign sources, their presence throughout the world is due to the fact that they were transmitted between various regions in the past.

From the fourteenth through to most of the nineteenth century, the only attempts to control the international spread of diseases were the imposition of quarantines on ships and passengers after they had arrived in port, and the requirement of bills of health (from officials in their last port of call). The expansion of international shipping in the early nineteenth century, as a result of the invention of the steamship, promoted periodic international pandemics, and in consequence the imposition of quarantines and the requirement of bills of health became more and more frequent. These regulations then caused a great deal of conflict between flag states and port states. As a result of conflict over quarantines, the first international health conference was convened in 1851. Over the following four decades there were many conferences on regulating quarantines and prescribing measures to prevent the spread of diseases. While conventions were formulated by a number of conferences, they were not ratified by enough states and were therefore not implemented. An important reason for the differences among states during these years was a lack of scientific consensus on how the diseases in question were transmitted. In the last two decades of the nineteenth century, there was significant progress in bacteriology which led to definitive findings on how cholera, plague, and yellow fever were transmitted. In the 1890s four conventions were formulated and approved, and these were subsequently integrated into the first International Sanitary Convention in 1903.

The International Sanitary Regulations (retitled the International Health Regulations in 1971) have been revised regularly over the years. Soon after the first International Sanitary Regulations were accepted in 1903, states created an organization to gather and transmit information, assist countries with health problems, and organize international meetings. This was the *Office International d'Hygiène Publique* (OIHP), created in 1907. In the interwar period, there were two major international health organizations, the OIHP and the Health Organization of the League of Nations. They were superseded by the World Health Organization (WHO) in 1946. Since the beginning of this century there has also been a very important health organization in the Western Hemisphere — the Pan-American Health Organization.

Over the past century of formal international health co-operation there have been tremendous strides in controlling the occurrence and spread of the key diseases that have ravaged the world in previous centuries. The International Sanitary/Health Regulations and the various health organizations have contributed significantly to the reduction of disease, but it is difficult to separate the effects of scientific progress and international co-operation. Following a major WHO smallpox eradication program, the disease was completely eliminated from the world in 1977—a remarkable achievement, given the fact that about a seventh of the European population died of the disease in the late eighteenth century. On this development Richard Cooper has remarked: "In proper historical perspective, the eradication of smallpox will be recorded as one of the two outstanding practical achievements—along with the splitting of the atom—of the twentieth century."[15] There are occasional minor outbreaks of cholera, plague and yellow fever, and, as occurred recently with the appearance of cholera in Latin America, news of it brings immediate international assistance. The international spread of venereal diseases has been significantly controlled by internationally mandated clinics in most important ports and airports. Malaria occurs infrequently now, and the incidence of tuberculosis and poliomyelitis has been reduced, most cases now occurring in the Third World. The WHO has been instrumental in co-ordinating international support for the control of these diseases.[16]

In the last decade international health problems and co-operation have achieved a much higher political visibility as a result of the spread of AIDS. In fact, a multinational survey in the late 1980s indicated that people thought that AIDS was the most important health problem.[17] There is unquestionably a feeling today that AIDS is a common enemy, but as was the case with so many diseases prior to the twentieth century, international co-operation is stymied by the lack of scientific knowledge. The disease was first identified in the early 1980s. As of 1992 there are at least half a million cases of AIDS and another 8–10 million people with HIV infections who will eventually contract AIDS. By the year 2000 there will be around 40 million people who are infected, and about one million people will die each year. Approximately half of the cases are in Africa, and within the developed world the largest number of AIDS cases is in the United States.

The most important centre for sharing information on AIDS and helping countries with their control programs is WHO's Global Programme on AIDS. It sponsors many conferences. It has significantly contributed to the recognition that "If AIDS is to be controlled in any one country, it must be controlled in every country." An observation relevant to this comment has been made by another writer: "the challenge of coping with AIDS at all levels could give the world a new sense of planet-wide interdependence and responsibility for human survival and for the future."[18]

The international spread of diseases has increasingly been regarded as a transnational common enemy over at least the past millennium. It was, however, only very recently that scientific progress made international political action feasible. Until the past century, states could not make significant progress in building a control regime because they did not understand the etiology of the diseases. As the common enemies have become better understood and the means for combatting them have been invented, co-operation has grown. It is important to stress that states have come to see diseases as common enemies not only because they fear that the diseases will be transmitted across state boundaries but also because they fear the possibility that their international businessmen and tourists will contract the diseases abroad. This feeling of living in a global health community has recently been accentuated by AIDS, and one result is that "health may be conceptualized as a resource held in common, like the oceans, a resource that may be threatened worldwide and that requires collective action to protect."[19]

Conclusion

It is clear that important progress has occurred over the last century (and especially since 1945) in reducing the severity of international threats to life and health. Progress is particularly marked in the disease-control and military spheres, although humankind will not escape some periodic (but limited) disasters. New threats loom on the environmental front, but there is a good chance that the world will escape serious loss of life from these threats. However, to say that humans are presently in a very favourable position in comparison to past historical eras is not to say that real threats do not exist and will not arise regularly in future years. Like Sisyphus we cannot push progress to the summit of perfection, but with constant effort we can stay in the region of the summit most of the time and can mitigate any disastrous backslides.

Recapitulating, of the three threats that have been discussed, the greatest traditional foreign threat to human life — namely, *the spread of diseases* — has significantly been brought under control by scientific progress and international co-operation. However, co-operation must continue with regard to a range of traditional diseases, and in addition there is the new scourge of AIDS. The main international challenge is to help states control the internal spread of AIDS and, of course, to find a medical cure. *Military threats* have been around from time immemorial, but their magnitude has grown exponentially in this century. The nuclear revolution has greatly reduced the chances of war in the developed world, but there are still possibilities for limited international conflict in parts of both the industrialized and the third worlds. Perhaps the greatest actual threat of a recrudescence of warfare among industrialized countries stems from complacency and a sense that the impacts of international wars now are fundamentally local. There has been a growing recognition of international *environmental interdependencies* and a growing responsiveness among nations to the need to control the externalities of economic development. The more health is at stake in different environmental sectors, the greater the willingness of states to respond. Still, the challenges are immense, and there are tremendous obstacles because of the economic costs. If the effects of global warming are anywhere close to what are being projected by a good number of scientists, states are going to have to accept major constraints on economic development.

The Brundtland Commission wrote in 1987:

> Over the course of this century, the relationship between the human world and the planet that sustains it has undergone a profound change. When the century began, neither human numbers nor technology had the power to radically alter planetary systems.[20]

According to the Commission such population numbers and technological capabilities now exist and are certain to grow. From a recognition that humankind has created common enemies that threaten our lives and health, we must proceed to the adoption of co-operative control strategies. We can apply to these observations what Albert Einstein wrote concerning the atomic revolution: "we shall require a substantially new manner of thinking if mankind is to survive." At the centre of this mode of thinking must be the recognition that modern civilization is creating common enemies, has the power to control them, and must co-operate to realize fundamental human values.

Canada, like other countries, must devote considerable attention to inquiring how it can best contribute to controlling threats from the spread of disease, military technology and environmental damage. In the case of disease control it is obvious that the overriding problem is AIDS. While the spread is going to be largely within countries rather than across borders, it is unquestionably the case that the greater the number of people who contract AIDS from their own nationals, the greater the incidence of international transmissions. The Canadian government could perform a great service both to peoples in developing countries and to its own citizens if it launched a major international assistance program concerned with AIDS control in the Third World. Maybe we need significant government financial assistance to an organization such as *Médecins sans frontières* to mobilize the private medical and public health communities to go into areas of Africa, Asia and Latin America where there are serious problems.

The various strategies that Canada can pursue in reducing the possibility of war are many, and the key ones are those that have a long-range perspective. Canada can contribute to nuclear safeguard programs which will at least reduce nuclear proliferation. It can continue to be a major contributor to international peacekeeping and to peacekeeping forces. While specific military conflicts outside North America are unlikely to have short-term negative implications for Canada, the long-term international security environment is likely to be more favourable for Canada if the international community co-operates in controlling small military conflicts as they arise. The aim must be to encourage the growth of expectations that the use of military force is unproductive. Apart from contributing to peacekeeping and mediation by international organizations, Canada can also help to build a more stable international order by promoting respect for international boundaries and the growth of democratic governments. As has been indicated by a growing body of international relations scholarship, the reluctance of democracies to go to war with each other may be one of the most important pillars of international peace.[21]

Canada is now participating in international regimes and negotiations on a wide variety of environmental subjects. It is well placed to take a very strong role in international efforts to control marine pollution and radioactive pollution from accidents at nuclear power plants and from the disposal of nuclear waste. The ozone problem is on its way to solution, but the global warming issue is just beginning to emerge as a major international issue. Where Canada can play an important role is by monitoring different dimensions of the problem and generating regulatory proposals. As with so many of these threats from *common enemies*, what is required is the investment of resources in research and intellectual creativity over a long period of time.

To recognize that states have achieved major progress in protecting people's lives and health does not mean that there are not serious threats today. We have to remain constantly cognizant of the evolution of common enemies and devote considerable energy and resources to understanding and managing them. Complacency, or a naive notion that Canada can isolate itself from these problems, will inevitably wreak serious harm on Canadians over time. It cannot be stressed strongly enough that a long-term commitment to understand the international interdependencies in which we are inextricably involved and to generate innovative ideas for their management are required to protect Canadians and establish an ethical position for Canada in the international community.

11   Canadian Immigration Policy and Refugee Policy

Michael Shenstone

We need a global approach which tries to cope coherently with immigration and refugees, with world population growth, with poverty and underdevelopment, with international disorder and oppression, with the environment, and with barriers to trade and investment.

THE LATE 1980S AND EARLY 1990s have seen the mass movement of people, whether as refugees or traditional migrants, become a subject high on the foreign policy agenda of many countries. This is the case in Europe, and increasingly elsewhere in the industrialized world, while various developing countries are also concerned from their own perspectives. Migration issues now engage the attention of political leaders and foreign affairs officials much more than in the past, and are no longer the virtually exclusive preserve of Ministries of the Interior, Justice or Immigration.[1] This results from major developments in the international environment, which pose new challenges for Canadian policy abroad and at home.

International Developments

In the last few years there has been a vast increase in the numbers of people on the move. There are some eighteen-and-a-half million people who have had to flee their countries of origin (a million and a half more than a year ago), and perhaps twenty million internally displaced. Many millions more cross borders, or seek to do so, in desperate search of a better life; others flow from an impoverished countryside into monster urban agglomerations like Mexico City or Lagos, Nigeria. The movements involve all continents, and are from East to West, South to North, and South to South, with the latter of these three categories being much the largest, even though industrialized countries like Canada worry more about the first two. The causes of these huge movements are complex, and if anything, growing in intensity:

- civil unrest or actual civil war in many countries, and massive violations of individual or collective human rights in many others — problems which are likely to be with us for decades or more;
- deep and persistent poverty in much of the developing world, combined with growing awareness of the profound disparity with the countries of the North, and easier and cheaper means of getting there;
- social dislocations caused by increasing globalization of the world economy;
- in many regions, environmental degradation, resulting either from poverty or from hasty development efforts, causing problems likely to increase in the future, as Rio has shown (see Chapters 7 and 8);
- and looming behind these proximate causes of migration, and contributing indirectly but massively to most of them, the enormous and still largely unchecked increase in world population, ninety-five percent of which occurs in developing countries.[2]

One obvious result is that refugee determination systems in many Western countries are becoming swamped by claimants; Germany, for example, which received 256,112 persons claiming refugee status in 1991, had 438,191 in 1992, not counting some 200,000 who were given entry as "ethnic Germans." Over two million people have been displaced within the former Yugoslavia by the hideous events there, and well over 500,000 others are now in Western Europe. Irregular migrants from North Africa flood into France and other countries on the north side of the Mediterranean, while Mexicans pour across the U.S. border. Racist incidents are becoming more common, particularly in Europe, as evidenced by a series of ugly events in Germany, and in other countries such as Sweden and Spain. While there are still only four recognized "countries of immigration" (Canada, the United States, Australia and New Zealand), some European countries with populations already or soon to be in decline are in practice becoming the same thing, although they have not yet faced up to the fact. Before long, Japan will probably find itself moving in a similar direction.

Industrialized democracies now see that they are facing parallel problems: a world-wide blurring of the distinction between political refugees and economic migrants; high numbers of refugee claimants and irregular migrants; huge costs for reception and determination, perhaps totalling $8 billion or more; the growth of "asylum shopping" by claimants seeking the easiest entry or most generous benefits; and everywhere, low removal rates of those rejected. In consequence, efforts to co-ordinate policies have greatly intensified, both among the European Community countries, with their Dublin Convention and, for a subset of them, the stronger Schengen agreement (both supposedly to be ratified in 1993), and more widely. The Conference on Security and Cooperation in Europe (CSCE), the Organization for Economic Cooperation and Development (OECD), the Council of Europe and various special outgrowths of these, almost all with Canadian participation, have been active with a plethora of partly overlapping meetings, conferences and seminars. So far, however, they have little to show for them in most cases, despite the pressure they put on the same group of tired officials. Of particular importance for Canada are the sixteen-member "Inter-governmental Consultations on Asylum, Refugee and Migration Policies in Europe, North America and Australia," or "Informal Consultations," discussed further below.

At the United Nations in New York a major response to the worldwide extent of the refugee crisis and related situations has been the setting up, with vigorous Canadian support, of a new co-ordinating body, the "Department of Humanitarian Affairs" under a new Under-Secretary-General, the Swedish diplomat Jan Eliasson. It is doing well in systematizing relief appeals from different parts of the UN system and rallying support for them, but an effective co-ordinating role still eludes it, perhaps largely because of the inadequate financial and personnel resources it has been given, and its problems with large quasi-independent UN agencies such as the Geneva-based Office of the United Nations High Commissioner for Refugees (UNHCR). The latter, with 2,200 employees and annual expenditures approaching a billion dollars, continues as the world focal point for refugee protection, relief and resettlement. It is no longer seeking to expand the definition of a refugee enshrined in the 1951 Geneva Convention.[3] Instead, it is now stressing the fact that its own competence to afford protection extends in practice to persons displaced by armed conflict or generalized disorder, whether or not they are Convention refugees, and it is also developing new concepts of relief, protection and prevention activities *within* countries of origin.[4] Cases in point are its activities in Iraqi Kurdistan and particularly in the former Yugoslavia, where it has been very ably conducting the co-ordination of all international relief activities, as entrusted to it by the former UN Secretary-General before the Eliasson post was created. These developments in UNHCR doctrine, although put into practice on the ground, have so far been only tentatively accepted in principle by donor countries. They are important not only for the future direction of international refugee policy, but also for the very concept of state sovereignty.

Migration issues have not yet been seriously taken up at Economic (i.e., so-called "G-7") Summits, nor at essentially North-South fora such as the Commonwealth or La Francophonie. While developing countries are anxious for more help in coping with the large refugee burden that many of them bear, and resent what they see as Northern attempts to gang up against them on migration issues, they are far from unanimous in pressing for entry for their nationals. Some stimulate emigration to reduce unemployment or to benefit from émigré remittances (totalling perhaps $60 billion worldwide), others worry that immigration countries skim off their best, and still others either resist or encourage emigration of specific ethnic elements for political reasons—Serbian "ethnic cleansing" being only an extreme example. Because of all these cross-currents, migration may be one of the most contentious issues at the major 1994 International Conference on Population and Development to be held in Cairo.

The Canadian Environment

Mounting world migration pressures affect a wide range of Canadian policy objectives overseas, but come to Canadian public attention mainly in the form of what are seen as the persistently large numbers of refugee claims made in Canada, even though we receive only about four percent of the world total (See Table 11.1). While there is much continuing support for accepting significant numbers of genuine refugees, public attention has focused

Table 11.1
Asylum Claims Made in Canada

Year	Number of Claims	Top Countries
1989	20,267	Sri Lanka, Somalia, Lebanon, China, Iran, El Salvador
1990	36,196	Sri Lanka, Somalia, China, Bulgaria, Lebanon, El Salvador, Iran
1991	30,539	Sri Lanka, Somalia, USSR, China, Iran, El Salvador, Lebanon
1992	33,623	Sri Lanka, Somalia, CIS, Pakistan, Israel, Yugoslavia, Iran, India, China, Lebanon

Note: Most 1992 claimants from Israel are originally from the CIS (ex-USSR).

Source: Information provided by Employment and Immigration Canada.

on the following aspects: the cumbersome nature of our determination system (whose delays encourage further arrivals as well as eventual positive decisions after claimants have taken root); the difficulty of maintaining what officials describe as the "precarious balance" recently attained between claims received and claims disposed of one way or another;[5] the high costs of the system (upwards of a billion dollars annually to all levels of government); the significant proportion of claims ultimately determined to be unsubstantiated or fraudulent (now up to about forty percent, a figure which is nevertheless only half as high as the findings of other countries with similar judicial standards and similar refugee claim patterns); and, as elsewhere, the small proportion (perhaps ten percent) of those found not to be Convention refugees who are actually removed from the country.

All this has given rise to a feeling that immigration as a whole is not really under control and is not necessarily working in the country's interest. Nevertheless the government's target of 250,000 immigrants a year,[6] a level which makes Canada the highest per capita immigration country, has not been seriously challenged by the public; nor is there open criticism of the fact that some seventy percent of immigrants are now so-called "visible minorities," although Canadians are not as tolerant as they like to think they are (see Table 11.2). Of the 4.3 million immigrants living in Canada in 1991 most have come from the U.K. and other European countries,

Table 11.2
Landed Immigrants to Canada by Country
of Last Permanent Residence

Area	1992	%	1991	%	1990	%
Asia	127,449	55.4	119,997	52.0	111,739	52.2
Europe	41,006	17.8	48,056	20.8	51,945	24.2
Africa	17,554	7.6	16,087	6.9	13,440	6.3
Caribbean	13,345	5.8	12,922	5.6	11,689	5.5
Central America and Mexico	11,629	5.1	13,404	5.8	7,781	3.6
South America	9,449	4.1	10,582	4.6	8,898	4.2
USA	6,444	2.8	6,597	2.9	6,084	2.8
Australasia and Oceania	3,309	1.4	3,136	1.4	2,654	1.2
Totals	230,185	100.0	230,781	100.0	214,230	100.0

Note: Figures include accepted asylum claimants. 1992 figures are incomplete for November and December. Among linguistic groups, Chinese are much the largest (51,928 or 22.5 percent in 1992, taking Hong Kong, Mainland China and Taiwan together); runners-up among nationalities were India (11,880), Sri Lanka (11,720), Philippines (11,494) and Poland (11,260).

Source: Information Supplied by Employment and Immigration Canada.

but over 30 percent of the immigrants who arrived between 1981 and 1991 came from Hong Kong and four other Asian countries — see Table 11.3.

The overwhelming majority of immigrants go directly to, or end up in, our three largest cities, with the Toronto area receiving perhaps 100,000 annually; its immigrant population is now 38 percent of the city's total (see Figure 11.1). Studies indicate that immigration is at worst economically neutral in its effects, but more probably positive, although not dramatically so.

Thus, apart from the special high-profile issue of our refugee claim system, the basic problem for Canadian policy is not the national composition or the total of immigration, but the balance between its three broad categories:[7] a) family class and assisted relatives, who together make up close to half of the total, largely because most newcomers to Canada are now from developing countries where obligations to the "extended" rather than the "nuclear" family are the social norm; b) accepted refugee claimants

Table 11.3
Immigrants to Canada — Country of Birth
(top 10 countries)

Immigrants living in Canada in 1991:	
United Kingdom	717,745
Italy	351,620
USA	259,075
Poland	184,695
Germany	180,525
India	173,670
Portugal	161,180
China	157,405
Hong Kong	152,455
Netherlands	129,615
Total (all countries)	4,342,890

Immigrants arriving in Canada, 1981 to 1991:	
Hong Kong	99,540
Poland	77,455
China	75,840
India	73,105
United Kingdom	71,365
Vietnam	69,520
Philippines	64,290
United States	55,415
Portugal	35,440
Lebanon	34,065
Total (all countries)	1,238,455

Source: Statistics Canada.

and other humanitarian cases (plus refugees and others taken directly from abroad), comprising about seventeen percent of the whole (not counting others accepted in clearing up the backlog built up under the disastrous pre-1989 system); and c) independent and business immigrants, i.e., those actually selected by Canada for its own deemed requirements, who are only twelve and a half percent, with about another nineteen percent as their (non-selected) dependents. Of course those arriving in any of the three categories can and usually do soon start sponsoring those in the first, which thus grows in a compounding manner.

Figure 11.1
Immigrants as a Percentage of Census Metropolitan Areas, 1991

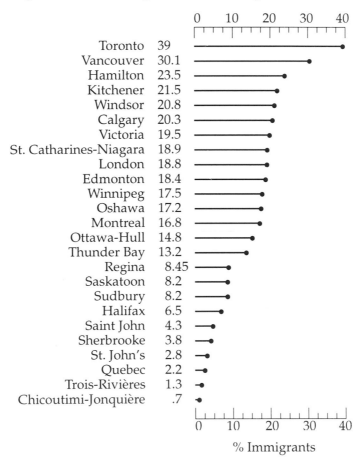

% Immigrants

A different kind of effect of recent immigration trends on Canada is the fact that the changing composition of our population is beginning to alter some of our foreign policy priorities. Canada's manifestations of official interest in the evolution of Hong Kong, and the close attention given to the political problems of Haiti, are two examples that come to mind. However, there is no automatic correlation between size of immigration from a given country and degree of foreign policy interest; many other factors are in play.

Canadian Policy Responses

Canada's reaction to current pressures at home and abroad on its policies is threefold: most conspicuously, "Bill C-86," a series of major amendments to the 1976 Immigration Act; a related international strategy of expanding co-operation, mainly with other industrialized countries; and the beginnings of an attempt to tackle the "root causes" of mass migration. Each seems reasonable, despite problems and weaknesses; but none should be expected to bring speedy solutions.

The Bill and Related Domestic Measures

Bill C-86 became law in December 1992. Its passage through Parliament was relatively smooth; a number of minor amendments were accepted in response to criticism, but there was little broadly-based political opposition to the measure in the country at large. Its provisions, together with associated regulations and plans, are intended to have the following effects, mostly but not entirely explicitly stated:

(a) to give somewhat more room, within the overall 250,000 annual total, for actual selection of immigrants by Canada and the provinces, and to enable the government to compel a small proportion of these "independents" to reside for a period of time in areas where they are deemed to be needed;

(b) to speed up the refugee determination process (in the interests of genuine claimants and as a discouragement to others); to make decisions more consistent, and inhibit unfounded or duplicate claims, while maintaining the acceptance of all genuine claims in Canada as well as a limited number of refugees abroad recommended by UNHCR for resettlement in Canada; and to provide a less *ad hoc* and more transparent system for dealing with humanitarian cases in Canada and abroad who are not Convention refugees;

(c) to restrain further growth in the family class (which had nevertheless been increased by 5000 to 100,000 in the recently revised version of the 1993 plan) by speeding the admission of spouses and minor children, but somewhat slowing decisions on parents and grandparents, and lowering "points" (i.e., priority in selection) given to assisted relatives;

(d) to discourage irregular migrants by additional control measures overseas (largely through visas and pressure on airlines),
   at borders (expanded search and anti-smuggling provisions)
   and within Canada (steps, including fingerprinting, to prevent
   multiple refugee and welfare claims, and—of particular importance—to increase the speed and percentage of removals
   of those rejected).

(e) alongside Bill C-86, to improve settlement help for all categories of immigrants, including dependants, largely through
   the allocation of more federal money for increased and more
   flexible provision for language training outside Quebec.[8] Language training is, laudably, no longer confined to preparation
   for the labour market, but is designed for "integration" and
   is accessible to all adult family members. The provinces have
   settlement activities of their own, of uneven extent across the
   country, and for constitutional reasons must carry alone the
   burden of educating immigrant children.

The new policy has been vigorously criticized by a number of
church, civil liberty and refugee advocate groups, although perhaps not as strongly as they criticized its predecessor, the system
which came into effect in 1989. The criticisms focus on human
rights arguments, and for some, a perceived anti-refugee and
anti-developing-country bent; for instance, it is claimed that measures favouring the nuclear over the extended family discriminate
against the new elements in Canada's population. In the view of
the present author, however, the policy is adequately balanced, basically fair and generally along the right lines; its passage should
help to preserve the credibility of immigration as a whole in the
eyes of a public increasingly critical of the abuses and cost of the
refugee system, while maintaining the essential humanitarian element of our policy, which rightly remains of importance to most
of us.

Some of the results will be modest, and not necessarily long-
lasting. Some argue that independents are important as part of
Canada's drive to restructure itself economically in a competitive
world; yet no more than ten thousand additional slots for independent immigrants will eventually result from the slight reduction
of preference for the non-selected family class. Measures to retain immigrants in specific localities for any length of time will

be of doubtful effectiveness and possibly vulnerable to legal challenge. Whether there will be successful legal challenges to any of the new control measures or the changes in the refugee determination system, is difficult to say. It is equally difficult to predict whether there will be a significant increase in the rate and speed of removals — which is essential as a deterrent to irregular migration — given the lack of specifics on how this is to be achieved, and the degree to which it may depend on the determination of a specific minister and the political circumstances of a specific government. Above all, it is likely that the ingenuity and desperation of refugee claimants and others seeking to come, the skills and persistence of their lawyers, and/or an increase in Canada's relative attractiveness (if our economy improves and social benefits are maintained) will eventually lead to the circumvention of our new policy, as happened with its predecessors. When, how, and to what extent this will take place, one cannot say, but take place it will. The pressures of the world outside will in the longer term make this inevitable. But such a probability is no reason not to improve the system now; the new policy does so.

International Co-operation

A key part of the government's strategy is to harmonize approaches with other like-minded countries, and in particular to achieve agreements for "responsibility-sharing." This means principally the curbing of "asylum-shopping," whereby individuals make refugee claims in several countries or pick the one that offers them the best prospects. The basic idea behind the proposed agreements is the "first asylum principle," i.e., that the first country with a good asylum system that a claimant enters should be responsible for hearing the claim. Canada's negotiating problem here is that we are basically the "demandeur," since most claimants go to other countries first, and are subsequently attracted here by the presence of relatives, our more generous medical and social benefits, or our higher claim acceptance rate. Our priority is to achieve an agreement with the United States, whence over a third of our claimants arrive; talks are slow, but Canadian officials say they are optimistic. Last year's hopes for an early collective agreement with the European Community countries, paralleling their Dublin Convention, have faded — Eurocentrism proved too strong — but the attempt is now being made to work towards agreements with a few smaller European countries as a start.

Meanwhile Canada, which for the past year-and-a-half chaired the "Informal Consultations" mentioned earlier, has been taking a vigorous lead, and with some success, in the process of making them an effective means of exchanging information and harmonizing approaches to all aspects of irregular migration, in the face of differing levels of interest by some of the other participants. Canada has rightly attached priority to retaining a clear link between the Consultations (as a "Northern" grouping) and the UNHCR (as an international organization comprising both North and South). Moreover, although Canada has not faced the same degree of migration pressure from Eastern Europe as has Western Europe, and the expected flood of "Slavic hordes" from the ex-USSR to the West has not materialized, we have joined with others in assisting some of the new governments to set up modern entry and exit control systems; this is a modest but worthwhile effort, which should be continued if the need persists. More broadly, further action to permit the new governments to succeed is important for many reasons; discouraging the desire to emigrate is only one of them.

In stressing the need for harmonization of policies by countries facing influxes of refugees and irregular migrants, Canada has hitherto avoided urging the Europeans to accept immigration as a fact, i.e., by giving permanent status and eventual citizenship to the foreigners they admit, instead of keeping most of them in a second-class limbo, where they are looked down upon. But Europe will eventually have to move in this direction if it is not to succumb to racial tensions, which would inevitably have negative repercussions for us all.

A possible new international migration challenge for Canada could arise in future as a side-effect of the North American Free Trade Agreement (NAFTA), even though it does not touch the issue of the freer movement of people, except with regard to business travel. In this context, it is useful that trilateral talks on asylum and related issues began last year between Mexico (which now receives many refugees from further south), the United States and Canada, with a good deal of parallelism in outlook emerging between Mexicans and Canadians. The nascent habit of consultation should be encouraged.

Canadian international refugee policy outside the sphere of "Northern" countries is focused on the UNHCR, except where the Palestinian refugees are concerned. For the purpose of meeting their needs Canada gives strong financial support to the UN Relief and Works Agency (UNRWA), and now presides very skillfully over the difficult "Middle East Refugee Working Group" as part of the U.S.-led peace process. As for the UNHCR, it receives from Canada a core contribution of nine million dollars, plus varying amounts (some $30 million in 1991) in response to its special appeals for various areas. The responses depend on how CIDA judges the appeals in relation to those of other relief agencies which seek Canadian funding, such as the International Red Cross. Whether Canada should give more to international refugee relief as a whole, as is urged by some eminent Canadians, is a difficult question. Because the total aid budget has been capped and is to be reduced by ten percent, any increase in the "International Humanitarian Assistance" sector, now two percent of the whole, would have to be at the expense of another, perhaps of equal or greater priority.

Canada has made a number of specific, well-formulated suggestions for badly needed administrative and financial reforms in the UNHCR; the task will have to be continued. We have also pointedly warned, at the 1992 session of the UNHCR Executive Committee, that the new UN Department of Humanitarian Affairs will only work "if all concerned UN agencies, including the UNHCR, give it their full support." Unconsciously illustrating the problem, Mrs. Ogata, the UN High Commissioner, had used the more patronizing term "collaboration" instead of "support" in her statement. A major policy issue has been raised for Canada by Mrs. Ogata's call for specific endorsement of the UNHCR's "new protection focus on the country of origin," described in its Note on International Protection (see note 4 to this chapter). In this author's view, Canada should do more than saying lukewarmly, as it did at the Executive Committee, that it is "impressed" by the UNHCR's "pragmatic" approach. This is an area in which difficult policy questions will have to be resolved, for instance, with regard to the role of international organizations in providing protection after repatriation (cf. Kurdistan) and other such questions affecting sovereignty. Our policy on refugee issues should be consistent with our increasing emphasis, notably in the peacekeeping context, on the fact that "sovereignty can no longer be absolute or

exclusive. The world is too complex for this kind of absolute . . . ,"
as the Secretary of State for External Affairs has put it.[9]

Our efforts, whether undertaken with other "Northern" countries or within UN organizations, should be part of a broader
strategy of fostering sympathetic understanding of, and greater
attention to, movement of people, including refugees, as an integral part of the complex of basic political, economic and social
issues with which the international community now has to deal.
This will require a stronger effort at the political level, and not one
which is confined to the Department of Employment and Immigration. We should constantly seek opportunities to raise migration
issues, and their relationship to other key problems, at Summits,
at the UN General Assembly, in the many multilateral organizations (political, economic and developmental) to which Canada
belongs, and in our bilateral contacts with countries in all parts of
the world. This is not yet being done as systematically as would
be warranted by the importance of these issues to Canada and to
the international community.

Tackling "Root Causes"

Above all, what is needed is a collective effort to understand and
try to deal with the fundamental and long-term causes of the migration phenomenon, in a comprehensive approach. There are
tentative beginnings in this direction, both in Canada and internationally. Last year saw a start on long overdue efforts to look at the
problem jointly on the part of senior officials of the three government departments most directly concerned, i.e., Employment and
Immigration, CIDA and External Affairs and International Trade
Canada. So far, however, these efforts have not been pushed very
far. There is, for example, nothing in preparation within or alongside the Canadian government apparatus remotely on the scale of
the July 1990 report of the high-level bipartisan U.S. Commission
for the Study of International Migration and Cooperative International Development, entitled "Unauthorized Migration: An
Economic Development Response." Its farsighted findings, which
dealt with trade, aid, and investment in conjunction with migration, concentrated on the Western Hemisphere, but have important
lessons for the whole world concerning the broad, long-term approach that is necessary.

Canada has, however, taken some modestly useful initiatives internationally. One of these, starting in late 1991, has been to promote, within the Informal Consultations, a "Country Assessment Approach," whereby groups of Consultation member-countries work jointly with selected countries of origin of asylum-seekers or migrants "on various development measures which might provide an alternative to emigration or facilitate repatriation." The idea was originally to be called the "Country Consortium Approach" but this proposal had to be altered at the insistence of countries wary of strengthening the Consultations by the use of a title for the initiative reminiscent of World Bank operations. The emphasis is to be on short-or medium-term measures with potential for early effect. Five target countries were initially selected (Romania, Albania, Ghana, Sri Lanka and the Commonwealth of Independent States), and Turkey has since been added. So far, however, the discussions have been limited in scope, as have decisions for action, and developmental considerations have not figured largely in them. Refugee-producing countries in true crisis, notably Yugoslavia and Somalia, have not yet been tackled by this experimental mechanism, because of the immediacy and huge size of their problems. The jury is still out as to whether the "Approach" will produce tangible results on a significant scale, but it is certainly useful as a means of encouraging practical international co-operation on specific migration issues in specific situations and it is, in the process, providing broader lessons for the future.

A start is also being made with more general international discussion of "root cause" issues, for instance at the OECD, and at a pioneering UNHCR-ILO (International Labour Organization) meeting last May with government and academic representatives on "International aid as a means to reduce the need for migration"; Canadian academics as well as officials participated in this discussion. Canada has taken this a step forward by sponsoring, with the OECD, a major conference on "Migration and International Cooperation" in Madrid in March 1993, to stimulate further thinking and action by governments and the international community generally on the broad issues.[10]

The task of educating governments and interested members of the public to pay heed to the complex nature of the basic problem will require years if not decades. The difficulty is illustrated by the preparations for the 1994 Conference on Population and

Development mentioned earlier. So far, preliminary discussions among the developed-country participants, all grouped in the intergovernmental "European Population Conference" being held in Geneva just before the Canada-OECD conference in Madrid, have dealt quite adequately with the Conference's migration theme. But to the disappointment of Canadian participants these discussions have been slow to come to grips with the wider relationships between migration and other world issues. It will be a challenge for Canada to keep these relationships to the fore in the preoccupations of European and other policymakers, before and during the 1994 Conference, as well as in other international fora where long-term issues are debated. Otherwise the international debate will degenerate into North-South controversy along sterile traditional lines.

There are of course no easy or quick answers to the problem of migration. The U.S. Commission mentioned earlier made the sage comment that

> . . . while job-creating economic growth is the ultimate solution to reducing . . . migratory pressures, the economic development process itself tends in the short to medium term to stimulate migration by raising expectations and enhancing people's ability to migrate. Development and the availability of new and better jobs at home, however, is the only way to diminish migratory pressures over time.[11]

Doris Meissner, in the article cited in note 10, comments that the shorter-term stimulus to migration is related to the fact that "development is inherently disruptive, forcing workers out of subsistence jobs into new areas of economic activity." Moreover, as Canadian officials have pointed out to colleagues in the Informal Consultations, development assistance is of little use in checking emigration in conditions where the outflow is due to war or to human rights infringements by governments, firstly because aid becomes difficult or impossible during hostilities, and secondly because there are few countries where it is large enough to give immediate leverage over despotic regimes. Also, since potential asylum-seekers are almost by definition at odds with their governments, the latter are unlikely to use development aid to help dissident groups. Specific targeted aid could well be appropriate in certain instances, but it is not yet clear how.

Such questions will need much more intensive study than they have hitherto received, if immigration and overseas development policies are to complement one another to good effect, particularly in the shorter term. It will take decades of patient effort before economic conditions in the main migrant-producing developing countries advance, and population growth rates fall, to the point where remaining at home becomes universally more attractive than trying one's fortune abroad. In the meantime, additional countries may emerge as large sources of migration. Sustained progress in human rights and democratization, the flavour of the year in aid policy, is desirable to check outflows, as well as for other reasons, yet even here there are ironies. It was only after human rights in Albania and Romania advanced to the point where their citizens were relatively free to leave, that Albanians and Romanians became major migration "problems" for other countries. What will Canada and other countries do when the day comes, as it eventually will, when China liberalizes to the point where it permits, or conceivably even encourages, mass emigration? The temptation to seek outlets abroad for China's surplus population may grow if current efforts to reduce Chinese population growth stall, as some experts believe is happening.

Trade is a particularly important and difficult policy issue for Canada and other countries facing migratory pressure. The North American Free Trade Agreement (NAFTA) is criticized because jobs may be lost to Mexicans, yet only if they are employed will they wish to stay at home. Migration factors do not now enter into the calculations of Canadian or any other trade policy experts,[12] but should be seriously considered in future when trade negotiations are envisaged. Of course, this is easy for salaried officials and professors to say, but not easy for those whose jobs may be at risk; and employment transferred from Canada to, say, Mexico, may reduce Mexican migration pressure on the United States rather than on Canada, where it does not yet exist. But the problem is broader than that. Like other rich countries, we must wonder whether we can indefinitely count on "having it all": an immigration policy that keeps our intake of people to a trickle on the world scale of things (however large we may think it by our standards), and at the same time a trade policy that inhibits the ability of people abroad to earn their living from us. As the relative and absolute total population of developing countries increases still further in the coming century, this practical and ethical dilemma will sharpen for us. It will be even more acute for the officially "non-immigration" industrialized countries, i.e., those of Western Europe, and Japan.

One can also draw a connection, although a more tenuous one, between our efforts to tackle root causes of migration and our policy on the international environment. Even here the issues are not simple. Initiatives to slow climate change or prevent desertification may help to prevent future mass flight from coastal or arid areas, but others aimed at the environmental side-effects of rapid development, such as indiscriminate use of polluting fuels like soft coal or overuse of fertilizers or of scarce water resources, may slow job-creating growth in the shorter term, however desirable such measures may be for other reasons.

The conclusion to be drawn from these complexities is that, just as the migration phenomenon is so closely interwoven with other current world issues, so any Canadian policy to deal with it over the longer term must be integrated with our efforts in other spheres. We need a global approach which tries to cope coherently with immigration and refugees, with world population growth, with poverty and underdevelopment, with international disorder and oppression, with the environment, and with barriers to trade and investment. Canada's impact on any of these can only be modest, but it will be enhanced if we endeavour to see that inconsistencies are kept to a minimum and that our policies in each sector complement, to the extent possible, those in others, as well as taking into account parallel efforts, or the lack of them, outside Canada. Above all, we must be prepared to stay the course over decades. If we and others do not, our successors risk being overwhelmed by factors which will be beyond our control.

12 Les Nations Unies, le maintien de la paix et le Canada

Albert Legault[*]

La paix enlisée

Au MOMENT D'ÉCRIRE CES LIGNES, le président George Vassilou et le leader turc Rauf Denktash viennent de conclure deux semaines de négociation sur l'unification de Chypre, mais sans succès. Leurs pourparlers reprendront en mars 1993. Au Cambodge, les Khmers Rouges refusent toujours les plans de démobilisation et de cantonnement de l'ONU, tandis que le ministre indonésien des Affaires étrangères, M. Ali Alatas, estime que le Conseil de sécurité de l'ONU devra sous peu prendre les mesures "nécessaires et appropriées" pour faire respecter les termes des accords de Paris. En Yougoslavie, on discute toujours de l'aide humanitaire qui est acheminée à travers les corridors terrestres croates et peut-être, demain, depuis Belgrade, mais plusieurs observateurs se demandent si la Bosnie-Herzégovine existera encore, lorsque le président élu Bill Clinton assumera ses fonctions en janvier 1993. Il est probable qu'au même moment le Conseil de sécurité de l'ONU tentera de définir les modalités d'application des "zones d'exclusion" de vol au-dessus de la Bosnie, jusqu'alors peu respectées.

Au sein de la CÉI, les minorités ethniques continuent de se déchirer en Abkhazie, au Nagorno-Karabakh et en Ossétie du Sud. Dans les Républiques d'Asie centrale ainsi qu'en Afghanistan, les hostilités se poursuivent entre factions différentes, dont les plus virulentes se réclament du fondamentalisme musulman. Les négociations sont à un point mort au Proche-Orient, notamment entre Israël et la Syrie, tandis qu'en Somalie les gens continuent de mourir par milliers. Au Libéria, la guerre civile continue de faire rage et le Nigeria, le contributeur le plus important à l'ECOMOG (le Groupe de surveillance militaire de l'ECOWAS— Economic Community of West African States), tout autant que le Sénégal, menacent de s'en retirer. Ailleurs en Afrique, les hostilités ont repris en Angola, tandis qu'au Mozambique le Conseil de sécurité a autorisé, le 16 décembre 1992, l'opération ONUMOZ (Opération des Nations Unies au Mozambique). En Amérique latine, la démobilisation des groupes armés de la guérilla a été reportée au Salvador jusqu'en décembre 1992, au grand dam du président Alfredo Cristiani. Où que l'on regarde, la paix prend du retard. Elle s'est tout simplement enlisée.

Faut-il réinventer la roue ou réformer l'ONU?

Les efforts pour sortir de l'ornière la paix enlisée ne manquent pourtant pas. Dès janvier 1992, les membres du Conseil de sécurité se sont réunis au sommet à New York. Ils ont réclamé du Secrétaire général de l'ONU la production d'un rapport sur la diplomatie préventive, le rétablissement de la paix et le maintien de la paix. M. Boutros Boutros-Ghali a produit en juin 1992 son célèbre *Agenda pour la paix*,[1] et en septembre de la même année son *Rapport* annuel sur l'activité de l'Organisation. Plusieurs aspects essentiels méritent ici d'être soulignés.

La crise financière de l'Organisation

De tous les aspects déconcertants de l'ONU, sa situation financière est de loin la plus dramatique. Elle est due en partie à l'augmentation massive des dépenses de l'ONU depuis les lendemains de la crise pétrolière de 1973, au désintéressement des États-Unis face au rôle de l'ONU sous le gouvernement Reagan, ainsi qu'à la volonté de ce pays d'utiliser sa contribution comme un levier afin d'amener l'Organisation à réduire ses dépenses et à prévoir l'établissement d'un budget à croissance zéro, et à l'augmentation substantielle des coûts reliés aux opérations de maintien de la paix depuis les cinq dernières années.

L'augmentation massive des dépenses de l'ONU et la réduction inversement proportionnelle de la contribution des États-Unis au budget régulier de l'Organisation sont particulièrement évidentes. Durant la période 1946 à 1987, le budget régulier total de l'ONU totalise près de 11 milliards de dollars, 2,4 milliards ayant été assurés par les États-Unis, soit environ 22 pour cent.[2] Il est vrai que durant certaines années—les années 1968–70 et 1971–73—, la part américaine du budget régulier de l'ONU a oscillé entre 28 et 30 pour cent, mais dans l'ensemble la contribution des États-Unis s'est située en deçà des 25 pour cent qu'on était en droit d'attendre d'eux.

Afin de remédier à la crise financière de l'ONU, l'AGNU (Assemblée Générale des Nations Unies) a proposé dans sa Résolution 41/213 que tous les États membres acquittent "promptement et en totalité" leur quote-part, mais ce processus n'est pas encore entré dans les faits. De son côté, le Secrétaire général propose dans son *Rapport* annuel de septembre 1992 de réclamer des intérêts sur toute fraction des quotes-parts non acquittées, de porter à 250 millions de dollars le Fonds de roulement de l'Organisation, de prévoir un fonds de réserve de 50 millions pour les opérations du maintien de la paix, ce qui a été fait avec la Résolution 46/182, et de créer un Fonds de dotation pour la paix d'un montant de un milliard de dollars. Parmi les autres suggestions, notons la perception d'un droit sur les ventes d'armes, d'une taxe sur les voyages aériens internationaux, d'une exemption d'impôt sur les dons faits à l'Organisation, et de l'établissement d'une formule différente de calcul pour les opérations de maintien de la paix.

Les opérations de maintien de la paix, dont les prévisions de coût s'élèvent à 3 milliards de dollars pour la période de 12 mois en cours, représentent évidemment un fardeau très lourd. La participation américaine s'élève à un peu plus de 30 pour cent du budget d'imposition séparé, et celle du Canada à 3,11 pour cent.

L'une des propositions les plus originales avancées par le Secrétaire général a été de demander aux différents ministères de la défense d'assumer désormais les coûts des opérations du maintien de la paix. Aux États-Unis en particulier, le Congrès n'a pas manifesté un enthousiasme délirant face à cette proposition. Certains craignent ainsi que le Congrès ne perde son pouvoir discrétionnaire si les fonds venaient à être prélevés directement sur le budget du Pentagone. Dans son discours devant l'Assemblée générale des Nations Unies en septembre 1992, l'ex-président Bush s'est bien gardé de se prononcer sur le sujet, voire même de se s'engager financièrement pour résoudre la crise de l'ONU. Les milieux les plus réticents sont représentés par la droite conservatrice américaine. Le dernier rapport de la Fondation Heritage est significatif à cet égard.[3]

On y dénonce le rôle "imprudent" de l'ONU, le peu d'intérêt stratégique américain dans les grands conflits en cours au Cambodge ou en Yougoslavie, et l'incapacité de l'Organisation de faire "soit la paix soit la guerre" pour lesquelles, dit-on, elle est mal "équipée." Dans ce même document, on suggère de réduire à 25 pour cent au maximum le coût de la contribution américaine aux opérations du maintien de la paix. En revanche certains sénateurs, comme Paul Simon et Joseph Biden, se rangent carrément en faveur de l'organisation. D'autres éléments politiques comme M. Pell, ancien sous-secrétaire du Secrétariat international responsable de la rédaction de la Charte de San Francisco, et le *New York Times* se sont même prononcés, le second dans son édition du 1ᵉʳ septembre sous le titre *A Foreign Legion for the World*, en faveur de la création d'une armée permanente de l'ONU.

Le 7 août 1992, dans une interview accordée au journal *Die Zeit*, le Secrétaire général précisait que les États membres devaient encore 2 milliards de dollars à l'Organisation au titre de son budget régulier et à celui des opérations de maintien de la paix: 820 millions étaient dus par les États-Unis et 1,2 milliard par les autres membres, y compris l'ex-URSS. Les États-Unis pour leur part ont décidé de régler la question de leurs arrérages sur une période de cinq ans par tranches successives égales. En mars 1992, l'administration américaine a réclamé 350 millions de dollars pour l'année fiscale en cours, et 460 millions pour l'année fiscale 1993. La plus grande partie de la somme prévue pour l'année fiscale 1993 ne proviendra peut-être pas des amendements récents à la Loi sur l'aide étrangère, car dans le cadre du projet d'approbation des crédits du Département de la défense pour l'année fiscale 1993 (the fiscal 1993 Defense Department Appropriation), on prévoit d'affecter 300 millions de dollars pour les opérations de maintien de la paix. Les États-Unis, le principal débiteur de l'Organisation, paraît donc devoir s'engager dans la bonne voie.

Dans son édition de l'été 1992, le *Harvard International Review* livrait à ses lecteurs les vues du candidat démocrate à la présidence sous le titre "A New Covenant for American Security." Si Bill Clinton s'est prononcé en faveur de la création d'une force de réaction rapide pour l'ONU et de l'élargissement du Conseil de sécurité, qui devrait inclure le Japon et l'Allemagne, rien n'a été dit sur les obligations financières des États-Unis à l'égard de l'Organisation. Toutefois il faut s'attendre dans l'avenir à un appui plus soutenu et nuancé des États-Unis à l'égard des opérations du maintien de la paix, en dépit de la réticence marquée de nombreux membres du Congrès face aux obligations internationales des États-Unis.

De son côté, le Canada s'est acquitté dès la fin de l'année 1992 de la totalité de sa contribution financière à l'ONU pour l'année 1993. Il entend ainsi mettre en pratique ce qu'il réclame des autres États et ne se gêne pas dans de nombreux discours pour réclamer des États-Unis qu'ils s'acquittent le plus rapidement possible de leurs obligations financières auprès de l'ONU.

La diplomatie préventive, le maintien et le rétablissement de la paix

Dans l'ensemble, tous les auteurs s'entendent sur la notion classique du maintien de la paix. Selon les termes mêmes du Secrétaire général dans son dernier *Rapport*, il s'agit de "l'utilisation de troupes placées sous le commandement de l'Organisation dans le cadre d'opérations 'non violentes' avec le consentement des parties à un conflit, afin de maintenir la stabilité dans de nombreuses zones de tension de par le monde." La plupart des opérations du maintien de la paix, menées par l'ONU, ont eu lieu une fois qu'ont cessé les hostilités militaires, et que les parties se sont mises d'accord pour en faire respecter la cessation.

La diplomatie préventive se distingue du maintien de la paix à trois égards. En premier lieu, il s'agit d'éviter qu'un conflit ne dégénère ouvertement en une menace contre la "paix et la sécurité internationales." En deuxième lieu, il s'agit d'intervenir avant plutôt qu'après les hostilités. En troisième lieu, cela suppose que l'Organisation dispose au préalable d'une force d'intervention capable d'être rapidement déployée sur les lieux.

Certains auteurs souhaitent renforcer le rôle du Secrétariat en matière de maintien de la paix, tandis que d'autres souhaitent au contraire renforcer le rôle du Conseil de sécurité. Ceux qui souhaitent développer davantage le rôle du Secrétariat ont tendance à mettre l'accent sur trois points: le rôle de "leadership" du Secrétaire général;[4] l'établissement à l'intérieur du Secrétariat d'un petit secrétariat doté d'une structure permanente capable de dépêcher des éléments de paix dans une zone en conflit;[5] et le développement d'une capacité de renseignement destinée à permettre au Secrétaire général d'agir avant qu'une crise n'atteigne un point de non-retour.[6]

En revanche, ceux qui souhaitent renforcer le rôle du Conseil de sécurité mettent l'accent sur l'actualisation des articles 43 à 47 de la Charte qui autorisent le Conseil de sécurité à recourir à la force pour redresser les situations qui mettent en cause la paix et la sécurité internationales. Ces articles sont toujours aujourd'hui dans les limbes,[7] et d'après certaines déclarations du Secrétaire général Boutros-Ghali, la perspective d'une actualisation de l'article 43 de la Charte n'est pas pour demain.

Au Canada même, certains spécialistes n'hésitent pas à réclamer purement et simplement l'application inconditionnelle de la Charte de l'ONU. À leurs yeux, l'ONU n'a qu'à mener à bien la mission pour laquelle elle a été créée: maintenir la paix et la sécurité internationales. Geoffrey Pearson fait partie de ceux qui souhaiteraient voir l'Organisation prendre en main ses propres responsabilités, sans égard aux considérations géo-stratégiques qui continuent d'exister au lendemain de la Guerre froide. Il ne sert donc à rien de réinventer la roue ou de réformer l'Organisation. Tout ce qu'on lui demande, c'est de mettre en œuvre intégralement les dispositions de la Charte. Il reste toutefois que l'ONU de 1993 n'est pas celle de 1945, et c'est sans doute dans le but de répondre à ces principales préoccupations qu'au printemps 1992 les pays nordiques[8] et les pays membres du groupe CANZ (Canada, Australie et Nouvelle-Zélande) se sont réunis afin de présenter au Secrétariat une réponse conjointe, destinée à faciliter la rédaction du rapport *Agenda pour la paix* du Secrétaire général. Dans leur réponse conjointe, les pays nordiques ont proposé au Conseil de sécurité d'étudier la possibilité de dépêcher tôt dans la phase du pré-conflit des contingents armés, à titre de mesure dissuasive pour prévenir l'éclatement des hostilités. On souligne en ce domaine l'urgente nécessité d'établir une structure de commandement et d'organisation parfaitement intégrée (integrated organizational and command structure), avec la possibilité d'en arriver à des arrangements *ad hoc* en ce qui a trait au personnel à détacher auprès de l'Organisation ainsi qu'à celui qui pourrait être prêté par des États membres en cas d'opérations devant rapidement être mises sur pied. Des mécanismes de consultation *ad hoc* devraient également être créés pour répondre aux besoins du "peacemaking." On rappelle enfin que le Comité spécial des opérations de maintien de la paix a déjà suggéré d'importantes mesures pour améliorer l'efficacité et le coût-efficacité de ces opérations.[9]

En outre, les pays nordiques insistent sur la nécessité d'augmenter et de rationaliser la capacité de l'Organisation à colliger, analyser et à disséminer l'information relative aux menaces actuelles et potentielles à la paix et la sécurité internationales. On rappelle que les membres ont le "devoir d'informer" l'Organisation, et qu'ils devraient être encouragés à échanger de telles informations. On insiste enfin sur la nécessité d'établir un lien opératoire (an operative link) entre la cueillette des informations et les tâches dévolues au Secrétaire général ou encore au Conseil de sécurité.

Afin de compléter les données d'interprétation nécessaires au bon fonctionnement de l'Organisation, les pays nordiques encouragent aussi le Secrétaire général à avoir plus souvent recours à des missions d'enquête, en conformité avec la résolution 46/59, comme s'il s'agissait d'opérations routinières. Par ailleurs on encourage le Secrétaire général à mettre à profit la publication de son rapport annuel pour établir des appréciations à long terme des situations (forward-looking assessments) qui risquent de mettre en danger la paix. En outre, on rappelle au Secrétaire général que des moyens utiles ont déjà été suggérés à cet égard dans la résolution 43/51 de l'AGNU.[10] De la même manière, le Conseil de sécurité pourrait se réunir d'une façon informelle pour échanger par anticipation des informations sur les situations qui risquent de menacer la paix et la sécurité internationales. Cette procédure n'est pas nouvelle, mais elle méritait ici d'être rappelée, car comme l'a souligné le Secrétaire général dans son Rapport de septembre 1992, si le Conseil de sécurité s'est réuni 49 fois en tout durant l'année 1987, il s'est déjà réuni 81 fois au cours des sept premiers mois de 1992 seulement, en plus d'avoir tenu 119 séances plénières de consultations. Enfin notons deux idées essentielles avancées par les pays nordiques qui sont aujourd'hui en vigueur: la constitution d'une structure permanente au Secrétariat chargée des opérations de maintien de la paix et son fonctionnement 24 heures sur 24.

L'idée de constituer une armée internationale de l'ONU ne manque pas de partisans, mais il est clair à cet égard que celle-ci ne pourra être constituée que si les membres permanents du Conseil de sécurité en veulent bien. La difficulté majeure tient toujours au fait des structures de commandement et de contrôle d'une telle force. Si l'évolution récente de la politique américaine, en particulier le discours du président Bush à l'AGNU, témoigne d'un fléchissement heureux à cet égard, il reste que l'utilisation de cette force n'est envisageable que pour des opérations 1) de type limité et 2) qui ne touchent pas au cœur des relations fondamentales entre les grandes puissances, étant donné que l'unanimité des membres permanents sera requise pour son déploiement dans de telles opérations. La guerre du Golfe illustre bien par ailleurs, dans le cas de conflits majeurs, les implications d'une telle approche qui aurait supposé, pour son application, que le général Schwarzkopf eut été responsable devant le représentant désigné par le Secrétaire général de l'ONU!

En matière de rétablissement de la paix, la situation est toujours aussi délicate. Car il s'agit ici non seulement de tous les moyens de conciliation, d'arbitration et de médiation qui accompagnent les mesures de maintien de la paix et que le terme anglais désignait autrefois correctement sous le vocable du "peacemaking," mais aussi à proprement parler de l'imposition de la paix, souvent traduite en anglais par la formule du "peace enforcement." En ce domaine, la situation restera toujours ambiguë, car il est impossible de définir à l'avance les conditions qui pourraient justifier l'obligation de recourir à la force pour imposer la paix.

Deux précédents paraissent devoir cependant s'imposer. Il s'agit de l'aide humanitaire et du droit d'intervention pour protéger les minorités menacées de génocide dans les conflits internes. De plus en plus, le droit international semble évoluer vers l'obligation de prêter assistance aux personnes en danger, plus particulièrement dans le cas des populations civiles. La crise yougoslave est un exemple éclatant des difficultés multiples qui se dressent sur la voie d'une telle cause. En ce domaine, ce ne sont pas tant les moyens et l'organisation qui manquent, mais bien plutôt la difficulté de fonctionner dans un environnement hostile et dangereux, ce qui à nouveau soulève le problème du "peace enforcement."

Les cas d'intervention dans les conflits civils pour protéger les minorités menacées de génocide ou de "purification ethnique," comme c'est le cas en Yougoslavie, tendent à devenir de plus en plus nombreux. Cette situation vaut aussi pour les Kurdes dans le nord de l'Iraq et les populations chiites dans le sud de ce même pays. Pour des raisons compréhensibles, la Chine et l'ex-URSS ont toujours fait preuve de la plus grande prudence en ce domaine. Sur le plan du droit international, certains auteurs soutiennent avec éloquence le principe du droit d'intervention de l'ONU dans les conflits internes en avançant comme argument que le monde ne saurait rester coi dans les cas de crime contre l'humanité, sans encourir une forme de culpabilité.[11] Si de nombreux juristes ne mettent pas en doute la capacité d'intervention de l'ONU en la matière, il reste que la plupart soutiennent que de telles interventions ne peuvent avoir lieu que si la paix et la sécurité internationales sont menacées, c'est-à-dire une fois qu'a été invoqué l'article 39 de la Charte de l'ONU. Encore là, si l'application de tels principes est exigée dans l'avenir, elle ne pourra l'être qu'avec l'accord des membres permanents du Conseil de sécurité.

La décentralisation du maintien de la paix

Durant l'année en cours, 12 opérations du maintien de la paix se poursuivent de par le monde. À la fin du premier semestre 1992, il y avait 38,144 militaires, 2,461 membres de police et 9,461 civils travaillant dans le cadre de ces opérations, soit un total de 50,006 personnes. De plus, le Secrétaire général s'est engagé dans plus de 75 missions d'enquête, de représentation et de bons offices. Dans sa première conférence de presse en mars 1992, le Secrétaire général s'est prononcé en faveur d'une décentralisation des opérations du maintien de la paix. Cette attitude vise non seulement à faire supporter par des organisations régionales une partie du coût des opérations — cette tendance existe aussi au sein d'autres organisations internationales, telle l'AIEA (Agence internationale de l'énergie atomique) — mais aussi à donner corps au chapitre VIII de la Charte qui encourage le développement des organisations de sécurité régionale.

Le 28 octobre 1992, l'AGNU s'est prononcée par consensus sur la nécessité de renforcer les liens de coopération entre l'ONU et la CSCE (Conférence sur la sécurité et la coopération en Europe). Par ailleurs un projet de loi devant le Parlement russe prévoit la création d'un groupe d'experts entre l'ONU et la CSCE qui pourrait se pencher sur ces problèmes, tout autant que sur les questions relatives à la conduite d'opérations de maintien de la paix entre l'ONU, la CSCE, la CÉI, et qui ne soient pas reliées à des "mesures coercitives ou d'emploi de la force." Le président Eltsine a d'ailleurs parlé de fonctions "subsidiaires" par rapport à l'ONU.

L'expérience des organisations régionales a sans doute été plus fructueuse durant l'époque de la Société des Nations que sous les Nations Unies. De plus, le conflit yougoslave a démontré l'incapacité de l'Europe et de ses institutions à régler les conflits aux portes de l'Europe. La CSCE est peut-être ici l'organisme dont il est fait le plus souvent mention en matière de sécurité régionale.

À la défense de la CSCE, notons qu'à l'origine cet organisme avait été créé dans le contexte des relations Est-Ouest, et non dans le cadre des procédures plus générales de la résolution des conflits sur une base régionale. Ceci n'a pas empêché la CSCE de se doter d'un Comité de hauts fonctionnaires et d'un Centre de prévention des conflits à Vienne. De plus, la CSCE se réunit au sommet à tous les deux ans, et une fois l'an au niveau ministériel. La dernière réunion ministérielle a eu lieu à Stockholm à la mi-décembre 1992.

La CSCE est intervenue activement en nombre d'occasions. Elle a dépêché des officiers de douane en Hongrie, en Bulgarie, et en Roumanie, et agira peut-être demain de la même manière en Albanie, pour surveiller l'embargo déclaré contre la Serbie et le Monténégro; elle a constitué des missions d'enquête au Kosovo, en Macédoine, et au Nagorno-Karabakh; et elle a envoyé des représentants en Géorgie, pour évaluer la situation en Ossétie, dans la République de Moldova, et dans quelques-unes des Républiques d'Asie centrale. En outre, elle s'est engagée, dans le cadre de la résolution 771 du Conseil de sécurité, à faire la lumière sur la question des crimes et atrocités commis en Yougoslavie. Depuis l'exclusion de la Yougoslavie de la CSCE en juillet 1992, cet organisme fonctionne désormais sur la base du "consensus moins un." Une nouvelle procédure est cependant à l'étude où l'organisation fonctionnerait sur la base d'un "consensus moins deux," c'est-à-dire que les 51 participants officiels pourraient s'entendre pour commander aux parties en conflit—d'où la formule consensus moins deux—de se soumettre à des procédures de médiation, d'arbitrage et de conciliation. Cette procédure ne serait certes pas contraignante sur le plan juridique, mais elle indique la volonté très nette des Européens de faire progresser le dossier de leurs structures et institutions en matière de règlement pacifique des différends.

Il reste toutefois que la CSCE ne dispose ni d'un secrétariat permanent, ni de structures décisionnelles efficaces, ni d'une organisation adéquate qui lui permettrait de s'engager dans des opérations du maintien de la paix. L'OTAN a certes accepté de devenir le "bras armé" de la CSCE, si le besoin s'en faisait sentir, mais il est bien évident que dans de telles situations, les décisions ne pourraient être prises qu'au cas par cas, ce qui augure mal de l'avenir de la décentralisation du maintien de la paix.

En règle générale, toutes les institutions régionales souffrent des mêmes maux. Elles n'ont pas de fonds suffisants pour s'engager dans de telles entreprises; elles ne disposent pas de pouvoirs décisionnels efficaces en vertu desquels les États accepteraient dans certains cas qu'un directorat—en l'occurrence le Conseil de sécurité dans le cas de l'ONU—agisse en leur nom en cas de menace à la paix et à la sécurité internationales; enfin, elles ne bénéficient d'aucune infrastructure capable d'exercer des sanctions militaires pour les cas où la paix serait bafouée. Si l'OTAN devait un jour intervenir au nom de la CSCE, c'est parce qu'elle l'aurait elle-même ainsi décidé. C'est donc dire que pour l'instant le chapitre VIII de la Charte reste ce qu'il est, c'est-à-dire tout au plus un bel espoir.

Le maintien de la paix et la presse canadienne

Durant l'année 1992, les grandes questions relatives à la paix et à la sécurité internationales n'ont pas laissé indifférentes les grandes agences de presse canadiennes. Il est intéressant de nous interroger dans un premier temps sur la répartition de l'information en ce domaine et de voir ensuite quels sont les profils d'intérêt de la presse canadienne à l'égard de ces grandes questions.

Le maintien de la paix et l'information internationale

Hormis le journal *La Presse* de Montréal, toutes les sources d'information que nous avons analysées sont en anglais. La période couverte s'étend du 1ᵉʳ janvier 1992 au 31 août 1992, soit les 8 premiers mois de l'année. Les réseaux d'information électroniques auxquels nous avons eu recours sont *Infomart Online* et *InfoGlobe*. Quant aux descripteurs, nous en avons utilisé trois, à savoir les termes "peacekeeping," "peacemaking" et "preventive diplomacy." Les sources disponibles en accès direct par ordinateur nous ont permis de dépouiller 16 quotidiens, y compris *La Presse* de Montréal.

Deux éléments nous paraissent ici importants. En premier lieu, la plus grande partie de l'information est concentrée dans la province de l'Ontario, car aurions-nous ajouté cinq journaux régionaux à ces sources que la liste globale des documents n'aurait été portée qu'à 5,207 documents, comparativement aux 4,012 que

Tableau 12.1
Nombre d'articles et de documents sur le maintien de la paix
selon 16 sources pour la période du 1er janvier au 31 août 1992
N = 4,012

Entre 10 et 150 documents		Entre 250 et 350 documents	
WCNW	10	MTGZ	291
NTMC	22	GAM	331
NTFP	74		
WSNS	96		
Entre 150 et 250 documents		**Entre 350 et 1,150 documents**	
WINT	165	OTCT	352
WBIW	180	TOST	373
HBSP	197	WCPA	1,147
WIST	205		
KWRC	215		
TOSN	226		

Key:

GAM	*Globe & Mail, The*	TOSN	*Toronto Sun, The*
HBSP	*Hamilton/Burlington Specta-*	TOST	*Toronto Star, The*
	tor, The		
KWRC	*Kitchener-Waterloo Record*	WBIW	*Business Information Wire*
MTLP	*La Presse*	WCNW	*Canadian Newswire*
MTGZ	*Gazette, The* (Montreal)	WCPA	*Canadian Press Newswire*
NTFP	*Financial Post, The*	WINT	*Inter Press Service*
NTMC	*Maclean's Magazine*	WIST	*Windsor Star, The*
OTCT	*Ottawa Citizen, The*	WSNS	*Southam News*

Source: *Infomart Online* et *Info Globe*.

nous avons obtenus en dépouillant les quotidiens accessibles par ordinateur (voir le tableau 12.2). L'addition de cinq journaux régionaux, dont l'un des Maritimes, deux des Prairies, et deux de Colombie-Britannique, donnerait la distribution suivante: *Halifax Daily News* [194], le *Calgary Herald* [264], *The Edmonton Journal* [323], *The Vancouver Sun* [253], et [161] pour *The Province* de Vancouver. L'information dans la province de l'Ontario représente donc le plus gros de l'information au Canada.

En deuxième lieu, il faut noter ici l'existence d'une source d'information majeure, à savoir le WCPA (Canadian Press Newswire). Les autres grandes sources d'information sont *The Toronto Star* et *The Ottawa Citizen*, ces deux journaux étant talonnés de près par *The Gazette* et *The Globe and Mail*. Notons enfin que la plupart des journaux cités dans le quadrant inférieur gauche du tableau 12.2 accordent à peu près la même importance à la couverture de presse des questions du maintien de la paix et de la diplomatie préventive.

Cette distribution des sources témoigne de l'intérêt élevé porté à ces questions par la presse anglophone et canadienne, car l'utilisation des mêmes descripteurs pour la même période de temps auprès du *New York Times* aurait permis de recueillir 416 documents, soit un nombre plus élevé de 10 pour cent par rapport au quotidien anglophone qui recueille le plus grand nombre de mentions, à savoir *The Toronto Star*.

Les profils d'attention de la presse anglophone

Comme le démontre le tableau 12.2, une part importante de l'actualité est consacrée au trois grandes questions suivantes: le rôle du Canada dans le domaine du maintien de la paix, le rôle de l'ONU, et d'une façon un peu étonnante, le rôle du Japon.

Nous avons codé deux fois ce dernier élément, car il touche aussi directement aux aspects organisationnels du maintien de la paix. Chose surprenante, l'Allemagne est citée presque trois fois moins que le Japon en la matière. Il n'existe aucune explication à ce phénomène, sinon de penser que le Japon est considéré, plus que l'Allemagne, comme ne faisant peut-être pas assez sa part en matière d'opérations de maintien de la paix. Il est vrai qu'une part importante du débat est transmise par les organes d'information des milieux d'affaires, et qu'à ce titre le Japon est peut-être par habitude une cible de choix. Car même si le débat constitutionnel était d'une importance capitale à Tokyo, il ne l'était pas moins à Berlin, ce qui laisse supposer que dans les préoccupations canadiennes, Tokyo vient bien avant Berlin.

Il faut aussi noter l'intérêt élevé de la presse canadienne pour toutes les questions qui touchent à la réorganisation du maintien de la paix en général, les questions européennes venant en premier lieu, suivies des questions relatives au maintien de la paix au sein du Commonwealth et de la CÉI qui recueillent dans les deux cas le même degré d'intérêt.

Sur le plan des conflits, la Yougoslavie occupe évidemment l'avant-scène de l'actualité. Le Cambodge vient au second rang, puis les problèmes du Proche-Orient, et enfin la Somalie. Par

Tableau 12.2
Profil d'attention dans la presse canadienne
en matière de maintien de la paix*

Les grandes questions du maintien de la paix au Canada;			n = 787
Le Canada et le maintien de la paix			482
Les Nations Unies et le maintien de la paix			189
Le Japon et le maintien de la paix			114

Aspects organisationnels;				n = 365
Le Japon et maintien de la paix	114	CÉI et maintien de la paix		22
La réunion au sommet du Conseil		CSCE et maintien de la paix		22
de sécurité des Nations Unies	57	Commonwealth et maintien		
L'OTAN et maintien de la paix	61	de la paix		9
Eurocorps/CEE/Allemagne		Russie et maintien de la paix		9
et maintien de la paix	41	OUA et maintien de la paix		6
G 7 et maintien de la paix	24	ASEAN et maintien de la paix		3

Profil d'attention pur les conflits majeurs;			n = 2326
Yougoslavie	1,912	Somalie	73
Cambodge	174	Arménie/Azerbaïdjan	57
Proche-Orient (Israël/Palestine,		Afrique du Sud	31
Israël/Liban; Israël/Syrie)	92		

Profil d'attention pour les autres conflits;			n = 153
Liberia	19	Thaïlande	16
El Salvador	18	Afghanistan	15
Géorgie (Ossétie)	18	Moldavie	12
Haïti	16	Sierra Leone	12
Liban	16	Iraq	11

Les données ont été codées d'après les sources mentionnées dans le tableau 12.1.

ailleurs, il est étonnant de constater que la plupart des autres conflits retiennent une attention à peu près également distribuée.

Le Canada et le maintien de la paix

Notre objectif dans cette partie de l'étude est double. En premier lieu, nous souhaitons brièvement couvrir la participation canadienne aux opérations de maintien de la paix au cours de l'année écoulée. Nous verrons ensuite quels sont les problèmes qui découlent de cette participation accrue et les débats qu'elle soulève au sein des milieux politiques.

La participation du Canada aux opérations de maintien de la paix

Si certains milieux politiques et financiers espéraient une situation plus rose pour le Canada au lendemain de la guerre froide, ils ont dû déchanter très vite. Le retrait de nos troupes de Lahr, qui devait représenter une économie de un demi-milliard de dollars sur cinq ans, à subitement été remplacé par un engagement massif du pays dans les opérations du maintien de la paix.

En Yougoslavie, le Canada a dépêché en janvier et février 1992 des observateurs pour participer à la mission entreprise par la Communauté européenne, ainsi que des observateurs militaires pour faire partie de la mission de liaison militaire des Nations Unies. En mars, il confirme sa participation à l'opération de la FORPRONU (Force de protection des Nations Unies) dans une proportion de 1,200 casques bleus, ainsi que sa volonté de fournir des observateurs de police constitués depuis des éléments de la GRC, et à la fin d'août 1992, le Canada approuve le déploiement du NCSM Gatineau en Adriatique pour surveiller l'embargo décidé par les Nations Unies contre la Serbie et le Monténégro. En septembre 1992 le Canada accepte d'affecter à nouveau 1,200 hommes — en provenance de la base de Gagetown — à ce qu'il convient désormais d'appeler FORPRONU II, qui sera déployée en Bosnie, afin d'y garantir l'acheminement des secours humanitaires. Enfin, à la fin de l'année 1992, le Canada donne son feu vert à la participation de 900 militaires canadiens à l'opération Rendre l'Espoir en Somalie.

Entre-temps, le Canada refusera de reconnaître la Bosnie-Herzégovine, se ralliera à l'embargo décrété contre l'ancienne Yougoslavie, versera une aide de 5,25 millions de dollars en faveur des victimes du conflit, et participera aux missions d'aide humanitaire destinées à porter secours aux populations tenues en otages à Sarajevo.

Au Cambodge, plus de 100 membres des Forces armées participent dès mars 1992 à la MIPRENUC (Mission préparatoire des Nations Unies au Cambodge), nombre qui sera porté à environ 215, en juin 1992. En Somalie, le Canada accepte en août 1992 de contribuer aux opérations d'aide humanitaire en s'engageant à dépêcher 750 militaires dans la région de Bossasso, pour la plupart en provenance du Canadian Airborne Regiment de Petawawa. L'opération *Rendre l'Espoir* approuvée en décembre 1992 viendra modifier la zone de déploiement prévue pour les soldats canadiens qui seront dès lors intégrés à la force dirigée par les Américains en Somalie. En outre, le Canada projette de maintenir jusqu'en juin 1993 le contingent de ses 575 militaires au sein de la force des Nations Unies à Chypre, et environ 175 autres sur les hauteurs de Golan. Si on ajoute les autres contributions mineures du Canada au Sahara occidental, au Salvador, en Afghanistan et en Angola, il y aurait ainsi un total d'environ 5,000 militaires canadiens qui feraient office de "casques bleus" de par le monde au début de l'année 1993. Le Canada fournit ainsi une part importante de l'ensemble des "casques bleus" du monde; sa contribution le place au premier rang mondial, même si en Yougoslavie, la France a une représentation militaire plus importante que celle du Canada.

Si l'on tient compte du fait que les Forces canadiennes comptent environ 80,000 éléments, et qu'il faut prévoir un haut niveau d'engagement afin de former, d'entraîner le personnel de relève, et d'en prévoir la rotation, l'Armée de terre canadienne serait désormais taxée jusqu'à son extrême limite. Ainsi, les seules opérations du maintien de la paix mettraient à contribution directement ou indirectement plus de 13,000 militaires canadiens.

Les débats politiques

Trois aspects méritent ici d'être soulignés. Le premier a trait à la réorganisation de l'ONU, le second à l'éventualité d'un recours à la force pour "garantir" la paix, et le troisième aux ressources disponibles au Canada pour répondre à ses obligations en matière de maintien de la paix.

La réorganisation de l'ONU

Fidèle à sa conception de la diplomatie multilatérale, le Canada a soutenu dès les débuts de la Conférence de San Francisco le renforcement des pouvoirs de l'Organisation mondiale. En pleine guerre froide, le Canada a joué un rôle décisif dans la constitution de la première Force d'Urgence des Nations Unies (FUNU), et plus récemment il a obtenu en 1988 le prix Nobel de la paix pour sa participation extensive à toutes les opérations de maintien de la paix entreprises sous l'égide de l'ONU.

Il ne faut donc pas s'étonner que le soutien canadien aux opérations des "casques bleus" soit toujours aussi prononcé. Dans le texte préparé par les pays nordiques dont nous avons analysé ci-dessus les principaux éléments, il est clair que le Canada soutient corps et âme l'établissement au sein du secrétariat de l'ONU d'une infrastructure permanente chargée d'administrer et de gérer tous les aspects relatifs au maintien de la paix, y compris les fonctions de renseignements qui vont de pair avec la conduite de ces opérations. En janvier 1992, le Parti libéral du Canada a produit sous la plume de Lloyd Axworthy son *Rapport sur le Canada et l'ONU au XXIème siècle.* Parmi les mesures concrètes pour appuyer le Secrétaire général dans ses tâches, le Parti libéral suggère de renforcer les pouvoirs de renseignement du Secrétariat, grâce à l'établissement, si besoin est, de collectes d'information par satellite, et d'un Secrétariat permanent au maintien de la paix. De plus, le Parti libéral s'est prononcé en faveur d'une diplomatie préventive plus appuyée et a suggéré le recours plus fréquent à des médiateurs spéciaux. En ce domaine, il n'y a donc pas de différences fondamentales entre la position défendue par le gouvernement et celle soutenue par le Parti libéral.

Le recours à la force?

C'est cependant sur le plan des interventions de l'ONU que les débats deviennent plus nuancés. En effet, le Parti libéral souhaite la création de "zones bleues" habilitant l'ONU à intervenir pour protéger les droits de la personne, plus particulièrement en Croatie ou en Haïti. Le Parti libéral s'est aussi prononcé en faveur de l'établissement d'une cour pénale internationale qui serait saisie des atteintes au droit international et dont les auteurs ne sont pas des États. Il n'est cependant jamais allé aussi loin que certains critiques du côté du NPD, comme le député Sven Robinson, qui souhaitaient l'été dernier que les "casques bleus" se fraient un chemin par la force en Bosnie pour secourir les populations affamées. Dans sa déclaration de juillet 1992 sur la crise yougoslave, le Parti libéral s'est contenté de demander une réunion extraordinaire du Comité d'état-major de l'ONU pour étudier "toutes les solutions militaires" susceptibles de mettre fin au conflit.

Ce problème déborde largement le cadre des partis politiques. Du côté du gouvernement la prudence est de mise, car tout comme il a refusé de retirer son ambassadeur de Yougoslavie pour protéger la vie des militaires canadiens en fonction dans ce pays, il s'est toujours abstenu de préconiser une action plus musclée, de peur de mettre en danger ses propres troupes déployées en Croatie ou en Bosnie. Cette attitude sera défendue avec vigueur par l'ancien chef d'état-major de la FORPRONU, le général Lewis Mackenzie, qui ne s'est jamais gêné, tant à Washington qu'au Canada, pour dire que la paix ne pouvait être imposée, si les parties en conflit ne la voulaient pas.

En réalité, la crise yougoslave est l'occasion d'un débat nouveau et il est clair que le recours à la force ne saurait être exclu du revers de la main face à une situation qui se détériore de jour en jour. Le problème se pose en Yougoslavie avec la décision de l'ONU d'imposer le principe d'une "zone d'exclusion" de vols aériens en Bosnie, mais aussi en Somalie où il est de plus en plus difficile d'acheminer vivres et secours.   Plusieurs experts comme John Mackinlay en Angleterre ou C.R. Nixon au Canada préconisent le déploiement de forces rapides beaucoup plus lourdes et mieux armées pour exécuter les missions humanitaires ou de maintien de la paix qui pourraient leur être confiées.[12] L'ancien ambassadeur du Canada à l'ONU, Stephen Lewis, a déclaré pour sa part à la mi-septembre que le recours à la force pourrait être nécessaire pour ramener la paix, lorsque "le chaos est si extrême que la vie de chacun est mis en péril."

En réalité, depuis la crise du Golfe, trois choses sont apparentes. Il existe des opérations qui dépassent largement toutes les capacités que l'ONU pourrait espérer rassembler autour d'elle. Dans ces conditions, seule une coalition multinationale peut restaurer la paix et la sécurité, et celle-ci sera nécessairement sous le commandement militaire du plus fort ou des deux ou trois plus forts des États participants. En deuxième lieu, si le désert est un lieu de prédilection pour les armes intelligentes et les opérations aériennes de grande envergure, cela n'est manifestement pas le cas en Yougoslavie. Les démocraties sont vieillissantes et rien n'indique qu'elles aient tant soit peu l'intention de s'engager dans de grandes batailles terrestres. Elles peuvent à la rigueur intervenir lorsqu'elles n'utilisent que leur potentiel aérien et naval et qu'elles doivent faire face à une armée de paysans, contrôlé de surcroît par un peloton d'exécution, mais les règles du jeu changent complètement lorsqu'il s'agit d'intervenir dans des terrains montagneux, contre des militaires qui connaissent et contrôlent bien le terrain. Les deux actions d'importance militaire jusqu'à maintenant entreprises par l'ONU en Yougoslavie sont les "zones d'exclusion" de vols en Bosnie, et la surveillance de l'embargo dans la mer Adriatique. Personne n'a envie d'en découdre avec les Serbes, alors que durant la Seconde Guerre mondiale, même les 37 divisions déployées par l'Allemagne n'en sont pas venues à bout.

En troisième lieu, la crise yougoslave démontre qu'il existe des cas qui sont intermédiaires entre le maintien de la paix classique et le rétablissement de la paix par la force. C'est en ce domaine en particulier que les moyens d'intervention de l'ONU doivent être renforcés. Les conditions qui règnent en Yougoslavie et en Somalie sont tout à fait différentes. Il est possible que des zones entières puissent être "sanctuarisées" en Somalie; la tâche est plus difficile en Yougoslavie. D'ailleurs, dès que les tirs reprennent ou que les cessez-le-feu sont rompus, l'acheminement des convois humanitaires cesse.

L'ONU se limite donc à l'essentiel. Elle tente de sauver la face et fait tout ce qui est en son pouvoir pour soulager les civils et les populations affamées. Elle fait cependant aussi beaucoup plus. Elle a développé une doctrine d'intervention dans les conflits internes, elle a soumis la Yougoslavie à des sanctions qui l'isolent totalement du système international, et elle continue de préparer ce que l'on pourrait appeler la posture de l'après-guerre: déploiements navals destinés à maintenir la pression sur l'ex-Yougoslavie, contrôle de douane aux frontières terrestres, et constitution éventuelle de tribunaux qui pourraient se prononcer sur les crimes de guerre et le non-respect des conventions internationales sur son territoire. Sur ce dernier point, la ministre Barbara McDougall a déjà précisé qu'elle avait l'intention de convoquer une réunion de la Commission de droit international de l'ONU pour étudier ces questions. Rappelons qu'une telle hypothèse avait déjà été soulevée dans le passé en ce qui a trait aux "crimes de guerre" de Saddam Hussein. Chose certaine, on ne saurait ici totalement désespérer. En effet, il existe d'autres cas où des pays sortis victorieux d'une guerre ont dû rétrocéder des gains ou encore des territoire acquis par la force des armes, une fois les hostilités terminées. Faute d'un recours massif à la force, c'est à peu près tout ce que peuvent encore espérer les démocraties: gagner sur le terrain diplomatique, faute de ne le pouvoir militairement.

Disponibilités et ressources

Depuis quelque temps déjà, le débat est bien engagé sur les "surengagements" du Canada en matière de maintien de paix. Geoffrey York du *Globe and Mail* a fait récemment le tour de la question sous le titre *The Price of Peace*.[13] Quatre interrogations semblent dominer le débat. Les militaires canadiens sont-ils suffisamment formés et entraînés pour maintenir la paix? À quel prix et durant combien de temps le Canada pourra-t-il maintenir de tels engagements? Le Canada ne risque-t-il pas d'être entraîné contre son gré dans la spirale de la violence? Le Canada ne devrait-il pas se retirer de certaines opérations?

Sur le plan de la formation, le libéral Jean Chrétien a déjà proposé depuis mars 1990 que le Canada "offre les installations voulues pour former les gardiens de la paix internationaux." En septembre 1991, le premier ministre Donald Cameron de la province de la Nouvelle-Écosse, a proposé au premier ministre du Canada de faire de la base de Cornwallis un centre d'entraînement international pour les soldats de paix.[14] Outre que ce projet en particulier vise à maintenir ouverte la base de Cornwallis, tout comme probablement celle de Fort Dix lorsque le président Bush a suggéré la même idée dans son discours du 21 septembre devant l'AGNU, il semble qu'au ministère de la Défense on juge ce projet peu pertinent, puisqu'aucun pays ne s'est encore porté volontaire pour financer un tel centre de formation. Sur le plan de l'entraînement, le MDN (Ministère de la défense nationale) a reconnu certaines insuffisances mais juge adéquats la formation et l'entraînement des soldats canadiens à leurs missions de paix, en dépit de l'existence de certains rapports internes dans le passé qui dénonçaient l'insuffisance de la formation des militaires.[15]

Pendant combien de temps le Canada pourra-t-il tenir ses engagements? Pour plusieurs, comme le professeur Joel Sokolsky du Collège militaire royal de Kingston, le Canada s'est engagé dans de telles opérations sans même discuter. Selon ce spécialiste, un débat important s'impose sur la question. Pour Dan Middlemiss de Halifax, le Canada doit apprendre à dire non. Pour le général Lewis Mackenzie, les forces canadiennes sont taxées jusqu'à leur extrême limite et, selon lui, le Canada devra bientôt réfléchir à tous ces problèmes, car il ne pourra autrement répondre à des crises intérieures d'envergure, si celles-ci devaient se présenter. La critique la plus acerbe vient du professeur Jack Granatstein. Ce dernier dénonce en effet l'insuffisance de la préparation des forces de la Réserve qui sont de plus en plus mises à contribution pour participer à ces opérations, et le danger d'exposer inutilement les fils de la nation dans des opérations dangereuses. Le maintien de la paix, selon lui, est devenu un "substitut à la pensée et au développement d'une politique." Il est vrai que 500 membres de la réserve servent aujourd'hui dans des opérations de maintien de la paix et qu'aucune loi ne protège leur retour au travail, sauf dans de rares exceptions.

Sur le plan du financement, il est clair que la contribution canadienne est coûteuse, car elle s'élèvera sans doute à plus de 200 millions de dollars pour l'année en cours, d'autant que le Secrétaire général a demandé à ce que les régions concernées, c'est-à-dire l'Europe, assument une plus grande part du coût des opérations en Yougoslavie. Ceci vaut aussi pour le Canada, puisqu'on lui demande, comme à Chypre, d'assumer le coût de ses opérations. Cette façon de voir n'a guère été appréciée par la ministre Barbara McDougall lors de la présentation de son discours à l'AGNU en septembre dernier. En dépit des coûts élevés des missions, le maintien de la paix est toujours aussi populaire au Canada, car il correspond aux forces profondes de la société canadienne qui entend secourir les nations pauvres, tout autant que les populations innocentes détenues en otages dans les guerres civiles.

Le véritable problème n'est pas financier. Il tient aux maigres ressources humaines dont dispose le Canada pour assurer ces missions. Le Canada devrait donc s'employer à définir avec le plus de précisions possibles les conditions de sa participation aux opérations, et sa volonté très nette de s'en retirer si le mandat de ces opérations devait évoluer vers un recours systématique à l'emploi de la force. C'est peut-être là la meilleure des garanties dont le Canada devrait se prévaloir dans l'avenir.

Quant à Chypre, si le retrait des contingents de l'ONU devait donner lieu à une reprise des hostilités dans l'île, il est probable que l'on frappera à nouveau à la porte du Canada pour lui demander de bien faire. Quant à bien faire, il aurait peut-être mieux valu rester là jusqu'à ce que la situation politique ait été dénouée. Certains éléments politiques, comme le député John Brewin, ont dénoncé comme "irresponsable" la décision du Canada de se retirer de la FNUC (Force des Nations Unies à Chypre). Jean Chrétien, pour sa part, a estimé que si le Canada n'a pas les moyens d'être à Chypre, il ne comprend pas pourquoi il accepte alors de nouveaux engagements ailleurs. Quoi qu'il en soit, le Canada a bien précisé que le but de son retrait de la FNUC visait à accélérer le processus des négociations sur l'île, et que le retrait canadien ne signifiait ni la fin de l'opération ni l'éventualité qu'une autre plus petite soit constituée.

Conclusion

Dans un article paru dans le *Los Angeles Times* du 1er novembre 1992, Stanley Meisler, correspondant du *Times* à l'ONU, écrivait à propos du Secrétaire général: "it is still too early to tell whether he will be a great secretary general in the mold of Dag Hammarskjold, ineffectual like most of the others or somewhere in between; too early to tell whether he is truly independent or just plain stubborn, whether his analyses, in the long run, will prove practical or professorial." Les dés sont joués. L'Organisation dispose désormais d'un nouveau leader, souvent distant mais habile, et qui pour l'instant a décidé de jouer l'avenir de l'Organisation sur les triples crises du Cambodge, de la Yougoslavie et de la Somalie. Selon que l'Organisation réussira ou échouera, un ordre nouveau s'établira ou s'écroulera.

Dans l'ensemble, beaucoup d'eau a coulé sous les ponts depuis la fin de la guerre froide. L'ONU a été renforcée, le train du maintien de la paix est sur ses rails. Les réunions successives des membres permanents du Conseil de sécurité le rapport récent *Agenda pour la paix*, tout autant que le dernier *Rapport* du Secrétaire général, font la preuve d'un dynamisme encore jamais vu au sein de l'Organisation. Le Canada le premier se félicite de la recrudescence des activités de l'ONU en matière de paix.

Au niveau national, un débat s'impose pour les Canadiens, concluait le *Globe and Mail* du 15 décembre 1992. Les questions devraient porter sur les modalités de la participation canadienne à des opérations du maintien de la paix, sur les conditions du recours à la force, sur le coût et les modes de financement de ces opérations, ainsi que sur leurs rôles.

Si l'histoire sert ici à quelque chose, nous pourrions peut-être conclure que le Canada a toujours eu le cœur sur la main, que ses ressources sont limitées, et qu'il vaudrait mieux, en cas d'opérations de coercition ou d'imposition armée de la paix, se limiter à des opérations maritimes ou aériennes. Nos ressources de haute technologie nous permettent d'agir ainsi, mais il serait dommage que le Canada engage ses précieuses ressources humaines dans des opérations terrestres de redressement armé de la paix.

13   Security and NATO

Andrew Cohen

Three years after the fall of Communism, NATO is still an army without an enemy. The arrival of peace has been harder on the alliance than the threat of war; for the first time, NATO is questioning its founding principles. Is it still the foundation of the security architecture of Europe? Is there life beyond the Berlin Wall and the Fulda Gap? Is it an expensive, sentimental anachronism in a unipolar world?

SINCE THE END of the Second World War, the focus of Canada's relationship with Europe has been the North Atlantic Treaty Organization (NATO). No other association has tied this country so closely to the democracies of the northern hemisphere. For Canada, NATO has always represented an early and enduring commitment to the internationalism of the post-war era. Most tangibly, the presence of Canadian soldiers on the continent has been a measure of this country's belief in an interdependent world, for which it has been willing to pay in blood and treasure.

The commitment, however, has come to mean less in the 1990s than it did in the 1940s. The success of NATO ensured that Canada suffered no loss of life even as it suffered a loss of face. While Canada has provided fewer troops and reduced military spending in the last decade, it has always preserved enough credibility to remain at the table in Brussels and explain its delinquency. In announcing its withdrawal from Europe in 1992, however, Canada changed its relationship with NATO, although it was not immediately clear how. On the one hand, it was said that leaving Europe would deny Canada a real voice in the alliance, a consequence of "no-pay, no-say." On the other hand, it was also said that leaving Europe would invite an overdue assessment of Canada's place in NATO in the context of other pressing international obligations.

Canada's decision to pull out of Europe was made in a climate of growing self-doubt within the alliance itself. Three years after the fall of Communism, NATO is still an army without an enemy. The arrival of peace has been harder on the alliance than the threat of war; for the first time, NATO is questioning its founding principles. Is it still the foundation of the security architecture of Europe? Is there life beyond the Berlin Wall and the Fulda Gap? Is it an expensive, sentimental anachronism in a unipolar world? The search for answers, both in Canada and beyond, will animate the alliance in this decade and may be its salvation in the next.

The Decision to Pull Out

On February 25, 1992, the federal government announced that it would withdraw Canada's remaining forces in Europe by 1994. The decision disappointed its allies but should not have surprised them. In reality, the move had been expected since September 17, 1991, when Defence Minister Marcel Masse said that Canada would close its two military bases in Germany — Lahr in 1994 and Baden-Soellingen in 1995 — and withdraw its remaining 6,600 soldiers. At that time, Masse promised that Canada would leave an emergency force of 1,100 troops and two squadrons of CF-18 fighter planes in Europe. Subsequently, Prime Minister Brian Mulroney and Secretary of State for External Affairs Barbara McDougall reaffirmed the need to keep troops on the continent to maintain the trans-Atlantic link. Canada had been in Europe since 1951, they declared solemnly; to decamp now would be irresponsible and isolationist.

Five months later those reservations had vanished. Now Defence Minister Marcel Masse declared that this tiny force of infantry, tanks and artillery would not have made a soupçon of difference anyway. "It's not because we had 1,110 forces in Europe that we had a political voice," he said. "It is because we are a member of NATO and people know we are committed to Europe." Manfred Woerner, the Secretary General of NATO, said he understood the need for fiscal restraint but regretted the withdrawal "given the political and military importance of the presence of Canadian forces in Europe." From Bonn, London and Washington came stronger expressions of disappointment.

Surprisingly, though, these pro-forma declarations reflected a wider discontent. In April, at a NATO meeting in Lisbon, the "simmering displeasure...burst into the open."[1] The United States,

Holland, Luxembourg and Turkey attacked Canada's decision. One Canadian diplomat, surprised by this outpouring of invective, called it "Canada-bashing." The Helpful Fixer was not used to this kind of hostility but Ottawa was still unfazed. "I don't feel the slightest bit of shame," sniffed Jeremy Kinsman, soon to be appointed Canada's Ambassador to Moscow. "We have left behind 100,000 in European wars. I don't see why there is a huge issue right now about our reluctance to continue to station military troops in Europe."[2] At another NATO meeting in Alberta in May, Britain proposed that Canada leave 300 troops in Europe in a multinational contingent. But even this suggestion of a token rear guard was rejected.

The criticism from abroad was a little mischievous. Everyone knew that Canada was a minor player in NATO and its proposed brigade would have been inconsequential. The issue was symbolism. The Europeans feared that the United States would follow Canada and withdraw its forces from the continent, which would have a greater economic than strategic impact. If Washington was already halving its forces in Europe to 150,000 by 1995, so the Europeans worried, it might decide to go all the way. But the Americans did not often consult Canada on security questions. If the alliance was going to unravel — and this was now a legitimate fear — the catalyst would not be the withdrawal of Canada's garrison in the Black Forest.

While foreigners protested, Canadians were unconcerned over this shift in policy. War was unlikely in Europe, they said, so why remain there? Canada was keeping pilots in warplanes trained to strike targets in friendly countries, and soldiers in tanks trained to defend borders which had disappeared. The only real debate was among the professionals.[3] Critics of the decision argued that it was important "psychologically" for Canada to stay in Europe. If a nation already has a force in place, they said, reinforcements can meet an emergency; if forces are not there, the decision is qualitatively different. They also worried about a loss of influence. As Alex Morrison put it: "The next time we speak up we can legitimately be told to pipe down because we didn't put our money where our mouth was." In contrast, supporters of the decision said it was long overdue, pointing out that Canada could now focus on other areas of international security, such as peacekeeping. They called the Europeans hypocritical for attacking Canada for cutting its defence budget while many of them were doing the same.

The government, for its part, maintained that Canada could always return to the continent. "When NATO was founded, our troops were not in Europe," said McDougall. "We brought them back in response to a crisis, and we will do that again." In that sense, it was fair to argue that Canada was not abandoning NATO. It would still contribute a battalion, with pre-positioned equipment, to serve with either the NATO Composite Force or the Allied Command European Land Force in Norway; it would continue to join air and naval forces in operations in the Atlantic; it would maintain a dedicated brigade and two squadrons of CF-18s in Canada which could be sent to Germany in 24 hours; it would provide about 100 persons to the NATO early warning system and about 200 persons to staff headquarters in Brussels. Meanwhile, Canada would still guard its borders and contribute to arms verification and other programs. While there was doubt that Canada could send soldiers to Europe in a hurry — a scepticism expressed by a parliamentary committee in June, which noted that Canada had had to rent transport ships in past exercises — the thrust of the government's argument rang true. Whether in Europe or not, Canada would continue to pay its dues and fulfil commitments to the alliance.

The announcement in February came after months of bureaucratic wrangling. The soldiers in the Department of National Defence (DND) wanted to leave Europe to reallocate resources elsewhere while the diplomats in the Department of External Affairs wanted to stay in Europe to show the flag. The brigade announced the previous September was a clumsy compromise which the Department of Finance ultimately scuttled. The news came in a few lines in the federal budget, which suggested that defence policy was being made by sharp-nibbed beancounters. Indeed, it was left to Donald Mazankowski — not Marcel Masse or Barbara McDougall — to explain Canada's retrenchment. "The world has changed a great deal," he said, more a rationalization than a revelation.

True, closing both bases in Europe would save about $900 million a year (it costs $150,000 to keep a family in Germany) and help cut $2 billion from the defence budget over four years. But if the government knew these costs five months earlier, why did it not pack up then? Was it uncertain about its long-term commitments? Jeremy Kinsman argued that the government acted later in response to the failed coup d'état in Moscow in August and the deepening recession at home. But the recession had already bitten in the fall and the coup took place before Masse's announcement in September; if it indicated anything, it meant that the bear had not been declawed and Canada should remain in Europe after all. The more likely reason is that the government never knew what to do with the brigade and needed some window-dressing to placate its allies. When asked about the brigade's function in October, 1991, for example, Canadian senior officials in Germany simply shrugged.

In any event, Canada was withdrawing from Europe after four decades on guard. It would not leave with crowds cheering and bands playing. Rather, it would steal away in the hollow of the night on little cat feet. There would be no one left to turn out the lights but few would be burning, anyway. The château had become a *pied à terre*, and now even that was being abandoned because the rent was too high.

Having loosened but not severed its ties, Canada rushed to affirm its loyalty to the alliance. In the near future, Canada would have to think about its relations with Europe and its new role in a renewed organization. Some said Canada should abandon NATO altogether. This was no longer a radical idea. Even Escott Reid, one of those imaginative diplomats who had helped to found the alliance, suggested in 1987 that NATO had outlived its usefulness.[4] In Parliament, the New Democrats had long been urging complete withdrawal.

One reservation about leaving Europe was the danger of hurting Canada's economic interests. The European Community (EC) is Canada's most important trading partner after the U.S. (total trade was $25.8 billion in 1991) and its second largest source of foreign investment ($30.8 billion in 1991). Critics said that Canada would lose trade, particularly when Europe became a single market in 1993. But the argument sounded more persuasive than it was. In 1980, Canadian exports comprised twelve percent of total European imports; in 1990 they comprised eight percent. Keeping troops in Germany had not dismantled the protectionist Common Agricultural Policy or halted challenges to Canada's trade practices under the terms of the General Agreement on Tariffs and

Trade (GATT). Nor had it stopped European trawlers from flouting quotas on northern cod. The EC and Canada did agree in 1992 to end their lengthy dispute on overfishing on the Grand Banks. But the lesson here was that as Canada's presence in NATO had not prevented the dispute, its withdrawal had not resolved it. In the end, Canada would succeed in the European market on the strength of its diplomats and entrepreneurs, not its soldiers.

Now that Canada had promised not to abandon NATO, what role would it play? One recurring suggestion has been to expand NATO's mandate. Technically, the alliance has always had a political function; under Article 2 of the North Atlantic Treaty it was supposed to foster political, economic, social and cultural cooperation among its members. The clause has been ignored and some argue that Canada could lead an effort to revive it ("Article 2 is an idea whose time has come," says Canada's Ambassador to NATO). But while Canada has saluted the political role which NATO might play, especially by extending its offices to the new democracies of Eastern Europe, it has not talked much about institutional reform, as it has at the United Nations. This is an issue to which Canada might well address itself.

A more pragmatic proposal is to make Canada's base at Lahr a centre of operations for international peacekeeping. Canada could seek official authorization from NATO (as well as the UN and the Conference on Security and Cooperation in Europe — CSCE) to transform the base into a staging point and a site for training multinational forces in peacekeeping or humanitarian relief. The Liberal Party, which is promoting the idea, believes it would not only restore faith in Canada's commitment to European security but pioneer a co-ordinated UN response. "Lahr was closed for budget reasons," says Lloyd Axworthy, the party's foreign affairs spokesman. "It could be given new life for good policy reasons."[5]

The proposal is worth considering. It would make use of a base which is to be abandoned anyway. At a more symbolic level, it would enable Canada to take a leading role in the development of peacekeeping and "peace-enforcement," as the Secretary General of the United Nations describes the next challenge to the international community. As Canada detaches itself from NATO, this is where it will probably shift its resources.

New Tensions in Europe

While Canada was reassessing NATO in 1992, there was growing unrest across the continent: a rightist revival in Germany, a civil war in Yugoslavia, the splitting of Czechoslovakia, continuing instability in Russia and in the former republics of the Soviet Union. The end of the Cold War was supposed to end hot wars in Africa, Asia, and Latin America; in some places, it did. In Europe, though, it brought only more conflict. Ironically, the chaos brought a curious longing in some quarters for the old order. Balladeer Leonard Cohen caught the mood sardonically in his song, "The Future": "Give me back the Berlin Wall," he sings. "Give me back Stalin and St. Paul. I've seen the future, brother. It is murder."

This pessimism was unthinkable when Communism began crumbling in 1989. Over the next two years, as the Soviet Union itself disintegrated, the bureaucrats in Brussels were considering new ideas for NATO. At every ministerial meeting, the heads of government would consecrate NATO as the cornerstone of the European security architecture, a word which implied something more permanent than events in Europe indicated. That a handful of rival institutions were growing in stature — the CSCE, the Western European Union (WEU), the Franco-German Corps — did not seem to matter. NATO happily continued to assert its relevance. There was a surreal touch to the drilling of soldiers on empty bases, in a kind of shadow boxing. The alliance was like the lumbering prehistoric creature which could not get its body and its mind to act together; by the time the head had warned its legs of danger, the predator had pounced.

No one disputed that ambiguous dangers had replaced clear ones. NATO had to have a greater purpose than keeping the Americans in, the Russians out, and the Germans down. With the bi-polar world gone, the alliance would have to address a post-Communist era of smouldering ethnic hostility. As Manfred Woerner said in 1991: "Our character will profoundly change because the big threat has disappeared — the threat of a massive attack by the Soviet Union. What remains are risks. What remains is the instability and insecurity around us." Russia, for example, could still destroy the United States in thirty minutes. Its attachment to democracy was questionable. When its foreign minister rose at the CSCE in December to say that Russia was withdrawing support for the UN, the delegates shivered. It was a hoax, but nonetheless a brief, chilling reminder of the Cold War.[6]

In the future, Europe will present a catalogue of different but deadly threats, including an accidental nuclear explosion or the failure of a nuclear reactor, weapons proliferation, and mass migration from Eastern Europe and North Africa. The greatest immediate danger is the spread of domestic conflicts across borders, provoked by nations intervening to help their compatriots. Unfortunately, there are many possibilities for this "internationalization" of ethnic conflict: Albanians in Kosovo and Macedonia, Poles in Lithuania, Romanians in Moldova, Hungarians in Romania and Slovakia, Turks in Bulgaria, Russians in republics outside the Russian Federation. Suddenly it is nationalism, rather than expansionism, that is the danger. The contagion is not Communism, but racism and xenophobia.

In this environment the strategic doctrines of "forward defence" and "flexible response" are obsolete. The edge of NATO's power will be a highly mobile "rapid reaction force." But as long as NATO remains a defensive alliance — it cannot respond militarily unless one of its sixteen members is attacked — it will have to broaden its mandate to meet threats beyond its borders. Defining this new collective security will be a new test of the new NATO.

In 1992, NATO began to reinvent itself. The effort actually had its roots in the Rome Summit of November, 1991, the first since the collapse of the Soviet Union. There, NATO confidently declared "a new chapter" in its history. It conceded that security could not be guaranteed by one institution alone and invited help from the members of the CSCE, the EC, the WEU and the Council of Europe. Its "New Strategic Concept," however ambiguous in places, underscored the uses of political power to promote peace. At the same meeting NATO agreed to reduce its nuclear capacity by 80 percent and to cut its conventional forces. The most important aspect was that, in creating the North Atlantic Co-operation Council, NATO forged political contacts with Hungary, Bulgaria, Czechoslovakia and other countries of Eastern Europe, which were grateful for the invitation. While NATO stopped short of offering them membership, associate or full, or extending its security guarantee to them, the creation of the Council showed a willingness to think big. More and more, it seems that expansion will be the salvation of the alliance. Offers of membership to fledgling states will strengthen the growth of democracy on the continent and extend the security zone. The key to stability in Europe, as one commentator put it, is "a more and better NATO."

At Rome, the declaration was heavier on political intent than military strategy. There was nothing about a turbulent Russia, a rearmed Ukraine, an unstable Hungary or the growth of Islamic fundamentalism in North Africa. Nor was there much on European defence. No doubt NATO wanted to remain the guardian of continental defence while still operating under an integrated command. This called into question the balance between a distinctive European body and an association with North America. The British and Italians favoured a bigger role for the WEU, which could involve itself in peacekeeping outside NATO's boundaries, while NATO itself would look after European defence. The Germans and the French wanted a greater association with the European Community. Having the Eurocorps — the joint army founded by France and Germany — operate both inside and outside the NATO area would double its responsibilities.

The cracks in the alliance were showing here. The French and Germans wanted European defence to be European, not American. No wonder George Bush told NATO: "If you don't really want us, tell us." There was a growing body of opinion in Europe which wanted to leave NATO to itself, while giving other institutions a mandate to address civil war and ethnic upheaval. The United States sensed this, and asked whether it was finally time to part company.

The instability which haunted NATO erupted in March, 1992 in Nagorno-Karabakh, and the alliance was soon drawn into a discussion of how to stop the fighting. While NATO was not expected to end the conflict, this kind of intervention foreshadowed its prospective role. In April, at the first meeting of the North Atlantic Co-operation Council, the defence ministers of NATO met their new counterparts to discuss exchanges and joint military exercises. The prospect of peacekeeping was raised. Once again the Organization proclaimed "a new chapter" in its history, but again, no memberships were offered and no security guarantees were extended. In June, NATO signed an arms control treaty with the countries of the former east bloc. The signatories agreed to cut their stockpiles of tanks and artillery. Ironically, the treaty limits the arms these new republics can use not against the West, but against themselves.

NATO and the Crisis in the Balkans

Throughout the winter and spring, while NATO contemplated its future, fighting in Yugoslavia intensified despite the efforts of the EC and the UN. By early 1993, some 17,000 people had been killed, 100,000 were missing and 1.7 million were refugees, the largest number of homeless people since the Second World War. The epi-centre of the violence was the city of Sarajevo, in Bosnia, which was under daily bombardment by Serbian gunners. The horror of widespread rape and "ethnic cleansing" perpetrated against Bosnian Muslims evoked memories of the Holocaust, but the in-ternational response was tepid. The strange indifference recalled Mark Twain's view of the weather: "Everyone complains about it," he said, "but no one does anything about it."

Yet here was the threat NATO had been anticipating. This was not a drill. This was not an exercise. After all the murmuring in Brussels about a region of ethnic instability, mass migration and civil strife, here was the triad of evils at work in Yugoslavia. The fighting was not in North Africa or in the Middle East, but in the centre of Europe in NATO's backyard. For the alliance, the war in Yugoslavia should have been a godsend. A fitful, feckless organization now had purpose, a chance to flex its muscles before they atrophied.

At a ministerial meeting on June 4 in Oslo, the alliance con-demned the killing in Yugoslavia and endorsed the diplomatic efforts of the UN, the EC and CSCE. Its most important move was to support the sanctions imposed by the UN on Serbia and Mon-tenegro. "We are determined to make those sanctions effective and will continue to work to ensure that their objective is achieved," the ministers said. Still, NATO offered only moral support. When the United Nations debated armed intervention beyond peace-keeping, NATO was squeamish. An organization eager to trumpet its legions was unwilling to send them into battle. The Secretary General liked to say what NATO could do if given the chance, but as the talking went on, so did the killing.

In July, NATO took a first step in Yugoslavia: it dispatched seven ships to the Adriatic Sea to enforce the economic sanctions intended to stop the flow of materiel fuelling the conflict. Because NATO had no authority to stop and board the merchant ships, its force could be no more than a deterrent and the blockade was ineffective. On November 16, the United Nations voted to tighten the embargo and NATO agreed "to halt, inspect and verify" suspicious cargo. But while the UN had sent 10,000 UN troops to guard the relief convoys bringing food to Sarajevo, the UN and NATO still refused to authorize direct military intervention to halt the Serbian offensive or to supply arms to the Bosnians for self-defence. Woerner said of the alliance's response: "We are still not ready to handle this kind of post-Cold War crisis in a satisfactory way."

This was largely true. The trouble was that the cost of failure in Yugoslavia would be greater for NATO than the UN or the EC, both of which had also narrowly circumscribed their mission. The difference was that neither the UN nor the EC had something to prove, as NATO did. Whatever might be the UN's problems of money or authority, its future was not in question. And whatever the divisions over its direction, the European Community was not going to fade away. NATO had more fundamental problems. The end of the Cold War had affected it more than any other international body. "We don't need Yugoslavia to provide the rationale for our existence," said Woerner. Maybe not. But while Woerner could not admit it — nor could the mandarins determined to keep their jobs in Brussels — Yugoslavia represented a lost opportunity.

Had NATO been shrewder and quicker it could have turned a disaster into an advantage. A well-planned show of force, an early and effective blockade, a surgical aerial bombardment — all might have helped contain the conflict. More aggressively, it might have considered guaranteeing the borders of Eastern Europe, particularly those between Kosovo and Albania, Greece and Macedonia, and Bulgaria and Macedonia.

By early December, NATO did begin drawing up plans to act if the United Nations approved a ban on military flights over Bosnia-Herzegovina. Although there was no political will to deploy combat troops, NATO initially considered using air power to prevent Serbian aircraft from supporting their ground units and to hit Serbian artillery positions outside Sarajevo. To this end, the Netherlands — one of the strongest advocates of a military response — offered to send a squadron of F-16 fighters.

On December 11, at a meeting of NATO defence ministers, Woerner said that the alliance was prepared to intervene in Yugoslavia but only if asked to by the United Nations. He promised "to do what was necessary," including armed intervention. At the same time Woerner warned of the dangers of winter, the threat to UN forces on the ground and the effect on the humanitarian relief effort. Here, then, was NATO's move to intervention — less a step forward than a sliding, shambling and shuffling walk. A week later, the foreign ministers of NATO agreed to "support" the UN in enforcing a flight ban. They did not say how they would enforce the zone or respond to a reported 225 ceasefire violations. The vagueness reflected the alliance's difficulty in reaching a decision. While the United States, supported by Turkey and the Netherlands, had pushed for warplanes to shoot down the Serbian aircraft, the alliance's statement was more ambivalent. This was the politics of restraint, which had characterized NATO's approach from the beginning.

The debate continued in the winter and spring of 1993 as diplomats worked feverishly to forge a peace settlement. Whenever the opportunity arose, Woerner reaffirmed, in louder, more confident tones, NATO's intention to play a role. Whether it would be asked to fight was uncertain, but this willingness reflected a year of soul-searching. In the end, what was emerging was an alliance prepared to act on behalf of the UN or the CSCE because it was best equipped to do so. The Organization that had been formed to stop the advance of Communism was learning to cope with the world created by its collapse.

In more general terms, NATO had already begun broadening its mandate. The rapid reaction strike force of 250,000 soldiers was finally unveiled, although the terms of its use were undecided, and a slimmer, less cumbersome command structure was introduced. The deployment of the Eurocorps was also clarified; in an emergency, it would come under NATO command, ending fears that it would weaken the alliance by reducing the American role. Most important, NATO began drawing up formal plans for joint peacekeeping missions in Europe with the former countries of the Warsaw Pact. By 1993, the prospect of a reborn NATO, engaged in peacekeeping and fire-fighting, cheered its supporters. "We will still have the same vital Atlantic alliance in ten years," predicted Woerner confidently.

Whatever self-congratulation it might engage in, the Organization had a long way to go in ensuring its future. It still refused to consider early admission for Hungary, the Czech Republic and Poland, although that had been urged at the highest levels. Indeed, at his last meeting in December, 1992, U.S. Secretary of Defence Dick Cheney issued a blunt warning to the alliance about its continuing treatment of these new democracies as painted ladies. "A security organization that fails to address those concerns is not going to survive in the long term," he said. Regrettably, no one seemed to be listening.

Canada and NATO'S Future

That NATO was discussing peacekeeping and humanitarian intervention was particularly welcomed by Canada because both policies united its commitment to NATO and its commitment to international peace. The instruments of a reconstituted NATO had long been the instruments of Canadian defence and foreign policy. It was ironic that while Canada was considering a naval blockade or armed intervention in Yugoslavia as a member of NATO, it should find itself there already as a member of the UN peacekeeping force. Here, Canada could show NATO that its dedication to international security was broader than its membership in the alliance. The sceptics could see that as Canada was reducing one role it was increasing another. Fundamentally, it was finding new means to achieve ends NATO itself was now endorsing.

While Canada was reducing its green helmets in Western Europe, it was increasing its blue helmets in Eastern Europe. In April, it sent a contingent of 1,200 peacekeepers to Yugoslavia. Led by General Lewis Mackenzie, Canada secured the airport at Sarajevo and ensured that vital relief flights could land. The Canadians pushed through treacherous mountain passes and past roadblocks manned by twitchy gunners, and the world applauded. Canada also dispatched another 1,200 troops to Croatia, part of a broader effort which included sending observers, policemen and humanitarian assistance. It also accepted 13,000 refugees. This was not only goodwill but an assertion of national interest. "We are not in Yugoslavia by accident," said McDougall. "We are there because peace and security in Europe are essential to peace and security in Canada. We cannot overestimate what Europe means to Canada in terms of our political, economic and even environmental interests."[7]

Canada's eagerness to send more peacekeepers to Yugoslavia reflected its deepest impulses, which showed that NATO's loss could be the UN's gain. Ranking 33rd in the world in population, Canada provided ten percent of the world's peacekeepers, for which the demand was soaring. (In 1992, 4,300 of 45,000 peace makers were Canadians, second only to France.) Of course, Canada could only maintain a presence if its armed forces were adequately funded, which was no certainty anymore. In 1992, for example, Canada began withdrawing its 575 troops from Cyprus, where they had been since 1964.[8] Ottawa concluded that peacekeeping was harming peacemaking and that Greece and Turkey had come to rely too much on outsiders. Peacekeeping had become an end in itself, a substitute, as Barbara McDougall put it, for "political leadership, honourable compromise and negotiation." In leaving Cyprus, Canada was serving notice that such missions could not go on forever. It may be noted that Denmark, another one of the long-standing peacekeepers in Cyprus, also came to the same conclusion. But Canada's decision meant that while the country was withdrawing from NATO in Europe, it was also abandoning a peacekeeping mission which had successfully separated two members of the alliance.

The advantage of pulling out of Cyprus was that it enabled Canada to contribute forces to new or expanded UN missions, such as those in Macedonia, Mozambique and Cambodia. This was an important principle. Had Canada refused more peacekeeping requests in 1992, its withdrawal from NATO would have been a withdrawal from the world, as some feared it would be. But Cyprus was a retreat from peacekeeping, not a reversal. Canada intends to remain a leading peacekeeper, and knowing when to abandon foundering missions will ensure that. Canadians are proud of their role in peacekeeping and will support its expansion, if the request is made to undertake "peace enforcement" in Yugoslavia. It would be a foolish, myopic nation — particularly one that was in a crisis of national unity — that abandoned peacekeeping, the kindest face of its international personality.

The Shaky Prospects for NATO Renewal

As countries lash themselves together, seeking strength in association, international institutions are proliferating. The scaffolding erected after the Second World War is now supporting myriad institutions. Duplication is suddenly a threat to NATO. Like Canada, other members of NATO are seeking ways to cut budgets and find savings. Thus, as NATO tries to reinvent itself — as it must to survive — it will have to become something other than the UN, the EC, the WEU or the CSCE. The challenge will be to make itself demonstrably different. But to recast NATO as a wholly political body, however attractive that might be to a middle power like Canada, risks making it a copy of the EC, the CSCE, even the OECD; and if it is recast as a military body, it is likely to be a copy of the military component of the UN or WEU.

If NATO does not renew itself through an expansion of membership or a redefinition of purpose, it will fall apart in the 1990s. With its mission unclear and its resources drained, the sentry of Europe will stumble in the night. It cannot afford to miss opportunity, as it did in Yugoslavia, or to ignore the question of membership for the ambitious states of Central Europe, clamouring to get in. There are now faint signs that NATO has recognized the danger and has begun rethinking its raison d'être, but will its response be too little, too late? Up to now, its pace of reform has been glacial.

Canada, for its part, sees the future of NATO more clearly. It believes in NATO if necessary, but not necessarily NATO. Thus, it is keeping its options open. Having reduced its premiums, it has shrewdly decided to keep NATO around as an insurance policy. At the same time, it will continue to seek new ways, and new forms, to express its cherished commitment to a broader internationalism.

14 Canada and the Pacific

Brian L. Job and Frank Langdon

Asian states' perceptions of Canada as a minor and part-time player will not be easily overcome. Unlike the U.S., Canada will not automatically be invited to Asia-Pacific consultations. Only by consistently making its presence known, and by taking the lead on issues which directly affect its interests, will Canada be included and taken seriously.

THIS CHAPTER COVERS the international relations of the Asia-Pacific[1] region which are of most concern to Canada. It argues that Canada does not put sufficient effort behind its presence in the region to realize all of the benefits to be gained there both now and in the future. It also argues that, because of its important economic stake in the region, Canada has "security" interests concerning the Asia-Pacific, which may be summarized as any threats to peace and stability in the region that could disrupt regional economic expansion, growing prosperity, and trans-Pacific trade and investment flows. Thus, although the Canadian government has adopted the slogan of "Canada as a Pacific partner" and has stepped up its efforts in the region, this chapter proposes that Canada should adopt policies in the fields of foreign affairs, economics and security that would give more concerted attention to the Asia-Pacific.

The Atlantic-oriented bias that has pervaded Canada's world view in the post-World War Two era needs to be redressed. This bias, natural and even necessary for Canada in the two post-war decades, flowed from traditional cultural linkages and was cemented through the activist foreign policies pursued by the Pearsonian generation in their successful mission to secure a role for Canada in the Western alliance, the United Nations, and other major regional and international organizations. It was sustained by the Canadian business community whose preoccupation with the U.S. has made it slow to recognize, and react aggressively to, other global economic forces such as those in the Asia-Pacific. This is not to deny the efforts of those Canadian business representatives and government officials who have themselves worked in or with East Asia. These individuals have usually been well aware of the importance of the region to Canada and the benefits that could accrue to Canada if its interests there were vigorously and consistently pursued.

This is not an argument for redefining Canada's role as chiefly an Asia Pacific player, i.e., for swinging the pendulum in another direction. The challenge for Canadian leaders is to manage and balance (the key word) a whole series of new relationships in the post-Cold War world, including those with Central and South America. Furthermore, it is naive to assume that Canada can simply take on a predetermined role in the Asia-Pacific context. Asian states' perceptions of Canada as a minor and part-time player will not be easily overcome. Unlike the U.S., Canada will not automatically be invited to Asia-Pacific consultations. Only by consistently making its presence known, and by taking the lead on issues which directly affect its interests, will Canada be included and taken seriously. As one of the advanced economies in the region, and as a country with a strong reputation for effective international relations, Canada has considerable ability to do so. At the moment, the country faces significant difficulties in its domestic preoccupation with national identity, deeply rooted structural problems in its economy, and constraints due to the national deficit which mean few, if any, new financial or bureaucratic resources are available in Ottawa for new policies. However, these are not insurmountable obstacles to the creation of an effective Asia-Pacific policy outlook for Canada.

The present is an unusual time of uncertainty and flux for this region. New international economic and security institutions are evolving to replace the post-war Asia-Pacific order. By the end of the 1990s, however, these new regional institutions and patterns of relationships among Asia-Pacific states are likely to have settled in. Thus, Canada has an interest *now* in ensuring that the evolving regional order develops in ways that facilitate, rather than hinder or destroy, orderly, peaceful economic and political change in a region in which we have important interests. In 1993, this task assumes immediate importance. The American presidency has changed hands. The Japanese prime minister has recently revealed the directions of his country's new policies in Asia, especially towards

Southeast Asia. On the Canadian front, too, recent events have set the stage for action, including the signing of the North American Free Trade Agreement (NAFTA), the report of the Canada-Japan Forum 2000[2] and the successful conclusion of a recent Canadian initiative to promote multilateral security dialogue among Asia-Pacific states. A failure to grasp the opportunities of this decade could easily lead to Canada being counted out of, rather than into, the regional economic, political and security frameworks of the next century.

The balance of this chapter builds upon this line of argument, emphasizing Canadian economic as well as political and security interests in the Asia-Pacific. By way of introduction, however, brief consideration is given to the growing Asian dimension of Canadian society and the relevance of this phenomenon for Canada's foreign relations in the region.

Canadian Society and the Asian Fact

Since 1986, when immigration flows to Canada began to increase again, this country has added around three quarters of one percent (0.75%) each year to its population through the settling of foreigners as landed immigrants. In 1991, total immigration was over 228,500 persons; in the 1981–91 decade, some 1,238,000 persons came to Canada.[3] In historical perspective, this, of course, is not a new experience for Canada, most of whose population is within one or two generations of immigrant stock. What is distinctive about the current flows of people to Canada is the set of countries from which they originate. No longer does the majority of these persons come from the United Kingdom or other parts of Europe. The proportion of immigrants from these "traditional" countries has dwindled dramatically from levels of over 85 percent immediately after World War II to about 20 percent last year. As seen in Figure 14.1, their numbers have been replaced by people from the Americas, Africa, the Middle East, and most especially Asia. Throughout the last decade, the largest single group of immigrants to Canada has come from this last region — almost 50 percent of the total. In 1991 just under 100,000 persons from Asia gained residency in Canada.

When viewed as a cumulative process extending over the last decade and into the next, what we are experiencing is a broadening

Figure 14.1
Sources of Immigration to Canada, 1991

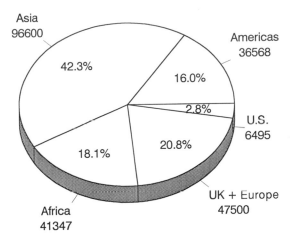

Source: Employment and Immigration Canada, Quarterly Statistics, Jan./Dec. 1991 (preliminary).

Figure 14.2
Destination of Asia-Pacific Immigrants to Canada, 1991

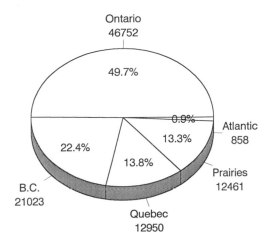

Source: Employment and Immigration Canada, Quarterly Statistics, Jan./Dec. 1991 (preliminary).

of the Canadian multicultural context. In particular, we are adding a significant Asian dimension. Several characteristics of Asian immigration tend to distinguish its societal impact. First of all, the settlement of Asian immigrants across Canada is quite highly concentrated. Almost 90 percent have gone to Quebec, Ontario, and British Columbia (Figure 14.2), and within these provinces have settled in the urban centres of greater Montreal, Toronto, and Vancouver. Second, Canada is attracting most of its investor and entrepreneur immigrants, i.e., its wealthier and business-oriented immigrants, from Asia. These individuals, in turn, have tended to settle in Ontario and British Columbia, with over half of 1991 "investor" immigrants choosing the latter province.[4]

Third, Asian immigration is having a significant impact upon the Canadian economy, in particular on the West Coast economy, but also on Canada's Pacific-oriented economic relationships in general. The single largest group of Asian immigrants to Canada has been from Hong Kong; about 25,000 individuals a year over the last five years. Many in this new Canadian community retain and capitalize upon their extensive familial and financial linkages throughout Asia. Thus, not only is the Canadian economy stimulated directly by their business and investment activity in this country, but Canada also indirectly participates in and benefits from the economic growth in Asia itself, especially in southern China and Taiwan.

To focus solely upon the economic aspect would be to miss the larger importance of the increasing Asian dimension of Canadian society. The growth of well-established, vibrant Asian communities will be felt in numerous ways by other Canadians — socially, economically, and politically. Ethnic Asian communities will seek to preserve their own cultural heritage within the Canadian fabric, just as previous immigrants to this country did and continue to do with their cultures. As a result, social services, education systems, and multiculturalism programs are having to expand their horizons, in both conceptual and practical terms. The impact of the Asian fact on Canadian society will become more pronounced in the next decade, as the cohort of young persons now in schools and universities take up positions in Canadian business and professional life.

However, what is most important for Canadian foreign policy is that new issues are brought on to the agenda and issues already there are given a new focus by Canadian officials and policymakers. For example, the Chinese government's treatment of its own citizens and its relations with Hong Kong have become and will remain of substantial concern to Canada, in part because vocal and politically influential segments of the population will demand that attention be given to this issue. As another example, the influx of Vietnamese refugees into Hong Kong and other Asian locations became a major international issue for Canada, as these people and their temporary providers pressured Canada to accept them in large numbers.[5]

In sum, not only does Canada have to develop new policies regarding the Asia-Pacific because of its national economic, political and security interests, as will be detailed below, but these policies have to be formulated within, and will have to reflect, a changing Canadian domestic context — one that is more attuned to, aware of, and connected with the Asia-Pacific environment.

Economic Aspects of the Asia-Pacific

Observers of world affairs contend that we are about to enter the Pacific Century, an era in which the states of Asia will increasingly determine the prosperity, peacefulness and environmental health of the globe. Such calls for attention to this region reflect a variety of developments and concerns, but particularly those oriented to economic growth, economic opportunities, and economic competition. Before proceeding to these considerations as they specifically concern Canada, certain underlying dimensions of the Asia-Pacific economy need to be reviewed. By the end of the current decade, 60 percent of the world's population, accounting for 50 percent of global production and 40 percent of global consumption, will dwell in the Asia-Pacific. Throughout the 1980s, Asia-Pacific was the only region of the world that sustained consistent economic growth, maintaining an average annual growth rate in excess of five percent. When one looks to future decades, what is even more important than the individual success stories of Japan, South Korea, and the other so-called Asian "tigers" is the broad overall foundation for economic growth established throughout the region. For instance, China has begun a process of economic transformation, which, if it continues at the rate of the last decade, i.e., at 9 percent of GNP growth per annum, could lead to China having one of the largest economies, if not the largest economy, in the world by 2010.[6] India, too, has embarked on dramatic economic reforms which, unless sidetracked by political instability, will make the country a significant member of the regional and global economies within the decade. Trans-Pacific trade, the engine of post-World War II recovery for the region, has been eclipsed by intra-Asian economic relations to such an extent that in 1992 intra-Asian trade exceeded trans-Pacific trade.

Japan figures most prominently in any discussion of the Asia-Pacific economy. It is the richest and most productive of Asian states, the only one to be a member of the Organization of Economic Cooperation and Development (OECD) and of the G-7. It has clearly established itself as a global, and not merely a regional, commercial, financial, and technical leader, having risen from a position in the 1950s in which it had 2 percent of the gross domestic product (GDP) of the world's most advanced countries (i.e., the OECD members), to 20 percent of their combined GDP today. In 1991, Japan's gross national product (GNP) was $4 trillion and that of the U.S. was $6 trillion. Foreign trade is, of course, critically important to the health of the Japanese economy. Japan currently accounts for about five percent of total world trade and, as constantly noted in the media, is running ever-larger trade surpluses with the U.S. ($43.6 billion in 1992), with Canada, and with Southeast Asia ($40 billion in 1991).[7] Structural features of both the Japanese and its trading partners' economies have made it difficult to address these imbalances, especially in the context of the recession of the last several years.

With the ending of the Cold War, Japan has increasingly shown signs of exercising its economic leadership within the Asia-Pacific region. By building economic relations with China and with Vietnam and by concentrating upon its already strong position within Southeast Asia, Japan has taken initiatives to ensure its dominant role in the Asian market place of the next century, and to reduce its future dependence upon access to less hospitable North American markets. Over the last five years a significant shifting of Japan's trading flows has taken place. Asia, rather than North America, is now Japan's largest export and import customer. During the recession of the early 1990s, Japanese foreign direct investment (FDI) declined substantially, but at a slower pace with respect to Southeast Asia than to North America (which for the moment remains the largest destination of Japanese investment.)

While the regional role of Japan has grown, the United States still carries significant weight. Although in the process of apparent long-term economic decline, it remains the region's other major trader and investor and still supplies significant portions of the investment in East Asia. In particular, trade access to the U.S. market is, and will remain, at least throughout this decade, critical to the economic health of Asian states, especially those countries in Southeast Asia which are just beginning to bring their manufacturing and industrial potential on stream. The U.S. has strong economic motives of its own for ensuring peace and stability in the region and for safeguarding the critical economic linkages between itself and key Asian states. What has been difficult for the U.S. president, and may become even more so, is the job of simultaneously fending off narrowly protectionist forces within the U.S. while achieving progress towards more open Asian national markets, particularly in Japan. Whether or not the Clinton Administration can walk this tight rope remains to be seen. There is currently a firming of political trends towards the formation of an East Asian Economic Grouping (EAEG) that could exclude the U.S., Canada, Australia and New Zealand and thus become the basis of a separate (yen) bloc led by Japan in competition with the North America Free Trade Area and the European Community. Washington, together with Ottawa, needs to act quickly to forestall such developments.

The most successful of the East Asian states, aside from Japan, are the new industrial economies (NIEs): Hong Kong, Taiwan, Singapore, and South Korea. Much of their growth was spurred on by aggressive export promotion. The investment and trade activities which the three predominantly Chinese NIEs, led by Hong Kong, have conducted in the central and coastal regions of China, have had a dramatically stimulative effect upon the economy of China as a whole. South Korea has followed the Japanese pattern in its development: the U.S. has played an important role in its recovery and export promotion strategies have been pursued aggressively. The remaining developing East Asian industrial economies (DAIEs) are Malaysia, Thailand, Indonesia, the Philippines, China, Cambodia, and Vietnam. They are in the process of transition to industrialization and regional interdependence. Malaysia and Thailand are the closest to the four NIEs. Laos will probably follow Vietnam, which is eager to improve its economy in spite of the present sanctions imposed by the U.S. Both North Korea and Myanmar are locked into rigid regimes which are unwilling to follow the example of the others in opening up their countries to foreign commerce and foreign presence for fear that such influences would undermine and eliminate their present political regimes.

Russia and China present striking contrasts in the manner in which their leaders have planned and balanced economic and political transformation in their societies. The former, having virtually lost control over economic and political forces, verges on the brink of economic chaos. Of the former Soviet Union, only Russia borders the Pacific. Its Far Eastern provinces have substantial, long-term economic potential but need assistance desperately. Japan appears to be positioning itself strategically for such opportunities. Thus, while their government provides only token humanitarian assistance to Russia (ostensibly because of deadlock with the Russians over the disputed northern territories), Japanese business groups are investing in resource development projects in Siberia and the maritime region. Authorities from Vladivostok have recently visited Canada as well, seeking joint ventures, investment, and aid. China, on the other hand, if able to manage a smooth leadership transition and to cope with the tensions arising from economic disparities within the Chinese population, may continue to head in a different direction. The main concerns of Beijing are that superheated economic activity, accompanied by inflation and by growing regional economic disparities within the Chinese population, will lead to potentially disruptive short-term crises over jurisdiction and control.

The Political Economy of Canada in the Asia-Pacific: Serious Concerns and Policy Priorities

Where does Canada fit into the Asia-Pacific economy? Although it is difficult to assess accurately the size of the Chinese and Russian economies, Canada's economy is probably the fifth largest in the region after those of the U.S., Japan, China and Russia. Canada is a valuable market for Asian exports and could be a source of capital and technology, as well as trade, for East Asian developing countries. Nevertheless, Canada's trans-Pacific economic presence, participation and influence remain far less than its comparative economic size would suggest. Its potential, of course, was greater several decades ago when its economy was larger than Japan's, and Canada was one of the wealthiest advanced countries in the world. While the overall value of Canadian trade has grown, Canada's portion of world trade is declining while its dependence on foreign investment remains. Canada's merchandise trade exports need to exceed imports in order to balance the current account. In the past this happened largely because of the vast amounts of relatively unrefined raw materials, (forest products, minerals, fuels, and agricultural products), that have historically made up the bulk of Canadian sales abroad. Canadians, however, have been concerned that as producers of "rocks and logs," they have not been able to realize the greater value-added profits of manufacturing and high technology production.[8] At the present time, the current account is in deficit, with the positive merchandise trade surplus far smaller than the negative invisible services deficit. As the last several years in Canada have shown, meeting the demands of a globally competitive market-place will require more resources and better methods of education and training, substantial capital investment programs and measures to cope with significant societal dislocation. Finally, Canada has been and will continue to be dependent on the maintenance of an open world economy and therefore upon the successful operation of institutions such as the General Agreement on Tariffs and Trade (GATT), the cornerstone of the liberal international economic order. The impasse of the recent negotiating rounds and the possible breakdown of the GATT, perhaps a higher probability event after the election of Bill Clinton in the U.S., has serious implications for Canada. If the exclusionary practices of trading blocs, such as the existing European Community (EC) or future blocs, e.g., the NAFTA or an East Asian bloc, were to dominate the international trading system, this would be a blow for Canada, which would like to maintain and expand its trade beyond North America. (The U.S. alone already accounts for over two thirds of Canadian exports and imports.)

In this context, Canada looks to the Asia-Pacific as an attractive economic partner, especially as a region in which the relative payoffs for an increased economic presence could be very high.

Figure 14.3
Canadian Exports to the Asia-Pacific, 1989–91

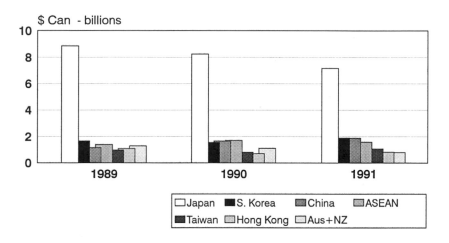

Source: Statistics Canada.

Figure 14.4
Canadian Imports from the Asia-Pacific, 1989–91

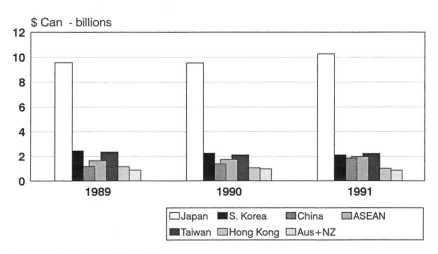

Source: Statistics Canada.

Canada's relationships with its key Asian trading partners for 1989–91 are set out in Figures 14.3 and 14.4. About 15 percent of Canada's imports and 10 percent of its exports are accounted for in this regional trade. While Canadian imports from the Asia-Pacific have increased, Canadian exports have decreased, with the net result being a negative balance of trade for 1991 of roughly Can. $5 billion.[9] Canada's most important trading partner in Asia is Japan, which accounts for roughly half of Canada's regional trade, and about 5 and 7.5 percent respectively of Canada's overall exports and imports. The most dramatic increases over this three-year period were registered in trade with China, which in 1992 is likely to surpass Taiwan as Canada's second-biggest Asian trading partner.[10]

Among the provinces within Canada, British Columbia has the largest trans-Pacific trade. Over two thirds of its trade is with Japan alone. B.C. was also the province which had the smallest proportion of its total external trade with the United States. With its large and growing Asian population, B.C. is the Canadian province with the closest ties to the dynamic East Asian subregion not only geographically, economically and politically but culturally as well.

When Canada considers its future economic relationships with the Asia-Pacific, three developments are of particular concern. Canada's first serious concern is its trade with the Asia-Pacific — the decline in its competitiveness and in the demand for its chief exports, i.e., natural resource products. A continuing trend of increasing trade deficits with the region is not healthy. Certainly, Canadian exports can become marginally more attractive as the value of the Canadian dollar falls. However, this is not a solution to the general problem of finding ways for Canada (a) to increase the value-added components of its natural resource products, while still sustaining demand for them, and (b) to increase the volume of manufactured goods, high technology equipment, and services sold across the Pacific.

Foreign investment represents a second concern. Canadian governments have wanted to increase foreign investment in Canada and to convince foreigners that this is a good place to invest. In fact, the Bank of Canada has worked to keep the dollar at a high value to attract investors and to keep down the rate at which Canada must borrow abroad in order to finance and service its foreign debt. The only important source of foreign investment funds in Asia-Pacific, aside from the U.S., is Japan. The outflow of funds from the latter country reached flood-like proportions in 1988 and 1989, after the G-7 economic ministers induced Japan to revalue its currency upwards. This enabled prize North American assets to be sold "cheaply" and encouraged indirect investment of enormous proportions. By March, 1992, Japanese portfolio investment in Canadian stocks and bonds reached \$49 billion, about \$3 billion higher than 1991.[11] There are two disquieting aspects to this picture. Canada is a relatively less attractive place for Japanese foreign direct investment (FDI) than is the U.S. From 1987 to 1989, the U.S. received an average of 45 percent of Japan's total FDI, but Canada received only 1.2 percent, 2.0 percent, and 1.3 percent for those years — that is significantly less than the 10 percent ratio that is usually applied when comparing the economies of the U.S. and Canada. Also, Japanese FDI in North America has fallen off dramatically in the last two years. In part, this is due to the severe business recession in Japan; but it also reflects the fact that the Japanese are increasingly viewing Southeast Asia as a more attractive environment for their investment.

Canadian government efforts have been concentrated on attracting foreign investment to Canada, not on directing Canadian investment to East Asia. Nevertheless, direct investment is an important concomitant of the trade that Canada hopes to secure by competing more effectively in Asian markets. Half of Canada's trans-Pacific trade is with Japan, and this indicates how important it is for the Canadian business community, if it wishes to maintain a substantial presence in Japan, simply to keep up with production methods and techniques and to stay abreast of market trends. However, Canadian direct investment in Japan is miniscule, only a couple of hundred million dollars — not enough to enable Canadians to collect the information on Japanese production they need, to manufacture in Japan themselves, to understand market conditions, or to find out how to compete with some of the world's most dynamic firms. The Canadian business presence has been, in practical terms, minimal to date, with certain exceptions such as the Council of Forest Industries of British Columbia, which maintains a Tokyo office. Canadian business attitudes are changing and the community is increasingly well-organized and active, assisted by the Canadian government through the expanded services of its new Tokyo embassy and the opening of consulates in most regional Japanese centres.

The third major Canadian concern is the danger that antagonistic trade and financial blocs throughout the world will undermine or replace the present relatively open international economic order. The principal threat presented by the nascent economic blocs is that they will gradually eliminate the relatively liberal global trading regime fostered by the GATT. Non-member countries fear that these blocs will reduce or exclude their trade and investment as a natural consequence of the increased trade among the members, their increased protectionism against outsiders, and their policies of subsidization which may give their products unfair advantages in global markets. Already, from Ottawa's perspective, the European Community, in conjunction with the former European Free Trade Area, not only leads a bloc of countries in Europe but also, under the terms of the Lomé Agreement, an additional group in Africa, as well as island nations in the Caribbean and South Pacific. Such a bloc presents impediments to Canadian trade and creates market problems for Canada through the agricultural subsidization policies of its members. In general, the growing fear is that a combination of factors, including severe friction over trade issues between the U.S., Europe, and Japan, will collapse the GATT negotiations and bring about self-defeating trade wars in which Canada, as a minor player, will not be able to maintain its position. More particularly regarding Asia, the concern in both Ottawa and Washington is that a trading bloc of Asian states will take form. Already the states of the Association of South East Asian Nations (ASEAN) have undertaken to establish themselves as a free trade area, and certain Southeast Asian leaders, especially Malaysian Prime Minister Mahathir have called for the establishment of an East Asian Economic Grouping or Caucus (EAEC) that would exclude the U.S., Canada, Australia and New Zealand. Japan and other states have publicly disavowed interest in any such association, but, as the negotiations on GATT have soured and as the dialogue with Washington has threatened to become more fractious, there have been subtle signals, including those given by Prime Minister Miyazawa during his recent visit to Southeast Asia, that Japan may begin to consider such a grouping more seriously.

From the Asian perspective, an additional reason for considering the formation of their own trading group is the creation of the NAFTA. Despite Canadian and U.S. assurances, this agreement is perceived as having discriminatory potential. For Ottawa, the NAFTA actually poses two sorts of dilemmas related to Asia. Canada not only has to convince Asia-Pacific states that the NAFTA does not hold the potential for excluding their access to North America; it must also protect its interests inside a NAFTA to ensure that member states, particularly the U.S., do not overtly or covertly structure their shared continental environment in such a way as to present the U.S. as a more attractive, less bureaucratically hassled place in which to invest than Canada. Recent U.S. behaviour concerning Honda plants in Canada that ship auto parts across the border cannot be seen as reassuring in this regard, either in Ottawa or Tokyo.

As a counter to the tendency of bloc formation to split the Pacific, the principal organizations which tie the Pacific Rim countries together are the Pacific Economic Co-operation Council (PECC) and the Asia Pacific Economic Co-operation (APEC) group. PECC is non-governmental (with officials acting in unofficial capacities); APEC has regular meetings of foreign economic and foreign ministers. Canada is active in both organizations. While the two organizations are mainly concerned with economic and political problems, proposals have been made to handle security matters in APEC, as the ASEAN Post-Ministerial Conference began to do in 1992.

In sum, two significant developments are occurring which are relevant to Canada's economic relations in the Asia-Pacific: first, Asia appears likely to continue as the economic engine of the world economy; second, increasing concentration of this activity within the framework of an Asian-oriented grouping could have troubling consequences for Canada, which, it can be argued, is already falling behind in the race to share in the growth and prosperity of the region.

The Evolving Asia-Pacific Security Order[12]

In the last two years, Ottawa has come to the realization that the maintenance of a stable and peaceful security order in the Asia-Pacific is important to Canada, first because the region's economic prosperity and growth is contingent upon the absence of hot or cold wars, and second because key elements of the success of several of Canada's major international policy goals, e.g., control of weapons proliferation, protection of human rights, and strengthened UN peacekeeping capacity, depend on what happens in the post-Cold War environment of the Asia-Pacific. This conclusion has in turn led to recent deliberations over the nature of Canada's security interests, broadly conceived, in the Asia-Pacific, particularly in the North Pacific. This is not a security policy debate in the traditional sense of an argument about the pros and cons of extending force commitments. Clearly, there is no relevant Canadian role of this sort to be played in Asia, nor is it feasible to envisage substantially enhanced Canadian Pacific naval capabilities. The questions being asked instead are whether or not Canada should play any role in the Asia-Pacific security context. If it should, does it have any comparative advantages to bring to bear? And finally, are there realistic possibilities for the establishment of multilateral processes that would advance the creation of an Asia-Pacific security community? A brief review of the parameters of the security context of the Asia-Pacific is in order before we focus directly on Canadian interests and policy options.

Asia-Pacific security relationships have never been strictly a bipolar affair, even during the Cold War; they have always been complex and multilayered — that is, local rivalries and the policies adopted to repel and deter local rivals have tended to spill over to complicate subregional and regional security relationships and vice versa. While almost all analysts are in agreement that the region is currently undergoing a transition towards multipolarity, they remain uncertain about the structure of this future regional system. Concerns are expressed about "power vacuums," ambitious regional powers, and the risks inherent in an "unbalanced" security environment. While international relations in the Asia-Pacific have become less dangerous, they are at the same time more unstable.[13]

The end of the Cold War, which in Asia was really the ending of two Cold Wars — between the U.S. and the Soviet Union, and between the Soviet Union and China, has brought significant change to the Asia-Pacific. Long-standing bilateral and subregional disputes have been settled, (e.g., China-Russia, and, albeit tentatively, Cambodia). Relations, official and unofficial, have been opened or revitalized across ideological barriers (e.g., South Korea with China and with Russia, Japan with Vietnam), largely on the basis of economic considerations. That perennial tension point, the Korean Peninsula, remains; but, here too, matters are proceeding in the direction of conflict resolution and non-aggression.

With these changes, however, have come uncertainties about the way in which the major powers in the region will define their new roles within this new post-Cold War, post-Gulf War environment. So far none of the leading countries, the U.S., China, Russia or Japan has been able to articulate its new roles in ways that have reduced ambiguity and removed doubts about its future commitments and goals. For Russia, this is perhaps most understandable, given that internal struggles over economic reform and the future of parliamentary rule have effectively paralyzed any sustained and coherent foreign policymaking process. Apart from concerns over the future of its residual nuclear capabilities and over the prospects of ethno-nationalist conflict overlapping its eastern boundaries in Central Asia, the current view of Russia is that it is not a player in Asia-Pacific security considerations.

Now that the U.S. is no longer worried by a Soviet threat, it lacks the strong incentive to continue provision of the expensive post-war security framework in the region—a framework which sustained U.S. dominance by maintaining the Pacific as an "American lake," and which gave Asian states a security umbrella under which their economic recovery could proceed without disruption and free of the burden of spending scarce resources on their own defence. Within key sectors of Washington, however, traditional policies and attitudes towards the Pacific are deeply engrained and resist rethinking. Thus, the U.S. has sought to assert its continued leadership position, while at the same time speaking of strategies of military drawdown, and complaining about defence burden sharing and unfair trading practices. The Bush administration's rather confused and fumbling efforts towards an Asia-Pacific policy were, as a result, characterized as "procrustean" and schizophrenic.[14] In the eyes of the American public, the real "threat" from the Pacific in the 1980s was the economic threat posed by the U.S.'s former Cold War allies—the "enemy" of the U.S. economy causing the displacement of American industry and employment.[15] With Bill Clinton's election signaling a rejection of Bush administration policies and a mandate for a

more domestically oriented and proactive economic foreign policy, the future of U.S. security arrangements and of U.S. economic
relationships with Asian states may be quite clouded.

Japan continues to hold to its defence relationship with the
U.S. — which both parties have seen as the "lynchpin" of the Asia-
Pacific security order — because it continues to regard this as the
most efficient mechanism for protecting Japan's current security
interests. The assumption of a new role in the post-Cold War
world is proving exceedingly difficult for Japan, because there is a
deadlock in its political system over defence and military matters,
and because any initiatives stir up worries throughout the region
about a resurgent and remilitarized Japan, as, for example, on the
occasion when the Japanese took on UN peacekeeping responsibilities in Cambodia. However, signs indicate that the Japanese
will be unwilling to sit on the sidelines and to confine their potential influence within the strictures of a U.S.-dominated partnership
for much longer, especially if trade disputes come to overshadow
their overall relationship. An example is the recent visit of Prime
Minister Miyazawa to Southeast Asia, on which occasion he made
it clear that Japan, as part of its strategy for achieving a more independent voice, would more actively support and participate in
the development of ASEAN's multilateral security agenda.

China, on the other hand, has sent clearer, but perhaps the
most troubling, signals about its regional role ambitions. With
the end of the Cold War, China is anxious (a) to avoid becoming part of any unipolar, U.S.-led global order, and (b) to assume
what it regards as its appropriate place within the geopolitical
context of the Asia-Pacific. Tension is also growing between the
U.S. and China over Beijing's violations of human rights, the reluctance of the U.S. Congress to extend most-favoured-nation trade
treatment, the arms race between China and Taiwan, and China's
contribution to weapons proliferation in the Middle East. China's
aggressive policy over the South China Sea islands and its air and
naval buildup puts it into confrontation with the Southeast Asian
nations, including Vietnam. To many observers, China appears
poised to assert regional leadership despite global pressures to
desist.

The prospect of leadership change in the key states of China,
North Korea and Vietnam only serves to complicate the picture.

In each case, aging leadership cohorts are attempting simultaneously to manage economic reform and to ensure that their political systems remain in place. This is almost certainly a vain hope in all three societies.

As far as weapons, and the militarism that surrounds their acquisition and deployment, are concerned, the Asia-Pacific region is distressingly "out of synch" with post-Cold War trends. With the exception of Russia and the U.S., defence budgets and military buildup continue to increase throughout the region — a region that is already highly militarized.[16] Even if we disregard North Korea's possible intention of acquiring nuclear weapons, there remain three nuclear powers in the region, the U.S., Russia, and China, and five nuclear actors if India and Pakistan are included. More troubling, however, are the volume and types of conventional weaponry that are being introduced into the region. China, for instance, by building up a blue water navy and acquiring in-air refuelling capacities appears bent on heightening substantially its ability to project its power. Smaller, but wealthy, actors like Taiwan and the states of Southeast Asia are accumulating large quantities of state-of-the-art weaponry, especially fighter aircraft, offering a disquieting prospect of nascent arms races.

Proliferation, a topic of priority for Canadian governments, remains a key problem. Within the region there is a volatile combination of states interested in acquiring weapons, e.g., China, Taiwan, with those that are highly motivated to sell almost any weapon or technology in order to gain hard currency, e.g., Russia, China, and North Korea. Stopping this activity will be very difficult. China has ignored pressures for termination of the sale of weapons; in Russia stopping the flow of weapons and the leakage of technology is probably beyond the capacity of the state. As is demonstrated by the recent U.S. sale of 150 F-16s to Taiwan, the profit and employment motives for states with large, established defence industries are potent forces in domestic political arenas.

But it is economics to which most analysts return when discussing the future security order of the Asia-Pacific. Over the next decade, economic factors and forces are seen as likely to exercise the most disruptive effects on the domestic and international relations in the region. The process of economic reform, certainly on the scale undertaken throughout Asia, is by its very nature a tenuous one. Societies have been radically disrupted. Governments are faced with the conflicting tasks of undertaking structural reform while increasing the supply of consumer goods, maintaining political control while simultaneously opening their societies to the presence and influence of foreigners, and managing conditions of economic disparity within and across their borders. China, India, Russia, Vietnam, and North Korea are all engaged in processes of economic transformation. For the Asian governments involved, Russia serves as an example of the anathema, i.e., failed economic reform coupled with loss of order. Thus, as has been seen in China, leaders will attempt to nurture economic restructuring while still clinging to authoritarian political systems. Already one can see signs of internal tensions between the rich south and the poorer northern interior. So-called "natural economic zones," centered upon Hong Kong and Taiwan and therefore detracting from Beijing's leadership, are flourishing in southern and coastal China — much to the concern of Chinese authorities.

In sum, there are portents of a possible, long-term deterioration of the security environment in the Asia-Pacific region. In the shorter term, there are two trouble-spots of particular concern, the Korean Peninsula and Indochina. Despite the promising initiatives in both North and South Korea that are aimed at limited co-operation, North Korea's loss of both Chinese and Russian support, which is going to South Korea, has apparently spurred its efforts to obtain nuclear weapons and longer-range missiles for its defence. As a result, it has come in the last two years into direct confrontation with the U.S., South Korea, and Japan. In Cambodia the promising Paris Accords and the efforts of the United Nations Transitional Authority (UNTAC) to restore peace are jeopardized by the resurgence and defiance of the Khmer Rouge. Not only are peace and stability threatened but also the larger reputation of the U.N. as an effective peacekeeping, if not peacemaking, institution in the post-Cold War, post-Gulf War, order.

To date, the solutions to security problems in the post-Cold War period have been tentative, relying on bilateral arrangements (e.g., Russia and China) and on subregional solutions, as in Korea and Cambodia. However, as is apparent in Indochina, these arrangements, in the absence of either regional security leadership or any solid multilateral framework to sustain and enforce commitments, can be very fragile. In conditions where the U.S. or other strong countries are no longer interested in guaranteeing the security of smaller allies through onerous and expensive policies of deterrence and forward defence, the smaller powers perceive a need to look to themselves and to each other for support. Hence, the prospect of regional multilateral security arrangements has become increasingly important and attractive to the smaller regional powers, especially in Southeast Asia. However, the major powers such as the U.S., Japan, and China, and possibly Russia, are reluctant to open themselves up to regularized multilateral consultation or joint action with the smaller countries.

Middle and smaller powers, like Australia, Malaysia and South Korea, have been advocating more extensive multilateral, co-operative security arrangements in the region. The ASEAN states have made the most direct moves in this sense, by beginning to include security matters overtly in their annual foreign ministers' meeting and to host conferences following on their post-ministerial meetings and involving the EC, U.S., Canada, Australia, New Zealand, and Japan as dialogue partners. In 1992 China, Russia, and Vietnam were also invited to some of the two sessions and to other informal ASEAN meetings.

In addition, the attitude of the U.S. and Japan is gradually becoming less overtly opposed to regular regional security strategies. U.S. official statements acknowledge the utility, even the necessity, of *ad hoc* multilateral coalitions to address crises; and according to U.S. unofficial stances exploratory steps towards multilateralism are viewed as positive. Japan, perhaps seeing the possibility that its relationship with the U.S. might be better managed in multilateral contexts, is responding quite favourably to ASEAN initiatives (as noted above) and is more receptive to proposals by Canada and Australia for more specifically focused North Pacific multilateral security fora.

Canada's Political and Security Interests in the Asia-Pacific

What does this all add up to for Canada, a country that has seldom been concerned with Pacific security during the Cold War, except to the extent that Soviet strategic nuclear forces threatened its territory? In contrast to its acceptance of an active security role in the Atlantic and Europe as a member of the North Atlantic Treaty Organization (NATO), Canada has been content to leave Pacific defence and Asian security management up to the U.S. Canada did take part in the Korean War, but this was essentially an extension of the Euro/Atlantic Cold War. Asia has also been the locus for Canadian peacekeeping and supervisory roles in Korea and Indochina, but these proved frustrating and accomplished little. Today, while Canada's economic stake in the region is obvious, it may be asked whether it necessarily follows that Canada has "security interests" in the region. The argument increasingly heard from analysts and from Ottawa is "yes," provided that one looks at Canada's "security interests" in the broader context required in the post-Cold War era. Put in another way, if one defines Canada's primary interests in security as the advancement of "co-operative security,"[17] and one considers that Canada's interests lie in being perceived as an effective actor in Asia-Pacific, the answer is "yes."

To be more direct, we posit that Canada has the following national interests concerning the Asia-Pacific:

- the advancement of Canadian trade and economic relations, and increased integration with East Asia through the maintenance of open regional economic systems;
- the maintenance of stable domestic, subregional, and regional environments in the Asia Pacific — environments of peaceful change in relations between ethnic and nationalist communities as well as states;
- the advancement of democratization and openness of government, in a framework of institutions that respect human life and freedoms — reflecting the long-standing Canadian concern for the advancement of human rights, broadly conceived;
- the improvement of the prosperity and well-being of populations;
- the employment of environmentally sound, sustainable development practices that conserve national and international resources; and most generally
- the creation of a security community — or security communities — in the region, involving decreased emphasis on military solutions to security concerns, resolution of proliferation problems, multilateral security dialogue and peaceful resolution of disputes.

When stated in this fashion, several conclusions can be drawn: First, Canada's security interests in the Asia-Pacific derive from its economic stakes in the region. That is, the "security" of Canada is seen to be advanced through the maintenance of stable economic and political conditions in the Asia-Pacific, conditions that facilitate the achievement of economic prosperity within Canada itself and conditions that remove the incentive to employ non-peaceful instruments of change. Canada cannot afford to remove itself from the security picture in the Asia-Pacific on the grounds that its interests are exclusively economic. As noted above, economic policy and security policy are not separable for the states in the region, either in their domestic affairs or in their foreign relations; (economic assistance, for instance, is a component of Japan's security policy in its relations with Russia, Vietnam, China, and North Korea). As a consequence, Asian states do not view such a separation as feasible or responsible for a state seeking to be an informed and engaged regional player. Finally, Canada cannot effectively promote a sense of community and of co-operative security in the region if it attempts at the same time to define its own relationships within the region narrowly, that is on premises contrary to its own stated broad definition of security.

It is, however, one thing to say that Canada has interests and another to say what can be done to advance them. The agenda for action in the Asia-Pacific context could be seen as overwhelming. Obviously, Canada should not spend its time either in spreading itself too thinly, trying to take on too many issues with too few resources, or overreaching itself by trying to assume a role larger than necessary or than would be accepted by its Asian counterparts. In other words, Canadian policies must be implemented with an eye to the following criteria: they are seen to advance Canadian interests directly; they are perceived as relevant and useful by the players in the region; and they are feasible within the constraints of Canadian finances and human resources, including the limited resources of the Department of External Affairs and International Trade Canada, and the Department of National Defence, the Canadian International Development Agency (CIDA) and related agencies.

What might be seen as Canada's "comparative advantages" that are relevant to the security relations of the Asia-Pacific? Where might Asian states expect Canada to be an involved player, or even to take the lead, in addressing outstanding problems? In an interesting way, Canada's history of effective diplomacy in multilateral contexts, including the UN and NATO, and especially in dealing with the U.S., is viewed by Asian states such as Japan and Korea as relevant to their own circumstances. More specifically, Canada is viewed as having particular expertise and resources relevant to the Asian scene — in peacekeeping, verification, surveillance, monitoring and associated confidence-reinforcing technologies, — in the organization, design, and delivery of development assistance programs. Thus, the Japanese have consulted with the Canadian military on peacekeeping training and with CIDA and the International Development and Research Centre on development aid; South Koreans have held workshops with Canadian experts with a view to introducing inspection regimes into the Korean Peninsula; and Canadian logistical planners have been involved in setting up the United Nations Transitional Authority (UNTAC) in Cambodia. Further specific application of Canadian expertise in the security field might be expected in resolving border disputes, in settling maritime claims, and more generally, over the long term, in the resource management, environmental regulation, and sustainable development areas. In this vein, CIDA has already established consultative projects in China.

The larger issue, however, is what policies should Canada take on for the purpose of fostering the establishment of the Asia-Pacific security community. Initial steps in this direction have been taken, beginning in 1990, when Joe Clark, as Secretary of State for External Affairs, began to promote what was labelled a "Canadian initiative for a North Pacific co-operative security dialogue" (NPCSD). The basic thrust of this initiative was to assert a more visible Canadian presence in the region "commensurate with its political and economic interests and its proven multilateral capabilities."[18] In effect, Clark's objective was to initiate the preliminary moves that could begin to nurture a security community in the subregion. Emphasis was placed on building slowly, on establishing working relationships among formerly non-communicating members of the subregion, on creating a "habit of dialogue," and on looking to the evolution from bilateral to multilateral co-operative security arrangements to fill the institutional vacuum of the North Pacific. Such an approach anticipated spill-over effects from other sectors into the more traditional security arena. This spill-over could be geographic; for example, the gradual extension of southern Pacific multilateralism northward, as in ASEAN's consultative process; or it could be functional, e.g., building upon the co-operation developed in economic organizations like APEC.

The Canadian strategy for an NPCSD was a novel enterprise in itself, (at least for Canada), in that it adopted a "two-track" approach: the first track involving governmental officials and the ongoing conduct of official diplomacy, the second track engaging non-governmental experts in interchange and debate on the wide range of co-operative security issues relevant to the North Pacific. On the first track, some Canadian diplomatic missions in Asia were concerned about the utility of taking on a "security dialogue" file in capitals where it would be received, at least initially, with scepticism. On the other hand, the second track, intended to lead to the building of informational bases and networks and to promote more sophisticated understanding of national attitudes and perceptions on Asian security matters among academics, expert analysts, and informed publics, was characterized by enthusiastic activity. Key second-track activities included a series of workshops held in Ottawa, Beijing, Honolulu, and Yokohama. A follow-up meeting is scheduled for Vancouver in March, 1993.

In the time elapsed since Clark's announcement, events have pushed forward the prospects for multilateral security consultations in the Asia-Pacific much more quickly than Ottawa could have imagined in 1990. To see how dramatically attitudes changed one only need consider the Bush-Gorbachev initiatives to remove all short-range and tactical nuclear weapons from their forces, especially those on Pacific naval forces. On the Korean Peninsula, the North and the South met to negotiate and, while serious divisions remain, a process leading to non-aggressive relations appears established. The ASEAN states have sought to expand considerably the scope of their security consultations so as to include, in one capacity or another, almost all states in the region. Indeed, the general attitude of most players has become more receptive towards the goal of multilateral consultation and consideration of frameworks for Asia-Pacific security. This should not be taken to mean that matters have progressed to the point where a multilateral, official institutional forum for the region as a whole or for the North Pacific subregion is in the cards. Certainly, both the U.S. and the Japanese, although their unofficial views are increasingly supportive, would not sanction such initiatives in their official statements. While Russia, and probably South Korea, would be eager to participate, Chinese reluctance to be involved could be assumed as well.

Ottawa is left, therefore, with the consideration of what steps should next be taken to advance its multilateralist agenda. Indications are that it recognizes the validity and relevance of participation in Asia-Pacific security and will continue the process commenced with the NPCSD.[19] This process will, however, go forward without a specific banner like the NPCSD and will not be focused exclusively on the North Pacific. A more general regional approach will be adopted, in line with the direction of recent moves by the Southeast Asian states and the policy interests of players like Australia, which largely share Canadian interests in advancing co-operative security in the Asia-Pacific. Ottawa will, of course, continue to support the ASEAN process and will be especially interested to see how the Japanese follow through on their recent endorsement of ASEAN as a regional forum for security consultation and on their call for the establishment of a commission for Indochina. Canada is also likely to be supportive of efforts to have APEC become a more active player on matters where there are security implications for economic relations and development. So far, however, the states which have mentioned APEC in this light, e.g., the U.S. and Japan, have not gone beyond making general, positive statements about the organization's potential, and Canada is unlikely to observe the lead on this front. Sustaining the momentum of the vigorous second-track approach commenced with the NPCSD will be a priority of Ottawa, which, while a bit nervous at times about academics and researchers "getting ahead" of the officials in their respective capitals, has realized the long-term advantages of having in place, and being able to call upon, a network of non-official experts with sophisticated knowledge about Asia-Pacific affairs.

However proactive Canada might be in advocating regional and subregional multilateral security consultation, the pace of these efforts will be dependent upon responses and attitudes in Beijing, Washington, Seoul, and Tokyo. But on more focused issues, Canada can bring relevant expertise to the two or three parties directly involved and progress is not so dependent upon orchestrating multi-party agreement. Accordingly, it appears that Ottawa is interested in becoming a more active player in respect to such security-related issues in the Asia-Pacific. Signs of this are found in Canadian participation in the Cambodian settlement, Canadian support for negotiations on maritime dispute settlements in the South China Sea, and in the initiatives mentioned in the recently completed Canada-Japan 2000 Report (most notably a proposal to establish a peacekeeping academy on the Canadian west coast).[20]

Finally, a necessary word about how the Canadian government's stated priority of the advancement of democracy, good government, and human rights is applied to the Asia-Pacific context. Advocacy of human rights has proven to be, and will remain, a contentious issue in Canada's relations with Asia, not only with those states labelled as violators, but more generally with the majority of Asian countries which do not agree with Western attempts to publicize and to use punitive measures — actions that they believe hinder, rather than enhance, the prospects for domestic change and regional harmony. The current Canadian government has sought to single out in "public diplomacy" countries like China and Myanmar. At the 1992 ASEAN Post-Ministerial Consultations, Barbara McDougall, for instance, not only singled out these countries for their poor human rights records, she chided the Association as a whole for not placing on its agenda an open discussion of the failures of the government of Myanmar. In response, ASEAN ministers signalled their views on this matter in their Joint Communiqué which stated that "environmental and human rights concerns should not be made as conditionalities in economic and development co-operation. . . . [B]asic human rights, while universal in character, are governed by the distinct culture and history of, and socioeconomic conditions in each country and that their expression and application . . . are within the competence and responsibility of each country."[21]

On the matter of human rights, Ottawa and Washington have generally seen eye to eye, with U.S. officials also pressuring the Asians to adopt a tougher policy towards countries like China and Myanmar. George Bush, however, had to fight hard to restrain the U.S. Congress from taking more aggressive actions against China. Congress tried to force Bush to withdraw most-favoured-nation status for China in order to punish it for the violations of human rights during and after the Tiananmen massacre. The new presidential administration may be both more vocal and tougher on human rights issues. During the election campaign, Clinton intimated that he would take specific steps to penalize China both for its human rights record regarding political dissidents and for related employment practices of state-owned enterprises.

Conclusion

Recently, the Canada-Japan Forum 2000 reported that Canadians and Canadian organizations familiar with and concerned about Japan overwhelmingly informed them that "the Canadian public did not attach adequate importance to the Canada-Japan relationship." They also noted that, "few Canadians seem to be aware of the consequences of such a relationship to their personal lives."[22] Certainly, if this is accurate regarding Canadians and their understanding of Japan, it is likely to be even more true of the Canadian public's appreciation of the remainder of the Asia-Pacific region.

It is, therefore, particularly important for Canada to reverse its reluctance to get more involved in the Asia-Pacific region and to adopt a more active and balanced foreign policy towards this important part of the globe. The success of the Clark initiative, for instance, confirms the value of such approaches and emphasizes the necessity for Canada to adopt perspectives that take account of the interrelated character of security and economic developments in the region. As was stated in our introduction, it is important that Canada not "drop the ball" at this moment. The momentum towards multilateralism in regional security affairs, both as a norm and as a process, is building. The Japanese government has already given, and the Clinton Administration is likely to give, an additional boost to this process that would be an important signal and energizer for the Asian states. It would be unfortunate, therefore, if at this juncture Canada was not seen as an involved participant. The process could and would readily go forward without Canada. If it did, the longer-term outlook for Canada's role in the Asia-Pacific would become less favorable.

The assessments in this chapter lead to the conclusion that Canada must conduct international relations with Asia-Pacific states which are *inclusive, engaging,* and *multilateral*. It is important for Canada to be included, i.e., to avoid being excluded from economic, political and security fora relevant to its interests. Perceptions of Canada as an outsider need to be countered. Being engaged means being consulted and being allowed to shape, rather than react to, policy initiatives. Multilateral contexts provide the most effective arenas for such inclusion and engagement. They are attractive to Canada because of its experience and tradition of effective diplomacy in such contexts and because, for a middle power, they are seen to provide increased opportunities for leverage and coalition building.

On the economic front, Canada has lost too much time preparing to deal competitively with the present East Asia, to say nothing of that region as it will be in the future. While the U.S. will continue to be the single most important influence upon Canadian policies, as it too focuses increased attention upon the Asia-Pacific, Canada will be drawn both directly and indirectly into closer economic and political interaction across the Pacific. Japan's importance to Canada will continue to grow. Its economy may well continue to sprint ahead, while the U.S. falls behind in a long-term decline. If the Asia-Pacific remains politically stable and comparatively peaceful, and the 1991–92 economic slowdown abates, East Asia could well become the sort of centre of the world's attention — economically, politically, and militarily — that Europe used to be.

Because we need whatever economic stimulus we can find in our external environment to help us reverse our internal economic malaise, East Asia, as the most significant area of dynamic growth, becomes critical to Canada. At present, there is a particular urgency about making a national effort to undertake effective policies towards, and in, this region. Canada has waited passively, except in a few notable cases, for Asian businessmen to come to us for our resource products and to bring their products to us. It is time for Canadians, in the public and private sectors, to bestir themselves and to confront the necessity and opportunities that will be presented by the twenty-first century in the Asia-Pacific.

Endnotes

Chapter One:

[No notes.]

Chapter Two:

1 See Peter Cook, "Referendum stalls recovery by at least six months" *The Globe and Mail*, October 26, 1992, pp. B1 and B4. Whereas a rise in interest rates immediately translates into postponed (and perhaps foregone) consumption and investment spending, a lower value for the dollar stimulates Canadian exports only after some time delay due to reaction lags, costs of adjusting production.

2 See Alexis Jacquemin, "Strategic Competition in a Global Environment," in *Trade, Investment and Technology in the 1990s* (Paris: Organization for Economic Cooperation and Development, 1991), p. 21.

3 For a detailed analysis of the federal government's "Competitiveness Agenda," see Michel Demers, "Responding to the Challenges of the Global Economy: The Competitiveness Agenda," in F. Abele, ed., *How Ottawa Spends, 1992–93* (Ottawa: Carleton University Press, 1992), pp. 151–190.

4 In Irene K. Ip and William B.P. Robson, "Avoiding a Crisis," *Proceedings of a Workshop on Canada's Fiscal Outlook* (Toronto: C.D. Howe Institute, February 1993), p. 11.

5 See Alan Freeman, "Japan frets over Canada's debt," *The Globe and Mail*, February 11, 1993, pp. B1 and B14.

6 For an analysis of the interrelationship between budget deficits and monetary policy see Fanny S. Demers, "The Department of Finance and the Bank of Canada: The Fiscal and Monetary Policy Mix," in Abele, *How Ottawa Spends, 1992–93*, pp. 79–124.

7 "U.S. auto makers drop dumping complaint," *The Globe and Mail*, February 10, 1993, p. B6.

8 See "U.S. talks tough on European trade," *The Globe and Mail*, February 2, 1993, p. B1; "Protectionisme: la tentation de Clinton," *L'Express*, 25 février 1993, pp. 42–46.

9 See John Saunders, "Canada wins time in wheat war," *The Globe and Mail*, February 10, 1993, pp. B1 and B6; "Steel duties criticized," *The Globe and Mail*, February 10, 1993, p. B6.

10 See "Support for BQ," *The Globe and Mail*, January 18, 1993, p. A4.

11 The model promoted by the Allaire Report was one of extreme decentralization according to which Quebec could allegedly stay within

the Canadian federation and enjoy all the benefits of sovereignty without bearing any of its costs. Alain Dubuc has qualified this as "souveraineté peureuse," i.e., wimpish sovereignty.

12 This section is based on Fanny Demers, Michel Demers and Murray Smith, *Oui pour renforcer l'union économique* (Ottawa: Centre de droit et de politique commerciale, octobre 1992), pp. 31–37.

13 See Pierre-Paul Proulx, "Comment" in Robin Boadway, Thomas Courchene and Douplas Purvis, eds., *Economic Dimensions of Constitutional Change*, Vol. 2 (Kingston: John Deutsch Institute for the Study of Economic Policy, Queen's University, 1991), p. 498.

14 This section is based on Fanny Demers, Michel Demers and Murray Smith, "Bring Back the Economic Union from the Back Burner," *The Financial Post*, May 27, 1992.

15 This argument is forcefully made by David Brown, "The Prosperity Initiative Report Reflects Public Opinion in Calling for More Joint Public and Private Sector Action," *Backgrounder* (Toronto: the C.D. Howe Institute, November 13, 1992).

16 Jim De Wilde, "How Partnership Pays Off," *The Globe and Mail*, January 24, 1992, p. A17.

Chapter Three:

1 The author is editor of *Canadian Foreign Policy*, a journal of Canada's international relations, and during 1991–92 was the Norman Robertson Research Fellow on the Policy Planning Staff at External Affairs and International Trade Canada.

2 See the Minister's discussion in Barbara McDougall, "The New Internationalism," *Canadian Foreign Policy*, Vol. 1, No. 1 (Winter 1992/93), pp. 1–6.

3 The term "good governance" means governing well and actually encompasses respect for human rights, the practice of democracy, and sound and responsible public administration. It turns on *how* a government governs and *what policies* it pursues. That Canada will give prominence and importance to promoting good governance in light of the "new internationalism" can be seen from numerous public statements by members of Cabinet. See for example Prime Minister Mulroney's speech at Stanford University, September 29, 1991; his speech at the Commonwealth Heads of Government meeting, Harare, Zimbabwe, October 16, 1991; and the Opening of the Chaillot Summit, November 19, 1991. See also a statement by the Honourable Monique Landry, Minister for External Relations and International Development, to the House of Commons Sub-Committee on Development and Human Rights, February 17, 1992, and a speech by the

Secretary of State for External Affairs, Barbara McDougall, McGill University, March 19, 1992.

4 In the aftermath of the collapse of communist regimes in Central and Eastern Europe in 1989, the Government set up a CIDA INC-like aid program (administered by DEAITC as a 'task force') that initially encouraged and supported the creation of democratic institutions and longer-term investment in a select number of Central and Eastern European countries. In the ensuing years the program's mandate has been expanded to include aid to the Baltics, Ukraine, Russia and some of the new republics in the Trans-Caucasus and Central Asia.

5 See discussion of Canadian aid opportunities in S. Neil MacFarlane, "Crisis and Opportunity in the Republic of Georgia," *Canadian Foreign Policy*, Vol. 1, No. 1 (Winter 1992/93), pp. 55–59.

6 For definitions of the terms see Report of the Secretary-General of the United Nations, "Agenda for Peace," June 17, 1992. "Preventive diplomacy" is action to prevent existing disputes from escalating into conflicts and to limit the spread of the latter when they occur; "peacemaking" is action (essentially peaceful) to bring hostile parties to agreement; "peace-keeping" is the deployment of a UN presence (military personnel and police) in the field, hitherto with the consent of all parties concerned; and "peace-building" refers to actions taken after a conflict to prevent its recurrence.

7 Lloyd Axworthy, "Canadian Foreign Policy: A Liberal Party Perspective," *Canadian Foreign Policy*, Vol. 1, No. 1 (Winter 1992/93), p. 14.

8 For a discussion of the changing nature of transatlantic relations see Evan H. Potter, "Canadian Foreign Policy-making and the European Community-Canada Transatlantic Declaration: Leadership or Followership?," *Policy Planning Staff Paper*, No. 92/6 (Ottawa: External Affairs and International Trade Canada, April 1992); and Conference Report, "The Troubled Partnership in Transition: A Report of a Conference on Europe's Security Dilemmas and the Transatlantic Relationship," April 30–May 1, 1992, sponsored by The Norman Paterson School of International Affairs, Carleton University, and the Edmund A. Walsh School of Foreign Service, Georgetown University.

9 See description of "key relationships" in Policy Planning Staff, "Foreign Policy Themes and Priorities: 1991–1992 Update," (Ottawa: External Affairs and International Trade Canada, December 1991), p. 15.

10 Daryl Copeland, "In Defence of Diversity: Towards the Legitimization of Dissent," *bout de papier*, Vol. 8, No. 4, 1991, p. 5.

11 This discussion draws on an interview with one of the authors of the report, John Halstead, and is cited in Evan Potter, " 'Storming' the Fortress of Canadian Foreign Policy: The Policy Commandos at

External Affairs," an unpublished paper completed while the author (Evan Potter) was a Research Fellow on the Policy Planning Staff.

12 However, following recent indications (January 1993) that the government plans to shift its foreign aid focus away from long-term development priorities to more short-term humanitarian relief programs and closer commercial ties with those countries most likely to achieve modern market economies, CIDA's resources may increasingly be shifted to DEAITC.

13 John Hadwen, "Whither the Canadian Foreign Service," *bout de papier*, Vol. 9, No. 1, p. 20.

14 See Andrew Griffith, "From a Trading Nation to a Nation of Traders: A Second Century of Canadian Trade Development," *Policy Planning Staff Paper*, No. 92/5 (Ottawa: External Affairs and International Trade Canada, 1992); and Andrew Griffith, "Straight Talk on Why Canada Needs to Reform its Trade Development System," *Canadian Foreign Policy*, Vol. 1, No. 1 (Winter 1992/93), pp. 61–85.

15 DEAITC News Release, "EAITC Streamlines Operations," February 26, 1992.

16 Letter from Reid Morden to all employees of the Department of External Affairs and International Trade, dated February 26, 1992.

17 Foreword written by Donald Mackay to a letter — also written by him — to Secretary of State for External Affairs Barbara McDougall and subsequently reprinted in *bout de papier*, Vol. 9, No. 2, 1992, p. 3.

18 Mackay, p. 4.

19 For an excellent analysis of the ramifications (i.e., principles of ministerial responsibility) of the allegedly irregular admission into Canada in 1991 of Mohammed Al-Mashat, the former Iraqi ambassador to the United States, see " S.I. Sutherland, "The Al-Mashat Affair: Administrative Accountability in Parliamentary Institutions," *Canadian Public Administration*, Vol. 34, No. 4 (Winter), pp. 573–603.

20 Letter from James H. Taylor (Under-Secretary of State for External Affairs, 1985–1989) to Michael Hart, Director of Economic Planning (CPE) at DEAITC, on the "Role of the Policy Planning Staff in the Formulation of Canadian Foreign Policy," dated May 27, 1992, p. 2; cited in Evan Potter, " 'Storming' the Fortress of Canadian Foreign Policy: The Policy Commandos at External Affairs," unpublished paper completed while the author was a research fellow on the Policy Planning Staff at DEAITC.

21 Taylor, p. 4.

22 The following arguments against the rationale for streamlining DEAITC activities are made persuasively by Donald Mackay in his letter to Barbara McDougall in *bout de papier*, Vol. 9, No. 2, 1992, p. 3.

23 John Kirton, "The New Internationalism: Implications for Canada's Foreign Policy and Foreign Service," *bout de papier*, Vol. 6, No. 4, 1989, p. 30.

Chapter Four:

1 Pierre Vincent, Parliamentary Secretary to the Minister of Finance, to the House of Commons, November 23, 1992. House of Commons Debates, p. 14019.
2 House of Commons Debates, Vol. 1, 1984, p. 7.
3 Department of External Affairs, Statements and Speeches, 83/18, October 27, 1983: "Reflections on Peace and Security," p. 2.
4 Bill C-32, Section 9, "An Act to Establish the Canadian Institute for International Peace and Security," June 28, 1984.
5 Gilles Grondin, "The Origins of the Canadian Institute for International Peace and Security," CIIPS Background Paper Number 6, August 1986, p. 5.
6 Bill C-32, Section 4.
7 Ibid, Section 29.
8 This section of the chapter is written by Geoffrey Pearson who was the author of the study by the Department of External Affairs, referred to earlier, and who was a member of the team of officials advising Mr. Trudeau during his peace initiative.
9 Dianne DeMille, "Challenges to Deterrence," CIIPS Conference Report, April 1986.
10 David Cox and Joseph Goldblat, "Debate about Nuclear Weapons Tests," CIIPS Occasional Paper 7, August, 1988; and Fen Osler Hampson, Harald von Riekhoff and John Roper, eds., *The Allies and Arms Control* (Baltimore: The Johns Hopkins University Press, 1992).
11 David Cox, "A Nuclear Freeze?," Background Paper, CIIPS, January 1986, and David Cox, "Trends in Continental Defence: A Canadian Perspective," Occasional Paper, CIIPS, December 1986.
12 Liisa North, "Negotiations for Peace in Central America," CIIPS Conference Report, April 1986; and "Measures for Peace in Central America," CIIPS Conference Report, December 1987; Lloyd Searwar, "Peace, Development and Security in the Caribbean," CIIPS Conference Report, August 1987.
13 François Lafrenière and Robert Mitchell, "Cyprus — Visions for the Future," A summary of conference and workshop proceedings, Working Paper 21, CIIPS, March 1990. Norma Salem, ed., *Cyprus, A Regional Conflict and its Resolution* (London: Macmillan, 1992). This book was begun by Dr. Salem and finished by Ron Fisher after her tragic death at an early age. "The Election Process in Namibia,"

Report of an International Round Table, CIIPS, July 1989. Deirdre Collings and Jill Tansley, "Peace for Lebanon? Obstacles, Challenges, Prospects," Working Paper 43, CIIPS, May 1992.

14 Boyce Richardson, *Time to Change* (Toronto: Summerhill Press, 1990).
15 Kenneth Bush, "Climate Change, Global Security and International Governance," Working Paper 23, CIIPS, 1990.
16 The papers which came out of these workshops were published in a special issue of *International Journal*, Vol. 45, No. 2 (Spring 1990) under the title Managing Regional Conflict.
17 For a list of Institute publications, see Appendix.
18 House of Commons, Minutes of Proceedings and Evidence of the Legislative Committee on Bill C-63, An Act to dissolve or terminate certain corporations and other bodies. Issue No. 4, June 4, 1992, page 4:6.
19 House of Commons Debates, 1992, Vol. 132, p. 7602.
20 Ibid, p. 127.
21 Department of External Affairs, News Release, July 27, 1992.
22 House of Commons Debates, Vol. 132, p. 9888, April 30, 1992.
23 See footnote 18. Minutes of Proceedings and Evidence of the Legislative Committee, Issue No. 4, June 4, 1992, p. 4:7.
24 CIIPS News Release, February 28, 1992.
25 Annual Report, 1991–92, Economic Council of Canada, p. 7.
26 G. Pearson, Memorandum, January 24, 1984, in possession of author.
27 See footnote 18 (Ernie Regehr), Minutes of Proceedings and Evidence, of the Legislative Committee, June 4, 1992, p. 4:39.

Chapter Five:

1 "The End of History," *The National Interest*, No. 16 (Summer, 1989). The article led to a lively debate in the pages of *The National Interest*, and also in the media and made Fukuyama's subsequent book, *The End of History and the Last Man* (New York: The Free Press, 1992), a best seller.
2 A handy introduction to globalization can be found in "The Business Implications of Globalization," Investment Canada Working Paper 1990–V. The three gurus of globalization are Robert Reich, *The Work of Nations* (New York: Alfred A. Knopf, 1991); Michael Porter, *The Competitive Advantage of Nations* (New York: The Free Press, 1990); and Kenichi Ohmae, *The Borderless World: Power and Strategy in the Interlinked World Economy* (New York: Harper Business, 1990).
3 While the GATT regime may have reflected these concepts, it was not built on them. Paul Krugman, in "Does the New Trade Theory Require a New Trade Policy?", *The World Economy*, Vol. 15, No. 4 (July,

1992), pp. 423–441, convincingly demonstrates that the GATT system is based on an enlightened mercantilism which posits that countries have an individual incentive to be protectionist but can collectively benefit from rule-based free trade. "GATT-think," while popular with officials and politicians, makes little economic sense. Perversely, however, it can lead to economically sensible policy. GATT negotiations have successfully incorporated the producer biases of most national trade policies into a set of rules that lead generally to freer trade. The process of getting there has been described by Martin Wolf as mercantilist bargaining. See his "A European Perspective," in Robert M. Stern, Philip H. Trezise and John Whalley, eds., *Perspectives on a U.S.-Canadian Free Trade Agreement* (Washington: Brookings Institution, 1987).

4 See Richard O'Brien, *Global Financial Integration: The End of Geography* (London: Pinter for the Royal Institute of International Affairs, 1992) for a discussion of the policy implications of global financial and capital markets.

5 For a discussion of changing theories to explain international trade and their application to trade policy, see Krugman, 1992. Also helpful are many of the chapters in Jorge Niosi, ed., *Technology and National Competitiveness: Oligopoly, Technological Innovation and International Competition* (Montreal: McGill-Queen's University Press, 1991).

6 The Uruguay Round is the eighth in a series of multilateral trade negotiations sponsored by the GATT. It was launched at Punta del Este, Uruguay in September, 1986 and is currently in its final phase. Its extensive agenda of trade and trade-related issues is the most ambitious yet in GATT's history and, if successful, would mark a substantive revitalization and modernization of the GATT regime.

7 Strategic trade policy is the work of a group of academic economists exploring the theoretical possibilities of using government policies, such as subsidies, quotas and tariffs, to shift the gains from trade from one nation to another. While the theories have enriched our understanding of trade, the practical possibilities of applying strategic trade policy are extremely rare, a fact admitted by its students but not by policy advocates who have found in it a sophisticated rationale for protectionist policies. See Paul Krugman, *Strategic Trade Policy and the New International Economics* (Cambridge: MIT Press, 1986).

8 DeAnn Julius, Global Companies and Public Policy: The Growing Challenge of Foreign Direct Investment (London: Pinter for the Royal Institute of International Affairs, 1990), pp. 83–84.

9 I have in mind, for example, the application to the emerging policy issues of work similar to Rodney de Grey, *Concepts of Trade Diplomacy and Trade in Services* (London: Harvester Wheatsheaf for the Trade Policy Research Centre, 1990).

10 On the investment/trade interface and the scope for future negotiations, see Phedon Nicolaides, "Investment Policies in an Integrated World Economy," *The World Economy*, Vol. 14, No. 2 (July, 1991), pp. 121–137. See also Don McFetridge, ed., *Foreign Investment, Technology and Economic Growth* (Calgary: University of Calgary Press, 1991); Leonard Waverman, ed., *Corporate Globalization through Mergers and Acquisitions* (Calgary: University of Calgary Press, 1991); and Raymond Vernon and Debora L. Spar, *Beyond Globalism: Remaking American Foreign Economic Policy* (New York: The Free Press, 1989). The series of Working Papers prepared for Investment Canada also provides useful points of departure.

11 There is a significant amount of literature on the interaction between trade and innovation policies, particularly by proponents and critics of strategic trade policy. A good introduction is provided by OECD, *Strategic Industries in a Global Economy: Policy Issues for the 1990s* (Paris: OECD International Futures Programme, 1991) which contains papers by a number of international scholars.

12 Interest in the interface between trade and environmental policies has burgeoned in the past few years. Among the better collections of studies are Kym Anderson and Richard Blackhurst, eds., *The Greening of World Trade Issues* (New York and London: Harvester Wheatsheaf, 1991) and Patrick Low, ed., *International Trade and the Environment* (Washington: World Bank, 1992). David Runnalls and Aaron Cosbey, *Trade and Sustainable Development: A Survey of the Issues and a New Research Agenda* (Winnipeg: International Institute for Sustainable Development, 1992) provides an exhaustive set of references as well as a clear indication of the wide range of issues at stake. See also Michael Hart with Sushma Gera, "Trade and the Environment: Dialogue of the Deaf or Scope for Cooperation?" *Canada-United States Law Journal*, Vol. 18 (1992), pp. 207–234.

13 There is no shortage of literature on the competition policy/trade policy interface. A convenient and thorough introduction is provided by Derek Ireland, "Interactions between Competition and Trade Policies: Challenges and Opportunities," a Discussion Paper prepared in the Canadian Bureau of Competition Policy, November, 1992. For a good introduction to academic thinking about the role of competition policy in a globalized economy, see Thomas M. Jorde and David J. Teece, eds., *Antitrust, Innovation and Competitiveness* (New York: Oxford University Press, 1992).

14 This is the main theme explored by Robert Reich in *The Work of Nations*. It will be interesting to see what kinds of policies he will pursue as Secretary of Labour in the Clinton Administration and what impact they will have on the pursuit of U.S. trade policy.

15 Little useful work has yet been done on the analytical and negotiating challenges that will need to be met if governments are to negotiate rules of general application on social policy issues within the context of trade agreements. Steve Charnovitz, "The Influence of International Labour Standards on the World Trading Regime: A Historical Review," *International Labour Review* (1987) at p. 565 and "Environmental and Labour Standards in Trade," *The World Economy*, Vol. 15, No. 3 (May 1992), pp. 335–356 provide a start. See also Fred Wien, *The Role of Social Policy in Economic Restructuring* (Montreal: Institute for Research on Public Policy, 1991).

16 Serious analysis of the architectural challenges to be faced in modernizing the trade regime has not progressed very far. John Jackson, *Restructuring the GATT System* (London: Pinter Books, 1990) provides a start. Other work of interest can be found in Ernst-Ulrich Petersmann and Meinhard Hilf, eds., *The New GATT Round of Multilateral Trade Negotiations: Legal and Economic Problems* (Boston: Kluwer, 1989) and Jagdish Bhagwati, *The World Trading System at Risk* (Princeton: Princeton University Press, 1991).

17 For a discussion of the challenges posed by "deep" integration, see Robert Z. Lawrence and Robert E. Litan, "The World Trading System After the Uruguay Round," *Boston University International Law Journal*, Vol. 8, Fall 1990, No. 2 (Symposium on International Trade for the 1990s), at p. 247, as well as the commentaries by Rachel McCullough, Richard Wright and Michael Trebilcock that follow.

Chapter Six:

1 John Hagedoorn and Jos Schakenraad, "Inter-firm partnerships and cooperative strategies in core Technologies" in C. Freeman and L. Soete, eds., *New Explorations in the Economics of Technical Change* (London: Pinter Publishers, 1990), Tables 1, 2 and 3.

2 Martin Fransman, *The Market and Beyond: Cooperation and Competition in Information Technology in the Japanese System* (Cambridge: Cambridge University Press, 1990); Jonah Levy and Richard Samuels, "Institutions and innovation: research collaboration as technology strategy in Japan" in Lynn K. Mytelka, ed., *Strategic Partnerships and the World Economy* (London: Pinter Publishers, 1991), pp. 120–148.

3 Mika Aaltonen et al., *Promoting the Start-up of International Strategic Alliances of Technology-Intensive Companies* (Helsinki: Helsinki University of Technology, 1991); Lynn K. Mytelka, "Crisis, technological change and the strategic alliance" in Mytelka, ed., *Strategic Partnerships and the World Economy* (London: Pinter Publishers 1991).

4 John Alic, "From weakness or strength: American firms and policies in a global economy" in Mytelka, ed., *Strategic Partnerships and the World Economy* (London: Pinter Publishers, 1991a), pp. 149–166.

5 Lynn K. Mytelka, "Crisis, technological change and the strategic alliance" in Mytelka, ed., *Strategic Partnerships and the World Economy* (London: Pinter Publishers, 1991), p. 1.

6 For a discussion of these newer relationships in biotechnology, see Stephen Barley and John Freeman, *Technical Report: A Preliminary Analysis of Strategic Alliances in Commercial Biotechnology* (Ithaca, Cornell University, mimeo, 1990); for textiles and clothing see Lynn Mytelka, "States, strategic alliances and international oligopolies: The European ESPRIT programme" in Lynn K. Mytelka, ed., *Strategic Partnerships and the World Economy* (London: Pinter Publishers, 1991), pp. 182–210; for electronics see Dieter Ernst and David O'Connor, *Competing in the Electronics Industry, The Experience of Newly Industrialising Economies* (Paris, OECD Development Studies, 1992).

7 David Mowery, 1991, "International collaboration in the commercial aircraft industry" in Mytelka, ed., *Strategic Partnerships and the World Economy* (London: Pinter Publishers, 1991), pp. 78–101.

8 OECD, "Multinational Enterprises and the Structural Adjustment Process" (Paris: OECD Committee on International Investment and Multinational Enterprise, September 23, 1983); M.N. Baily and A.K. Chakrabarti, *Innovation and the Productivity Crisis* (Washington, D.C.: The Brookings Institution, 1988).

9 Christopher Freeman and Carlota Perez, "Structural crises of adjustment, business cycles and investment behaviour" in G. Dosi, C. Freeman, D. Nelson, G. Silverberg and L. Soete, eds., *Technical Change and Economic Theory* (London: Pinter Publishers, 1988), pp. 38–66; Michel Aglietta, *Régulation et la crise du capitalism* (Paris: Calmann Lévy, 1976).

10 Lynn K. Mytelka, "States, strategic alliances and international oligopolies: The European ESPRIT program" in *Strategic Partnerships and the World Economy* (London: Pinter Publishers, 1991).

11 OECD, *Main Science and Technology Indicators* (Paris: OECD, 1991).

12 Investment Canada, *Investing in Canada's Future: A Report on the Investment Forums* (Ottawa: Investment Canada 1992), p. 16.

13 Conference Board of Canada, *R and D Outlook* 1992, (Ottawa, 1991), p. 2.

14 Michel Delapierre, "Les accords inter-entreprises, partage ou partenariat? Les stratégies des groupes européens du traitement de l'information," *Revue d'Économie Industrielle*, No. 55, 1er trimestre, 1991, pp. 148–149.

15 Digital switching in the communications industry, for example, is not an incremental extension of earlier electro-mechanical switching

technology, nor could compact discs based on laser technology derive logically from earlier phonograph records.

16 J.M. Gibb, ed., *Science Parks and Innovation Centers: Their Economic and Social Impact* (Amsterdam, Elsevier, 1985); and F. Williams and D. Gibson, eds., *Technology Transfer* (Newbury Park, Ca., Sage Publications, 1990).

17 Levy and Samuels, 1991, pp. 120–148.

18 Unless otherwise indicated much of the data and analysis in this section is drawn from Mytelka, *Strategic Partnerships*, and from data in LAREA/CEREM's "ESPRIT" data base created by the author.

19 Million European currency units. The écu is equivalent to US $1.239.

20 Commission of the European Communities, *ESPRIT 1989 Annual Report* (Brussels, DG XIII, 1990), p. 4.

21 Michel Delapierre et al., *Cooperation between Firms and Research Institutes: The French Case*, prepared for the Eureka workshop on Collaboration between Enterprises and Research Institutes (Milan: Bocconi University, 1988); Lynn K. Mytelka, *Technological and Economic Benefits of the European Strategic Programme for Research and Development on Information Technologies* (ESPRIT), A Report to the Department of Communications, Government of Canada (Ottawa: July 10, 1990).

22 "Pre-competitive" means that the products had not reached the stage of commercial market acceptance.

23 The EUREKA, VISION 2000 and PRECARN case studies are drawn from an unpublished paper entitled "Strategic Partnering: Some Lessons for Latin America" prepared for the International Development Research Centre (Ottawa: IDRC, 1992). The EUREKA case study has been updated to include material relevant to Canada.

24 In addition to the EC and EFTA countries these include Turkey and most recently Hungary.

25 Eureka, *All On-going Eureka Projects* (Brussels: Eureka Secretariat, 30 October, 1991); Eureka, *The Report of the EUREKA Assessment Panel* (Brussels: Eureka Secretariat, 1991).

26 Eureka, The Report of the EUREKA Assessment Panel (Brussels: Eureka Secretariat, 1991), p. 25.

27 Eureka, All On-going . . . , p. 27.

28 Michael J. Geringer, "Formation and Management of Joint Ventures in Canada" (Ottawa: Investment Canada, July, 1989).

29 Jorge Niosi, "Technical Alliances in Canadian High-Technology." A presentation to the seminar "New Technology Policy and Technical Innovations in the Enterprise" organized by CREDIT and CREST (Montreal: October 28–30, 1992), pp. 18, 27.

30 Jorge Niosi and Maryse Bergeron, "Technical alliances in the Canadian electronics industry: an empirical analysis," *Technovation*, Vol. 12, No. 5, 1992, p. 313.

31 The LAREA/CEREM data base is available from the author.

32 Niosi and Bergeron, p. 314.

33 The details for this section are mainly extracted from PRECARN Associates, *PRECARN, a New Alliance* (Ottawa, 1991); PRECARN Associates, "A Precompetitive Applied Research Network," paper presented by Gordon MacNabb, President and CEO of PRECARN to the IDRC-sponsored workshop on Establishing a Link between Research Centres and Enterprises: The Role of R & D Partnerships (Ottawa: January 16–17, 1992); and PRECARN Associates, "PRECARN: Its Organization and Objectives" (Ottawa, 1991).

34 PRECARN, a New Alliance 1991, p. 1.

35 The details for this section are mainly extracted from *VISION 2000 Inc., A Framework for the Evolution of Personal Communications in Canada* (Ottawa: VISION 2000 program office, Department of Communications, 1991); VISION 2000 Inc., "Networking the Global Village," a paper presented by Susan Baldwin, Director, Research and Technology Policy, Communications Development and Planning Branch, Department of Communications Canada, to the IDRC-sponsored workshop on Establishing a Link between Research Centres and Enterprises: The Role of R & D partnerships (Ottawa: January 16–17, 1992); VISION 2000 Inc. "Opportunities for Partnering," (Ottawa, VISION 2000 Programme Office, Department of Communications, May 27, 1991); VISION 2000 Inc., Project Review Committee Terms of Reference" (Ottawa: Vision 2000 Programme Office, Department of Communications, undated); and VISION 2000 Inc., R & D Project Announcements (Ottawa, VISION 2000 Secretariat, May 24, 1991).

Chapter Seven:

1 Quote from Prime Minister Brundtland in the *Globe and Mail*, June 15, 1992, p. 1.

2 The World Commission on Environment and Development, *Our Common Future* (Oxford and New York: Oxford University Press, 1987).

3 *The Changing Atmosphere: Implications for Global Security*, Conference Statement, Environment Canada, June 27–30, 1988, p. 1.

4 Mrs. Brundtland's speech in Rio, quoted in *The Globe and Mail*, June 15, 1992, p. 1.

5 Quoted in *The Globe and Mail*, June 12, 1992, p. 1.

6 *Final Canadian Reports for the United Nations Conference on the Environment and Development* (Ottawa: Department of External Affairs and International Trade Canada, 1992), mimeo.

7 Ibid.

8 Ibid.

9 Ontario Round Table on the Environment and the Economy, "Restructuring for Sustainability," Toronto, 1992.

10 *Report of the National Task Force on the Environment and the Economy*, Canadian Council of Ministers of the Environment (CCME), 1987.

11 For details see: John Girt's "Common Ground" prepared for Wildlife Habitat Canada and his paper on "The Environmental Impact of Farm Support Policies in Ontario" prepared for the Ontario Round Table on the Environment and the Economy, 1992.

12 William Murray, Impact of Energy Assistance on the Environment, Library of Parliament, September 3, 1992, p. 3.

13 House of Commons, Minutes of Proceedings and Evidence of the Standing Committee on Environment, Issue No. 45, Monday, November 26, 1992, pp. 45–12.

Chapter Eight:

1 United Nations, Founex Panel Report 1972 (A/Conf 40/10, Annex 1, paragraphs 4–5).

2 *Sardar Sarovar: The Report of the Independent Review* (Ottawa: Resources Future International, 1992) p. 349.

3 House of Commons, Ottawa, Proceedings of the Sub-Committee on International Financial Institutions. Issue No. 4, col. 4:7, November 5, 1992.

4 *Our Common Future* (Oxford, 1987) p. 1.

5 *Canadian Aid and the Environment* (Ottawa: The North-South Institute, 1981) p. 59.

6 Ibid., p. 63.

7 See its 85-page booklet, Brian Hanington, ed., *CARE for the Earth: Insights from a conference on agro-forestry* (Ottawa: 1990).

8 Kenny Bruno, "The Corporate Capture of the Earth Summit" in *Multinational Monitor* (Washington D.C., July–August 1992).

9 Quoted by Adam Schwarz in "Back down to earth: Global summit fails to live up to ambitions," in *Far East Economic Review*, June 25, 1992, p. 61.

10 Ibid., p. 62.

11 Jeanine Ferretti, "Report on UNCED" from Pollution Probe, Toronto, June 23, 1992.

12 Sophia Murphy, "Reflections on the UNCED process," document for CCIC circulation, September 1992.

13 Andrew Clark, *GEF Briefing and Issues Paper* (Ottawa: North-South Institute, commissioned by the Canadian Council for International Cooperation, August 1992). This section draws heavily from his 20-page paper. See also Roy Culpeper's contribution, "Can the GEF avoid pitfalls as a general sourcing fund?" in the North-South Institute's Briefing paper *Brazil '92: Getting down to earth* (Briefing B33, 1992).

14 Ibid., p. 11.

Chapter Nine:

1 Report of the United Nations Conference on the Human Environment, Stockholm, June 5–16, 1972, U.N. Doc. A/Conf. 48/14, rev. 1.

2 For a survey of U.S.–Canada bilateral issues see Nigel Bankes and Lindsay Staples, *Canadian-U.S. Relations in the Arctic Borderlands* (Ottawa: Canadian Arctic Resources Committee and the Canadian Institute of International Affairs, 1991).

3 B. Maxwell, *Atmospheric and Climate Change in the Canadian Arctic: Causes, Effects and Impacts, Northern Perspectives*, Vol. 15, No. 5 (December 1987), pp. 2–6.

4 See N. Bankes, "Forty Years of Canadian Sovereignty Assertion in the Arctic, 1947–87," *Arctic*, Vol. 40 (1987), p. 285.

5 This is a recurring theme in Canadian Arctic international relations literature. See for example J. Kirton, "Beyond Bilateralism: United States Canadian Co-operation in the Arctic" in W.E. Westermeyer and K.E. Shusterich, eds., *United States Arctic Interests: The 1980s and the 1990s* (New York: 1984). It also has other resonances. For example, Canada has pursued both multilateral and bilateral initiatives in relation to the problem of acid precipitation. The Economic Commission for Europe has provided the multilateral forum and has allowed Canada to make common cause with Germany and the Nordic countries. See N. Bankes and Saunders, "Acid Rain: Multilateral and Bilateral Approaches to Transboundary Pollution Under International Law," *University of New Brunswick Law Journal*, Vol. 33 (1984), p. 155.

6 Revised Statutes of Canada, 1985, c. 0–7.

7 Law of the Sea Convention, Montego Bay, October 21, 1982 (1982), 21 Int'l. Leg. Mat. 1245, article 234, ice-covered areas.

8 Agreement between the Government of the United States and the Government of Canada on Arctic Co-operation, Ottawa, January 11, 1988 (1987), 28 Int'l. Leg. Mat. 141.

9 *Our Common Future.* Report of the World Commission on Environment and Development (Oxford: Oxford University Press, 1987).

10 See A.R. Lucas and E.B. Peterson, "Northern Land Use Law and Policy Development: 1972–1978 and the Future" in R.F. Keith and J.B. Wright, eds., *Northern Transitions* Volume 2 (Ottawa: Canadian Arctic Resources Committee, 1978).

11 L. MacLachlan, "Comprehensive Aboriginal Claims in the Northwest Territories," *Information North*, Arctic Institute of North America, University of Calgary, Vol. 18, No. 1.

12 *Northern Perspectives*, Vol. 21, No. 1 (1992).

13 *Canada's Green Plan*, Ottawa: Government of Canada, 1990.

14 *The Arctic Environmental Strategy: An Action Plan* (Ottawa: Department of Indian Affairs and Northern Development, 1992).

15 Robert F. Keith, "Environmental Strategies for the Circumpolar North: A Review of Canadian Perspectives and Initiatives," paper presented at the Second Conference on the Role of Circumpolar Universities in Northern Development, Tyumen, June 10–13, 1991.

16 (1973), 13 Int'l. Leg. Mat. 13.

17 Reproduced in (1991), 30 Int'l. Leg. Mat. 1627.

18 Geneva, November 13, 1979 (1979), 18 Int'l. Leg. Mat. 1442. The AES does contain several references to proposals to negotiate a toxics protocol to the LRTAP Convention, in addition to those already negotiated on the subject of sulphur emissions and nitrogen oxides.

19 R.L. Dryden, "Industry, Shipping Proposals and Science" in D.L. VanderZwaag and C. Lamson, eds., *The Challenge of Arctic Shipping* (Montreal, Kingston: McGill-Queen's University Press, 1990).

20 Convention on Biological Diversity, Rio de Janeiro, June 5, 1992, reproduced in (1992), 31 Int'l. Leg. Mat. 818.

21 Framework Convention on Climate Change, New York, May 9, 1992, reproduced in (1992), 31 Int'l. Leg. Mat. 849.

22 United Nations Conference on Environment and Development: Rio Declaration on Environment and Development, reproduced in (1992), 31 Int'l. Leg. Mat. 874.

23 *Agenda 21*, United Nations Conference on Environment and Development, 1992, final and advanced version.

24 T. Fenge, "National Parks in the Arctic: The Case of the Nunavut Land Claim Agreement," *Environments* (1993), in press.

25 *Supra*, note 22: "States have, in accordance with the Charter of the United Nations and the principles of international law, the sovereign right to exploit their own resources pursuant to their own environmental policies, and the responsibility to ensure that activities within their jurisdiction or control do not cause damage to the environment of other States or of areas beyond the limits of national jurisdiction."

26 Arctic Council Panel, *To Establish an Arctic Environmental Council: A Framework Report* (Ottawa: Canadian Arctic Resources Committee, 1991), p.23.
27 Donat Pharand. "The case for an Arctic Regional Council and a treaty proposal," *Revue Generale Droit* (1992) 23:163–195.
28 The Arctic Council Panel is composed of the Inuit Circumpolar Conference, Indigenous Survival International, Canadian Arctic Resources Committee, and Canadian Centre for Global Security. It is funded by the Walter and Duncan Gordon Foundation.
29 See Arctic Council Panel, *To Establish an International Arctic Council.*

Chapter Ten:

1 Hans J. Morgenthau, "The Danger of Thinking Conventionally about Nuclear Weapons," in Carlo Schaerf, Britian Holden Rein and David Carlton, eds. *New Technologies and the Arms Race* (New York: St. Martin's, 1989), p. 255.
2 On the evolution of co-operation to prevent war see John Lewis Gaddis, "The Long Peace: Elements of Stability in the Postwar International System," *International Security* Vol. 10 (Spring 1946), pp. 99–142; Emanuel Adler, "Seasons of Peace: Progress in Postwar International Security," in Emanuel Adler and Beverly Crawford, eds., *Progress in Postwar International Relations* (New York: Columbia University Press, 1991), pp. 128–73; Alexander L. George et al., eds., *U.S. Soviet Security Cooperation: Achievements, Failures, Lessons* (Oxford: Oxford University Press, 1988); George W. Breslauer and Philip E. Tetlock, eds., *Learning in U.S. and Soviet Foreign Policy* (Boulder, CO: Westview, 1991). For an analysis of general trends affecting greater co-operation see Mark W. Zacher, "The Decaying Pillars of the Westphalian Temple: Implications for International Order and Governance," in James N. Rosenau and Ernst-Otto Czempiel, eds., *Governance Without Government: Order and Change in World Politics* (Cambridge: Cambridge University Press, 1992), pp. 58–101.
3 Patrick Morgan, "On Strategic Arms Control and International Security," in Edward Kolodziej and Patrick Morgan, eds., *Security and Arms Control* (New York: Greenwood, 1989), p. 302.
4 Robert Jervis, "The Political Effects of Nuclear Weapons," *International Security*, Vol. 13 (Fall 1988), p. 83.
5 K.J. Holsti, *Peace and War: Armed Conflict and International Order, 1648–1989* (Cambridge: Cambridge University Press, 1991), pp. 287, 305, and 333.

6 Kenneth N. Waltz, "Nuclear Myths and Political Realities," *American Political Science Review*, Vol. 84 (September 1990), pp. 732, 739, and 744.

7 John Mearsheimer, "Why We Will Soon Miss the Cold War," *Atlantic Monthly*, Vol. 266 (August 1990), p. 37.

8 On future Third World conflicts see Brian L. Job, ed., *The Insecurity Dilemma: National Security of Third World States* (Boulder, CO: Lynne Rienner, 1992); Mohammed Ayoob, "The Security Problematique in the Third World," *World Politics*, Vol. 43 (1991), pp. 257–283; Barry Buzan, "New Patterns of Global Security in the 21st Century," *International Affairs*, Vol. 67 (1991), pp. 431–451.

9 Adler, "Seasons of Peace."

10 On the general development of international environmental issues and regulations see Lynton K. Caldwell, *International Environmental Policy* (Durham, NC: Duke University Press, 1990). On nuclear pollution see Peter Sands, *Chernobyl: Law and Communication* (Cambridge: Grotius, 1988).

11 R. Michael M'Gonigle and Mark W. Zacher, *Pollution, Politics, and International Law: Tankers at Sea* (Berkeley, CA: University of California Press, 1979); Bill Moyers, *Global Dumping Ground: The International Traffic in Hazardous Waste* (Washington: Seven Locks, 1990).

12 Concerning acid rain, ozone depletion and global warming see: Jutta Brunnee, *Acid Rain and Ozone Layer Depletion: International Law and Regulation* (Dobbs Ferry, NY: Transnational, 1988); C. Ian Jackson, "A Tenth Anniversary Review of the ECE Convention on Long-Range Transboundary Air Pollution," *International Environmental Affairs*, Vol. 2 (Summer 1990), pp. 217–226; Richard E. Benedick, *Ozone Diplomacy: New Directions in Safeguarding the Planet* (Cambridge, MA: Harvard University Press, 1991); Peter M. Haas, "Banning chlorofluorocarbons: epistemic community efforts to protect stratospheric ozone," *International Organization* Vol. 46 (Winter 1992), pp. 187–224; Michael Grubb, *The Greenhouse Effect: Negotiating Targets* (London: Royal Institute of International Affairs, 1989); Richard E. Benedick et al., *Greenhouse Warming: Negotiating a Global Regime* (Washington, D.C.: World Resources Institute, 1991).

13 Caldwell, *International Environmental Policy*, p. 6.

14 William MacNeill, *A World History* (Oxford: Oxford University Press, 1979), p. 178. On the history of plagues see William MacNeill, *Plagues and Peoples* (Garden City, NJ: Anchor Press/Doubleday, 1976); Geoffrey Marks and William K. Beatty, *Epidemics* (New York: Charles Scribner's, 1976).

15 Richard Cooper, "International Cooperation in Public Health as a Prologue to Macroeconomic Cooperation," in *Can Nations Agree?* (Washington, D.C.: Brookings, 1989), pp. 179 and 183.

16 Norman Howard-Jones, *The Scientific Background of the Sanitary Conferences, 1851–1938* (Geneva: WHO, 1975); Neville Goodman, *International Health Organizations and Their Work* (Edinburgh: Churchill Livingston, 1971); Michael R. Reich and Eiji Marui, eds., *International Cooperation for Health* (Dover, MA: Auburn House, 1989).

17 Norman L. Webb, "Gallup International Survey on Attitudes Towards AIDS," in A.F. Fleming et al., *The Global Impact of AIDS* (New York: Alan R. Liss, 1988), p. 347.

18 Jonathan Mann quoted in: Panos Institute, *AIDS and the Third World* (Philadelphia: New Society, 1989), p. 98, and John Platt, "The Future of AIDS," *The Futurist*, Vol. 21 (November–December 1987), p. 15. On the development of AIDS and international cooperation, see Nicholas Christakis, "Responding to a Pandemic: International Interests in AIDS Control," *Daedalus*, Vol. 118 (Spring 1989), pp. 113–34.

19 Christakis, "Responding to a Pandemic," p. 127.

20 World Commission on Environment and Development, *Our Common Future* (Oxford: Oxford University Press, 1987), p. 343.

21 Michael Doyle, "Liberalism and World Politics," *American Political Science Review*, Vol. 80 (December 1986); Carol R. Ember, Melvin Ember, and Bruce Russett, "Peace Between Participatory Polities: A Cross-National Test of the 'Democracies Rarely Fight Each Other' Hypothesis," *World Politics*, Vol. 44 (July 1992).

Chapter Eleven:

1 Administratively, Canada seems to be bucking the trend. In early 1992, the Government decided to concentrate responsibility for all international migration policy issues as well as operational functions overseas, together with the equivalent part of the foreign service, exclusively in the Department of Employment and Immigration, thus ending a shared arrangement with External Affairs that in most respects had been working very well. The move was officially described to personnel as helping to bring External Affairs "back to basics." This contrasted oddly with the fact that a scant four months earlier, the Government's *Foreign Policy Themes and Priorities Update* document of December 1991, issued by External Affairs, had listed among the five "themes that should be viewed as basic priority objectives underpinning the full range of our activities and programs" that of "encouraging the international community and key multilateral institutions to expand their involvement with the serious long-term problems of population growth and mass migration . . . "

2 The relationship between rapid population growth and emigration is a complex one; because of geography or social systems, nationals of

some high-growth countries do not yet migrate beyond their borders. But among areas which do produce migrants, only the former Soviet-bloc countries do not have rapid population growth; here, systemic breakdown and resurgence of raw nationalism are the main factors pushing people to move.

3 'Convention refugees' are those who "because of a well-founded fear of persecution due to their race, religion, nationality, membership in a particular social group or political opinions, are unwilling or unable to return to their country of nationality or former habitual residence." Proposed expanded definitions would go beyond individuals who fear persecution to include the huge categories of people fleeing from war or other forms of generalized violence; they have been strongly opposed by the UNHCR's developed country members, although there are African and Latin American precedents.

4 An important statement of this position is to be found in the UNHCR's 13-page *Note on International Protection* (UN General Assembly document A/AC.96/799 of August 25, 1992).

5 Among current claimants, some 6,000 yearly arrive having destroyed their documents or carrying false ones, thus adding greatly to the difficulty of deciding on their claims.

6 The target will be in effect for the first time in 1993. Whether it will be fully met is uncertain; somewhat lower targets for 1990 and 1991 were not achieved. In any case the net inflow will average out at somewhat less, say 210,000 or 220,000, because of those who move on or return home. Maintenance of this inflow will only slow and not prevent the eventual start of a decline in Canada's population some forty years hence, due to our lower-than-replacement fertility rate. A Commons committee was told in 1990 that each additional 60,000 immigrants per year would delay the decline by eight or nine years.

7 As simplified by the author for analytical purposes. For a more detailed and authoritative breakdown, see *Managing Immigration: a framework for the 1990s* (Employment and Immigration Canada, Ottawa, 1992), p. 14. This publication provides the official rationale and description of the new Immigration Bill, discussed later in the present chapter.

8 Quebec runs its own program. The amount of federal fiscal compensation it receives for this is not made known.

9 Address by the Honourable Barbara McDougall to the Empire Club of Toronto, November 12, 1992 (p. 2 of text as released by External Affairs and International Trade Canada).

10 The chairperson of the conference, Doris Meissner, a former U.S. official now with the Carnegie Endowment for International Peace, is

among other things the author of "Managing Migration," an article in the Endowment's quarterly *Foreign Policy* (Number 86, Spring 1992), which is one of the best general analyses of the migration phenomenon in its broad international context.

11 *Unauthorized Migration; An Economic Development Response, Report of the Commission for the Study of International Migration and Cooperative Economic Development* (Washington, D.C., July 1990), p. xiv.

12 A rare exception was contained in a September 1991 discussion of post-Uruguay Round problems by Hugo Paemen, the European Community's chief GATT negotiator; he "described the migration problem 'as a background societal one' centering on a choice that industrialized countries must make to either accept immigration or accept imported products from poorer countries so that the potential immigrants can stay home and work in domestic factories. Pressures will build, and as a result, 'we believe it would be wise for an international organization to deal with this problem" *The International Trade Reporter*, Current Reports, Vol. 8, No. 38, September 25, 1991, p. 1405; original reference from *Canada Among Nations 1992–93*, Chapter 7, p. 121. But Chapter 10 of the same volume, on NAFTA, makes no mention of the migration factor.

Chapter Twelve:

* L'auteur tient ici à remercier ses assistants, Isabelle Desmartis et Yves Goulet, pour leur précieux concours.

1 *Agenda pour la Paix* (New York, Nations Unies), juin 1992. Ci-après cité Agenda.

2 Ces chiffres sont tirés de Margaret E. Galey, "Reforming the Regime for Financing the United Nations," *Howard Law Journal*, Vol. 31, 1988, pp. 543–574.

3 "A United Nations Assessment Project Study," Heritage Foundation Reports, 13 October, 1992.

4 Inis Claude conclut dans un étude récente: "the world needs, and perhaps it deserves, to have a succession of individuals with exceptional character and creativity in the position of Secretary-General." Voir Inis Claude, The Ralph Bunche Institute on the United Nations, New York, NY, September 1991, cité dans *Peacekeeping and International Relations*, March/April 1992, p. 13.

5 Voir Robert C. Johansen, "UN Peacekeeping and Military Force," *Third World Review*, Vol. 12, No. 2, April 1990, qui écrit, p. 59: "A helpful innovation could be to create a permanent UN force, individually recruited by the UN from among individuals who volunteer from many nations. Such a force could be more effectively trained,

organised and employed to carry out the demanding tasks of peace-keeping and international policing than ad hoc forces. [. . .] UN forces could be used in anticipation of a crisis." Robin Hay poursuit de la même manière: "il faudrait créer aux Nations Unies un secrétariat particulier qui serait chargé des missions de maintien de la paix. Cela contribuerait à rendre le processus officiel et permettrait de préparer les nouvelles opérations de façon cohérente." Cité dans Robin Hay, "Les aspects civils du maintien de la paix," Ottawa, CIIPS (Canadian Institute for International Peace and Security), *Document de travail no. 36*, octobre 1991, p. 39. Voir aussi F.T. Liu, *United Nations Peacekeeping: Management and Operations*, New York, IPA, Occasional Paper No. 4, 1990, où l'auteur note l'importance d'intégrer tous les aspects du maintien de la paix, y compris le "peacemaking" et la logistique qui y affère, sous la direction du Bureau des affaires politiques du Secrétariat.

6 Une première initiative a été prise en ce sens avec l'établissement d'ORCI (Office of Research and Collection of Information), mais ce bureau a depuis été aboli, tandis que ses fonctions ont été fusionnées avec d'autres responsabilités du Secrétariat de l'Organisation. Plusieurs auteurs réclament pour l'Organisation l'établissement d'un système de surveillance par satellites.

7 Il semblerait que la Russie et la France privilégient la voie de l'article 43, tandis que les États-Unis s'y opposeraient. Voir Louis Gordenker, "International Organization in the New World Order," *The Fletcher Forum*, Summer 1991, pp. 71–86, plus particulièrement la page 74. Dans un rapport sur le rôle du Conseil de sécurité, David Cox conclut de son côté: "This suggests that the Gulf operation (and, by implication, Korea) are the exceptions in the context of prospective UN enforcement actions. Despite the comprehensive nature of the language of Chapter VII, the Security Council might be better able to direct enforcement actions in dealing with smaller scale aggressions, while leaving large military actions to the ad hoc arrangements which characterize the operation in the Gulf. In support of this view, it can also be argued that many threats to the peace confronting the Security Council will involve military forces considerably smaller than those deployed, for example, by Iraq." Voir David Cox, éd., *The Use of Force by the Security Council for Enforcement and Deterrent Purposes: A Conference Report*, Ottawa, The Canadian Centre for Arms Control and Disarmament, 1991, 59 pages. La citation est tirée de la page 4.

8 Le Danemark, la Finlande, l'Islande, la Norvège et la Suède. Dans le document soumis par le Canada devant ce Comité en mars 1992, Ottawa rappelle que la diplomatie préventive peut être développée comme "a tool which is available [. . .] in appropriate circumstances." On rappelle aussi que dans sa résolution 46/48, l'AGNU

"consider[ed] it useful for the UN to monitor global developments which may eventually be transformed into a crisis." Parmi les mesures destinées à améliorer l'efficacité des opérations de maintien de la paix, le Canada souhaite la création d'un corps international d'officiers de formation, le développement de procédures et de doctrines de soutien logistique communes, une meilleure coordination entre États en ce qui a trait aux unités d'affectation "stand-by," et la mise en œuvre de procédures standardisées pour établir la structure des bataillons, car la structure des forces varie selon qu'un bataillon est fourni par un pays plutôt que par un autre.

10 Il s'agit de la Declaration on the Prevention and Removal of Disputes and Situations Which May Threaten International Peace and Security and the Role of the United Nations in this Field.

11 "Standing by idly . . . carries with it the charge of guilt." Voir Jost Delbruck, "A Fresh Look at Humanitarian Intervention under the Authority of the United Nations," *Indiana Law Journal*, Vol. 67, Fall 1992, pp. 887–901. Voir aussi dans le même numéro l'article de Mary Ellen O'Connell, "Continuing Limits on UN Intervention in Civil War."

12 Voir en ce domaine John Mackinlay, "Powerful peace-keepers," *Survival*, Vol. XXXII, No. 3, pp. 241–251, et C.R. Nixon, "Point of View VIII," *National Network News*, Vol. 1, No. 17, 15 octobre 1992. C.R. Nixon est l'ancien sous-ministre du Ministère de la Défense du Canada.

13 *The Globe and Mail*, 12 novembre 1992.

14 Voir *CFB Cornwallis: Canada's Peacekeeping Training Center: A Blueprint for a Peacekeeping Training Center of Excellence*, préparé par les sociétés Common Security Consultants et Stratman Consulting Inc., Nouvelle-Écosse, mars 1992.

15 En particulier le rapport du directeur des opérations de maintien de la paix, le colonel Michael Houghton. Voir *The Ottawa Citizen*, 6 juin 1992 et *The Kitchener Waterloo Record* du 8 juin 1992.

Chapter Thirteen:

1 Jeff Sallot, "Nato Members gang up on Canada over pullout," *The Globe and Mail*, April 9, 1992, p. A2.

2 Kinsman made these comments at a seminar hosted by the Canadian Institute of Strategic Studies in June 1992.

3 See comments made by Alex Morrison in *The Toronto Star*, February 27, 1992, p. 21.

4 Interview with the author, June 1987.

5 Lloyd Axworthy, "Forging the forces into a peace force," *The Globe and Mail,* July 27, 1992, p. A19.
6 See William Safire in the *International Herald Tribune,* December 18, 1992, p. 4.
7 Barbara McDougall, "Peacekeeping in the Limits of Sovereignty," December 2, 1992, Statements and Speeches, 92/58 (Ottawa: The Department of External Affairs and International Trade Canada).
8 "Canada to withdraw troops from Cyprus," *News Release,* No. 231 (Ottawa: Government of Canada), December 3, 1992.

Chapter Fourteen:

1 "Asia-Pacific" here refers to the three subregions, the North Pacific (i.e., Northeast Asia plus Canada and the U.S.), Southeast Asia, and the South Pacific.
2 "Canada-Japan Forum 2000, Partnership Across the Pacific," Asia Pacific Foundation, Vancouver, December 1992, 27 pp.
3 The cited figures on immigration are taken from Alanna Mitchell, "Canada's Ethnic Patterns Changing," *Toronto Globe and Mail,* December 9, 1992 and from Employment and Immigration, Canada, *Quarterly Statistics, Jan/Dec 1991,* which gives preliminary figures for that year.
4 Figures concerning the destination of immigrants within Canada need to be treated carefully, as Employment and Immigration gives its data on the basis of port of entry. There is strong evidence, but no exact data, suggesting (a) that immigrants to Canada often relocate to other provinces after their official entry, and (b) that numbers of immigrants, having attained status within Canada, return to their home countries.
5 For a recent discussion of the relationship between immigration and foreign policy, see Diana Lahry, "Immigration and Foreign Policy: Separate Concerns?" *Behind the Headlines,* Vol. 50, No. 2 (Winter 1992/93), Canadian Institute of International Affairs, Toronto.
6 For an interesting discussion of the rapid rate of Chinese economic growth and of how reported, standard economic measures tend to under-report the actual size and rate of economic activity in China, see "When China Stirs," *The Economist,* November 28, 1992, Survey section. The estimate which foresees China becoming the world's largest economy is by Lawrence Sumners, the World Bank's chief economist.
7 Data on Japan's trade surpluses are found in *JEI Report,* No. 413, February 5, 1993, p. 3; and "Economic Regionalism: Japan's Role

in East Asia," *Canadian Chamber of Commerce in Japan Journal*, Vol. 6, No. 1 (Winter 1993), p. 20.

8 In 1992, the proportion of manufactured products exceeded that of natural resource products in Canadian exports for the first time.

9 The drop in the value of the Canadian dollar in the latter half of 1992 could have had a significant impact on Asia-Pacific export/import trade values. However, these figures were not available at the time of writing.

10 Preliminary 1992 trade figures, as reported in the *Toronto Globe and Mail*, February 6, 1993, p. B23. The same article also noted that Mexico was in 1992 a greater exporter to Canada than either China or Taiwan.

11 Canada-Japan Trade Council, "Japanese Portfolio Investment," *Newsletter*, September-October 1992, p. 34. Mark Russell, "Japanese Direct Investment in Canada," *The Canadian*, Vol. 3, No. 2, pp. 9–10.

It should be noted that Japanese FDI in Canada is dwarfed by flows from the U.S. and the U.K. For 1990, for instance, the amounts were 4.3, 80.5, and 17.5 billion dollars, respectively. Investment Canada, *Investment Subject to the Investment Canada Act* (number of received cases by principal province of activity for the period from January 1 to December 31, 1989, companies with significant Japanese equity participation only); and Mark, *op. cit.*, p. 8.

12 For a fuller discussion of the issues raised in this section see, Brian L. Job and Frank Langdon, *The Evolving Security Order of the Asia-Pacific: A Canadian Perspective*, NPCSD Working Paper No. 15, Centre for International and Strategic Studies, York University, North York, September 1992.

13 Richard Ellings and Edward Olsen, "A New Pacific Profile," *Foreign Policy*, No. 89 (Winter 1992/93).

14 Ibid., p. 116.

15 The five countries which accounted for most of the East Asian trade with the U.S. in 1989 also accounted for $83 billion of the U.S. trade deficit for that year. George Friedman and Meredith Lebard, *The Coming War with Japan* (New York: St. Martin's Press, 1991), p. 305, Table 11–1.

16 Andrew Mack and Desmond Ball, "The Military Build-Up in Asia-Pacific," *Pacific Affairs*, Vol. 5, No. 3 (1992), pp. 197–208.

17 The term "co-operative security" has come into use as national analysts struggle to come to terms with the definition of their security interests in today's post-Cold War world. What is involved is a realization that national interests and security are affected by factors that are not included in the traditional notions of territorial threat and military security. Thus, "co-operative security" is "mutual security," i.e., it cannot be attained unilaterally and needs to be addressed

through strategies of co-operative interaction. Threats to security will arise not only from interstate territorial disputes but also from domestic and regional instabilities caused by ethnic and cultural pressures. States' security interests are not separable from their economic interests, especially their interest in maintaining the conditions of domestic and regional political stability that are necessary for economic prosperity. In addition, the security agenda must be expanded to include so-called "unconventional" or "transnational" security threats, such as weapons proliferation, drug trafficking, terrorism and economic migration.

For an indication of the way in which Ottawa has come to utilize the term "co-operative security" when speaking of Canadian security interests, see "Foreign Policy Themes and Priorities: 1991–92 Update," External Affairs and International Trade Canada, Policy Planning Staff, Ottawa, December 1991. And, for wider discussion concerning the Asia-Pacific, see Geoffrey Wiseman, "Common Security in the Asia-Pacific Region," *The Pacific Review*, Vol. 5, No. 1, pp. 42–59.

18 *The Canadian Initiative for a North Pacific Co-operative Security Dialogue*, a Position Paper of External Affairs and International Trade Canada, December 3, 1990.

19 See Stewart Henderson, "Canada and Asia Pacific Security, the North Pacific Co-operative Security Dialogue, Recent Trends," External Affairs and International Trade Canada, Policy Planning Staff Paper 91/8, November 1991, for an earlier discussion of Ottawa's assessment of the NPCSD, and Paul Evans and David Dewitt, *The Changing Dynamics of Asia-Pacific Security: A Canadian Perspective*, NPCSD Working Paper No. 3, Centre for International and Strategic Studies, York University, North York, January 1993, for a recent update.

20 Asia Pacific Foundation, "Canada-Japan Forum 2000, Partnership Across the Pacific," December 1992, 27pp. Report of the joint committee of eminent Canadians and Japanese appointed by the Canadian and Japanese prime ministers to report on ways to improve the relationship between the two countries.

21 Joint Communiqué of the Twenty-Fifth ASEAN Ministerial Meeting, Manila, July 21–22, 1992.

22 Asia Pacific Foundation, Letter from Peter Lougheed, co-chair of Canada-Japan Forum 2000, to Prime Minister Brian Mulroney, December 1992, p. 4.

FC 242 G56 1993

Global jeopardy

FC 242 G56 1993

Global jeopardy

DATE DUE